Terry Fox, Switzerland, and “Elsewhere”

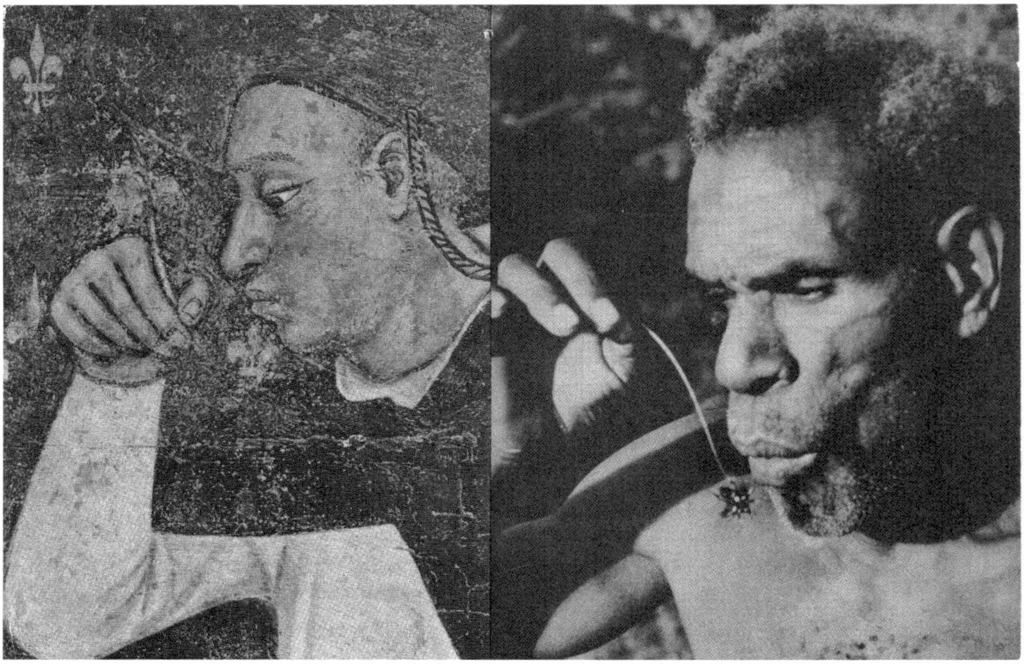

The eye is not the only glass that burns the mind.

Terry Fox, Switzerland, and “Elsewhere”

Edited by Michael Glasmeier
and Carsten Seiffarth

Kunstmuseum Bern
Terry Fox Association e. V., Cologne
Spector Books

Contents

Terry Fox, Switzerland . . .

. . . and "Elsewhere"

In memory of
Bernd Schulz (1941—2017)

Sound forester, philosopher, friend

Welcoming Remarks

The publication *The Eye's Not the Only Glass That Burns the Mind: Terry Fox, Switzerland and "Elsewhere"*—edited and published by Michael Glasmeier and Carsten Seiffarth, Kunstmuseum Bern, and the Terry Fox Association e. V. in Cologne—documents the symposium of the same name, held on May 5–6, 2017 during the Terry Fox retrospective, which was devoted to exploring the legacy of his ideas and body of work, as well as to the broader concept of his oeuvre. Not only was much-deserved homage paid to a brilliant and exceptional artist, who had recently been rediscovered, but a new chapter in art history was written in Bern. The art history that began with the friendship between Terry Fox and Elka Spoerri in the nineteen-seventies, continued with exhibition and performance activity at Jürgen Glaesemer's invitation in the eighties,[1] was deepened at Galerie Francesca Pia in Bern in the nineties, and was kept alive in recent years by Valerian Maly's ongoing attention and curatorial activity for the BONE Performance Festival. It was in this way that I, too, came into contact with the oeuvre of Terry Fox and the stories surrounding him. Since Marina Abramović's legendary solo exhibition in the late nineteen-nineties, I knew that the Kunstmuseum Bern was interested in performance art.[2] I had only just started to work here when my colleague Susanne Friedli organized a wonderful exhibition of the work of James Lee Byars,[3] in effect rediscovering another important performance artist from the seventies and acknowledging his contemporary relevance. Indeed, the Kunstmuseum Bern possesses an incredible treasury of work that deserves to be explored and investigated.

Like Terry Fox, James Lee Byars was a US artist who left behind artistic traces more extensively in Europe than in the USA. Both used the relatively new medium of performance to express themselves poetically, yet decisively, about life and contemporary events; both were interested in performance, language, and the voice.

Yet the differences between Terry Fox and James Lee Byars are instructive. Byars personifies the Baroque, the opulently sensual setting, his favorite colors being gold, red, black, and white; whereas to me, Terry Fox is the embodiment of the

1 *Die Gleichzeitigkeit des Anderen* (The Simultaneity of the Other), curated by Jürgen Glaesemer, Kunstmuseum Bern, 1987.

2 *Marina Abramović: Artist Body – Public Body*, curated by Toni Stooss, Kunstmuseum Bern, 1998. The exhibition later toured to Valencia (La Gallera), Alicante (Lonja del Pescado), and Ljubljana (Moderna Galerija and Cankerev Dom).

3 *I'm Full of Byars: James Lee Byars – Eine Hommage*, curated by Susanne Friedli, Kunstmuseum Bern, 2008–09.

Renaissance in his interdisciplinary, subtly enigmatic approach, conceptual density, and symbolic complexity. Like a Renaissance man, Terry Fox continually pursued his research and study of literature, music, and the visual arts throughout the ages. His materials, though, were quotidian: sound, blood, and the word.

Despite their differences, both artists represent the precious, albeit precarious, legacy of the art of the seventies. It was a period when it was important not to produce exclusively for the art market, to move out of the institutions, and to be committed to reflection on art, the times, and society. Dematerialization was a major aim. Away from the materials and techniques of the past, freighted with history and conventions and attributes, and toward freer, more direct expression, new experiments, a more interdisciplinary, spiritual movement. Both a new concept of making works and unconventional modes of thinking and acting were called for, and Terry Fox brought them into his art.

Terry Fox's extraordinary body of work, which obstinately defies artistic categorization and disciplinary pigeonholes (and in so doing stimulates us to new leaps of awareness), was honored in the retrospective, the symposium, and the publication now in your hands. As in the ancient sense of the word, the symposium was a gathering of friends, fellow travelers, the curious and the like-minded. The Kunstmuseum Bern was proud to be permitted to host the event, and thereby to point out one of Terry Fox's former artistic haunts, where history was written and, it is hoped, will continue to be written in the future.

A series of important occasions made this symposium and its publication possible. First of all, there was a level of collegial collaboration above and beyond disciplinary and institutional boundaries. I would like to express my thanks to Reto Sorg, the Robert Walser Center, Peter Schneemann, and the Institute for Art History of the University of Bern, as well as to the Bern University of the Arts and, of course, the Terry Fox Association e. V. in Cologne. The symposium and its publication received major funding from the Canton of Bern, the GegenwART Foundation, and the Johanna Dürmüller-Bol Foundation, without the support of which this project would never have been realized. Finally, my thanks to the symposium organizers Michael Glasmeier, Seraina Renz, and Valerian Maly. Their loyal and attentive dedication have ensured that this important oeuvre will not risk being forgotten in the future.

Kathleen Bühler
Kunstmuseum Bern

Translated from the German
by Andrea Lerner

The concrete is the wonder of reality, to which all theories must be oriented.

Marianne Gronemeyer

Only a few people know that Terry Fox's artistic journey began by chance. When he was sixteen years old, his uncle Alan, himself an artist and photographer, gave all his painting utensils to Terry: brushes, paints, and an easel. The photographic equipment went to Terry's twin brother, Larry. So it transpired that Larry became a photographer and Terry a painter—at first. It's well known that Terry Fox did not stop at painting. Throughout his entire life, he expanded his opportunities for artistic expression, in the process creating an oeuvre in which the boundary between art and life, between art and not-art, is a floating one. His work mirrors an attitude that unites apparent contradictions with the utmost ease: Terry Fox is discreet and provocative, a loner and yet connected, keeping to himself, yet very much present.

Although there are numerous descriptions, notes, and reflections by the artist on his works, the inner coherence of his complex oeuvre remains as yet largely obscure. In order to arrive at new and deeper insights, in May 2017 the Kunstmuseum Bern organized the symposium *The Eye's Not the Only Glass That Burns the Mind* in connection with their exhibition *Terry Fox – Elemental Gestures*. Most of the essays collected in this publication are based on the symposium lectures, where the main focus is on the "secluded" works and performances in Bern and Switzerland (keeping Ernst Jandl's "Anderwo"—elsew(h)ere—firmly in mind).[1] On the whole, the contributions follow fresh, previously undiscovered tracks, thereby opening up a field of reflection in which different perspectives on the oeuvre can resonate. All share a receptive point of view that starts from the concrete work. That's where their search for knowledge begins—not in the supposedly safe harbor of theory.

1 Ernst Jandl (1925–2000), experimental Austrian poet.

Unique to this collection of texts, too, is the linguistic and formal diversity in writing about art: from precisely detailed descriptive reporting on the work to a conversational protocol, from sketched recollections to a fragment and the first draft of an alphabetical list of key terms inherent in the oeuvre. The texts—all but one previously unpublished—offer new material and novel forms of interpretation, thus constituting the basis for future, more intensified research on this artist. It is to be hoped that publishing them in both English and German versions will also revivify an intensive examination of the art of Terry Fox in the United States.

The co-publishers of the publication are the Kunstmuseum Bern and the Terry Fox Association e. V. – a circle of the artist's friends and fellow travelers who are united in their desire to keep the oeuvre of Terry Fox alive. Since its founding in 2009, the TFA has gotten several projects off the ground, including *Recalling Terry Fox*, a series of events, concerts, and lectures, and it has been assisting with the compilation of a catalogue raisonné in collaboration with art historian Lisa Steib. The TFA was also behind the initiative for the major retrospective *Terry Fox – Elemental Gestures* (curators: Arnold Dreyblatt and Angela Lammert), which traveled to Berlin, Mons, Wuppertal, and Bern. In the autumn of 2015, the TFA organized the symposium *Terry Fox – Situations* at the Berlin Academy of Arts under the direction of Michael Glasmeier (concept) and Carsten Seiffarth (coordination).

Here I would like to specially thank Michael Glasmeier, founding member of the TFA. By focusing attention in his texts on the beauty of the incidental in the art of Terry Fox, on the freedom of the ephemeral and the subtle force of humor, he enriches thought about Terry Fox in his inimitable poetic way.

When quietness wants to prevail over loudness, special energies are required: I thank all the contributing authors for the success of the book at hand. My thanks to all sponsors and to the Kunstmuseum Bern, especially Birgit Achatz, Director of Sponsoring, for its comprehensive cooperation. A heartfelt thanks goes to Frieder Butzmann and Katja Teubner for the technical preservation and editing of sound documents. I thank Prill Vieceli Cremers for the design and Spector Books in Leipzig for supervising the publication.

My very special thanks goes to the volunteer production team: Michael Glasmeier for creative and editorial direction, Carsten Seiffarth for judicious management of the production, Valerian Maly for coordination with Bern, and Ingrid Beirer for careful editing and pragmatic supervision of all areas of the project. I thank Ron Meyers for advice and assistance with countless questions as to what went into the creation of individual works, including the extensive network of relationships to literary sources the artist used.

Here, now and forever, I thank Terry Fox for the fantastic gift he left us with his body of work.

Marita Loosen-Fox
Terry Fox Association e. V., Cologne

Translated from the German
by Andrea Lerner

THE EYE IS NOT THE ONLY GLASS THAT BURNS THE MIND:

A Title as Conceptual Space. In Lieu of a Preface

"One of the beauties of language is that, when it fails, its effectiveness becomes apparent, and it is capable of, while falling silent, intimating that it is there."

Robert Walser

When, in 1987, Terry Fox was invited to make a performance in the scope of the exhibition *Die Gleichzeitigkeit des Anderen* (The Simultaneity of the Other) at the Kunstmuseum Bern, it was perhaps the first time he had used the title *The Eye's Not The Only Glass That Burns the Mind.*[1] It is a title that, in its already manifesto-like beauty, poses certain riddles and, in its demonstrative length, appears to convey a poetic truth. Not only do we no longer know what happened in this performance,[2] but its title offers no further illumination on the matter.

Fox was never an artist of "Untitled" artwork.[3] Many of his works originated from and through language and can be described as poetically engaged situations. So the title of a work as a further level of reflection was absolutely vital to him, and it pays to take it more than seriously as part of the work itself. Indeed, since *The Eye's Not The Only Glass That Burns the Mind* is found in at least five other different works and contexts, yet without any hint as to its genesis, we have decided to follow the tracks of the title itself in works by Fox that are associated with this sentence. After the artist's passing, we started our quest in Los Angeles with Ron Meyers, who had been Fox's assistant for many years. In endless Internet searches, he was able to verify that this very clear but also very hermetic sentence originated from the epilogue to the second edition (!) of the poem *The Conflagration of London*, by a certain Simon Ford, which had initially been published anonymously in 1667 on the theme of the Great Fire of London from the year before.[4] For a researcher on a quest, that is a riddle wrapped in a mystery! Simon Ford, born around 1619 and died in Old Swinford in 1699, was a priest, theologian, politician, and author of countless sermons, but he also was famous for publishing long poems in English and

1 Cited here is the stylization given in the list of events from the accompanying exhibition catalogue

2 See the contribution "The Museum as a Resonating Chamber" by Michael Glasmeier in the volume at hand.

3 On titles of artworks, see for instance Tobias Vogt, *Untitled: Zur Karriere unbetitelter Kunst in der jüngsten Moderne* (Munich, 2006); Wolfgang Kemp, "Der Titel in Kunst (und Musik), Abteilung Moderne und Gegenwart," *Merkur: Deutsche Zeitschrift für europäisches Denken* (December 2010), pp. 1212–15.

4 *The Conflagration of London*. Poetically Described, Both in Latin and English. The Second Edition, with large Additions (London, 1667).

Latin, though he is primarily known to posterity, at least in literary circles, for his *Three Poems relating to the late dreadful Destruction of the City of London by Fire* .... The literary scholar Robert Arnold Aubin characterizes Ford thus: "He was a hard-grained, hard-hitting controversialist, ...; for he was for a season a Puritan among Royalists. And then for another season a Royalist among Puritans. Eventually, a Royalist among Royalists he found his reward."[5] It would be Aubin himself who, in 1943, two years after "The Blitz" (as the attack on London by the German Luftwaffe was known), once again brought Ford to light with his book *London in Flames, London in Glory*, and then first reprinted the poem in the book's second edition. Perhaps Fox was familiar with this publication.

Even if Ford's poem falls short of the elegance of the catastrophe poetry of John Dryden (1631–1700),[6] his text with its drastic tone mirrors the prevailing apocalyptic mood, when four fifths of the City of London were destroyed by infernal fire and around 100,000 residents became homeless, after having barely just survived the Great Plague in the late summer of 1666. Ford's language has something rushed, quickened, sensational about it; he availed himself of various methods in order to make this fire not only vivid, but also experienceable with all the senses. To this end, he also employed the microstructures of typecase, abbreviations, italics, et cetera, giving the verse printed in the 1667 edition the following form: "Th' *eye's* not th' *onely Glass* that *burns the mind*."

With such eccentric typography, certainly fitting to the Baroque, Ford touches on the laments of Jeremiah regarding the destruction of Jerusalem (586 BC) that were set to music with such sensational compassion by, for example, Marc-Antoine Charpentier or François Couperin, for the nighttime celebrations of the Baroque Holy Week—yet here taking the form of the catastrophic fire as spectacle in exceedingly glaring colors, sounds, noises, and smells.[7] Indeed, the engraving on the title page of *Conflagration* cites Horace's famous line "ut pictura poesis" (as is painting, so is poetry), a phrase which, since the Renaissance, has frequently lent itself to varied interpretation, and which in *Conflagration*, especially in the epilogue, is read as a triumph of poetry over painting.[8] In the rivalry between the arts, the paragone, the superiority of poetry is demonstrated, and then theoretically substantiated in Ford's epilogue, wonderfully titled *The Author to the Graver.* Here, Ford apparently made it clear to whoever illustrated the frontispiece that the horror of the fire, the screams and the noise, must not be rendered pictorially as such, in contrast to the writer who can verbally, even acoustically, mobilize the imagination. Later, he brings the illustrator back into play so as to relieve him from this predicament, as a visual designer of emblems, those multifaceted text-image symbols that so significantly shaped the pictorial, literary, and musical rhetoric of the time.[9] So with "THE EYE IS NOT THE ONLY

5 Robert Arnold Aubin, "The Conflagration of London," in *London in Flames, London in Glory: Poems on the Fire and Rebuilding of London, 1666–1709*, ed. Robert Arnold Aubin (New Brunswick, 1943), pp. 3–6, esp. p. 3.

6 See John Dryden, *Annus mirabilis* (1667; repr., Oxford, 1927).

7 See Margery A. Kingsley, *Transforming the Word: Prophecy, Poetry, and Politics in England, 1650–1742* (Newark and London, 2001), pp. 100–105.

8 On this general issue, see, for example, Antonella Braida and Giuliana Pieri, eds., *Image and Word: Reflections of Art and Literature from the Middle Age to the Present* (Oxford, 2003).

9 See Arthur Henkel and Albrecht Schöne, *Emblemata: Handbuch zur Sinnbildkunst des XVI. und XVII. Jahrhunderts* (Stuttgart and Weimar, 1996).

GLASS THAT BURNS THE MIND," we are not just immersed in the catastrophe of London, but also in its reflexive engagement with poetic-aesthetic reflection that actually suggests to the visual artist that he draft a rather dull emblem featuring a burning phoenix, et cetera, instead of a realistic painting. The catastrophe itself is to be left to literature.

So ultimately this treatise deals with the adequate rendering of an unfathomable reality, of the horror, the fright, the apocalyptic nature of the events, and naturally also the sense of helplessness—an experience that affects all senses of the body, not just vision, but hearing, to a surprisingly large extent. In fact, the word "burn" is referencing both a physical and a mental burning on a poetically symbolic level of corporeality and human sensory experience. The glass, here, stands for the medium as such, for perception impacted by media, as archaically experienced during that era through windows, spectacles, mirrors, microscopes, and telescopes. There is something inserted like a "burning glass" that ignites the mind, inspiring it to reflect on and fuel reflection itself. The glass also refers to the visual arts, which gives us a special vantage point, a unique detail view, so that reality can even begin to be conceived and reach our minds. Yet its power does not suffice, especially not for "those that *cannot see*."[10] In one of his first works, *What Do Blind Men Dream?*, Fox made a pact with a blind accordion player on the streets of San Francisco in 1969.

Arising in Ford's "The Author to the Graver"—besides the paragone and the emblem, besides the idea of illustration and art—is a rather astonishing anticipation of what Dick Higgins called "intermedia" in 1965. However, Ford here still unites the arts under the all-encompassing panoply of literature, while for Higgins all the arts freely fluctuated and were applied depending on the situation.[11] The eye, whose powers are terribly overrated today, was actually never the only medium to mobilize our minds. It merely pretends this were so. Fox made this point with an oeuvre that is situated at the margins of the barely visible. And thus Fox, in 1989, employed the simplest of means to immerse the Bern museum in sound, produced live amid the emblems, the rhetoric of the visible throughout the ages. Meyers, as researcher, interprets glass in the title as follows:

"The EYE is not the only GLASS that BURNS the MIND— the eye is at least three different kinds of glass: a WINDOW; a LENS; and a MIRROR:
1. a window ('the eye is the window onto the soul') through which, in 2 directions, the world is displayed to the soul/the mind, and the soul/the mind is revealed/unveiled to the world (making naked the soul to others).
2. a lens of the mind/soul which focuses sharply, clearly on objects and desires out in the world, and which (like a magnifying-glass, or a 'burning'-glass) brings these objects and desires (or objects of desire) back, in sharp focus, to the mind/soul where they are burned/etched into the mind/the memory, where they arouse/inFLAME the passions and emotions of the mind (Simon Ford speaks of 'the needy, the greedy eye').
3. a mirror which can reflect the world

10 See, among others, Peter Bexte, *Blinde Seher: Die Wahrnehmung von Wahrnehmung in der Kunst des 17. Jahrhunderts* (Amsterdam and Dresden, 1999).

11 See Dick Higgins, "Statement on Intermedia," http://www.artpool.hu/Fluxus/Higgins/intermedia2.html.

back to the world and maybe, from within, it reflects the image of the soul, the mind itself back to itself. I think, in this last case, this may be when the mind/soul remains hidden from others and even hidden from itself. It is a kind of DE-flection, a kind of clouding, a masking. And Terry had a passionate, long-time interest in all 3 materials: most especially Magnifying-Glasses and Mirrors."[12]

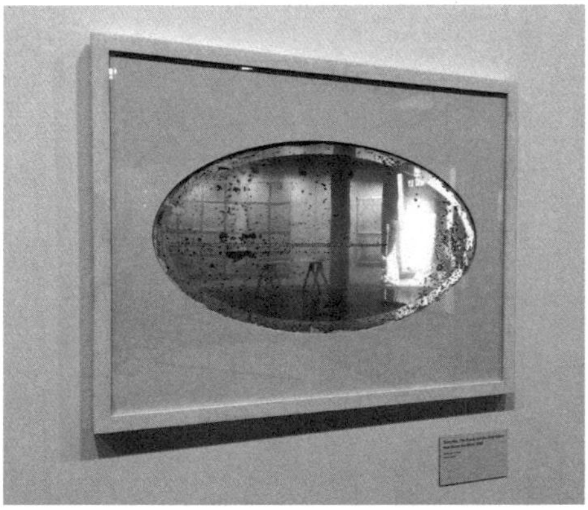

1 Terry Fox, *THE EYE IS NOT THE ONLY GLASS THAT BURNS THE MIND,* 1989, exhibition view Akademie der Künste Berlin, 2015, mirror, ink on paper, 38.5 x 59 cm, private collection, photo: Marita Loosen-Fox

As researchers, we discover a materialization, as it were, of such glass and mirror ideas and symbols during the year of the Bern performance in the wall object *THE EYE IS NOT THE ONLY GLASS THAT BURNS THE MIND* (fig. 1). The verse, like a discontinued horizontal line, gives rise to the title, not least because it appears in combination with an oval mirror, a rather blind one in this case. It projects—in writing along a strip—into the mirrored space, lending structure to the space in a minimal way.[13] Looking in the mirror, we find ourselves and the site confronted with the written line, which now seems like a sculpture, like a drawing in the realm of the mirrored.[14] A silent line that at the same time speaks, an imaginary sculpture that burns as language and once again indicates how precisely and cleverly Fox moved language out of the book and staged it as puzzle, rebus, metaphor, poetry, wit, and politics, especially in his later work. His teachers, were French poets like Arthur Rimbaud, Paul Verlaine, Stéphane Mallarmé, Antonin Artaud, Guillaume Apollinaire, Raymond Roussel, and Alfred Jarry—many experimental poets who, like Mr. Ford of the Baroque era, played with writing and poetry in an imaging and imagining way, navigating between speech and silence. The objective was to break through the alphabet phalanx aligned to visuality, as Hrabanus Maurus had already done with his *LIBER DE LAUDIBUS SANCTAE CRUCIS* from the second half of the eleventh century. Fox was in possession of a facsimile of this document, which is considered to be a first pinnacle of figural poetry since ancient times (fig. 2). Dick Higgins again comes into play here: he collected such figural poems under the fitting name "pattern poetry,"[15] a method of multiple layers, interlinkage, but also isolation of the literal, which was in turn picked up again by Fox in his written works.

Writing begs to become space. In 1990, Fox spelled out the verse in his German translation "DAS AUGE IST NICHT ALLEIN DAS EINZIGE GLAS DAS DEN GEIST

12 In an email to Marita Loosen-Fox in May 2016.

13 In a second edition, held in a private collection in the United States, the verse has been engraved directly into the glass.

14 On the art and cultural history of the mirror in general, see also Jurgis Baltrušaitis, *Der Spiegel: Entdeckungen, Täuschungen, Phantasien* (Gießen, 1986).

15 See Dick Higgins, *Pattern Poetry: Guide to an Unknown Literature* (New York, 1987). This book was also in Fox's possession.

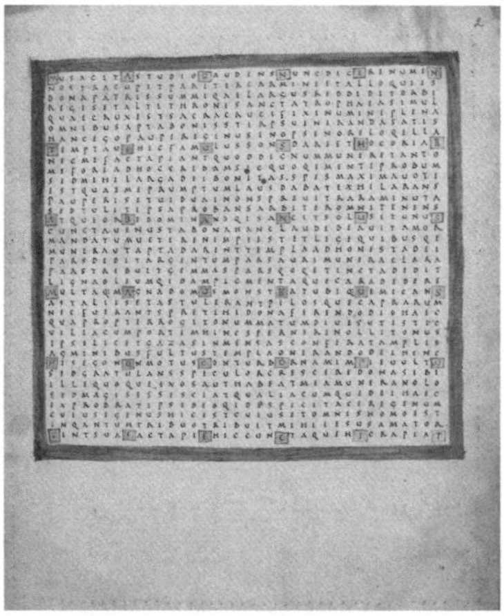

2 Hrabanus Maurus, *LIBER DE LAUDIBUS SANCTAE CRUCIS*, facsimile *CODEX VINDOBONENSIS 652*, Austrian National Library (Vienna and Graz, 1972), n.p.

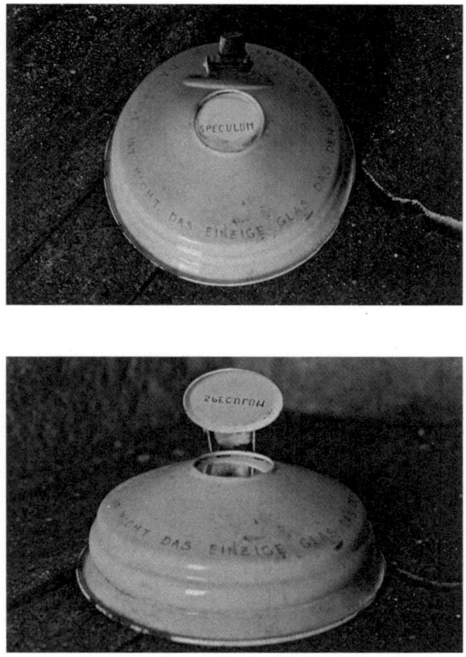

3 Terry Fox, *Locus Harmonium*, 1990, Furk'art, detail of an environment at the generator shed near Hotel Furkablick, photo: Marita Loosen-Fox, 1993

BRENNT" onto an agrarian object in his *Locus Harmonium*, inside a generator shed at Hotel Furkablick where the artist carefully applied poetry and small interventions (fig. 3).[16] An enameled funnel lid, marked with the now hardly readable sentence, had a clasp on which Fox wrote the word "SPECULUM" back to front, which was then readable in the mirror applied to the funnel opening. Speculum, here, tautologically refers to the mirror, but also to the medical implement. Fox was magically expanding the presence of a curious object by adding writing, yet without clarifying anything. Resonance arises between object and writing, leading in utmost purity to the poetry in which, according to our source Jean Paulhan (1884–1968), "all doctrine and rationale fail with nice regularity."[17] For Paulhan, poetry is distinguished by "indifference," which, however, shifts into the power of imagination. The aforementioned French classicists knew this, of course, and it ultimately lends impetus to that endless interpretation, the emphatic force of which Michel Foucault spoke. The act of interpretation links thought with empathy. Tellingly, in Bern it was Adolf Wölfli and Robert Walser who, each in their own way, confronted pictorial space through language: Wölfli with drawn writing and written drawing,[18] and Walser with an open, digressive treatment of the boundary between hearing and silence. Walser wrote: "I find it wonderful when, in a game, if a sound is barely audible, one therefore wishes all the more to hear it, listening with heightened eagerness. Similar

16 On this, see also the text by Max Wechsler in the volume at hand.

17 Jean Paulhan, *Schlüssel der Poesie und Kleines Vorwort zu jeder Kritik*, trans. Friedhelm Kemp (Cologne, 1994), p. 31.

18 On Wölfli, see the contribition by Konrad Tobler in the volume at hand.

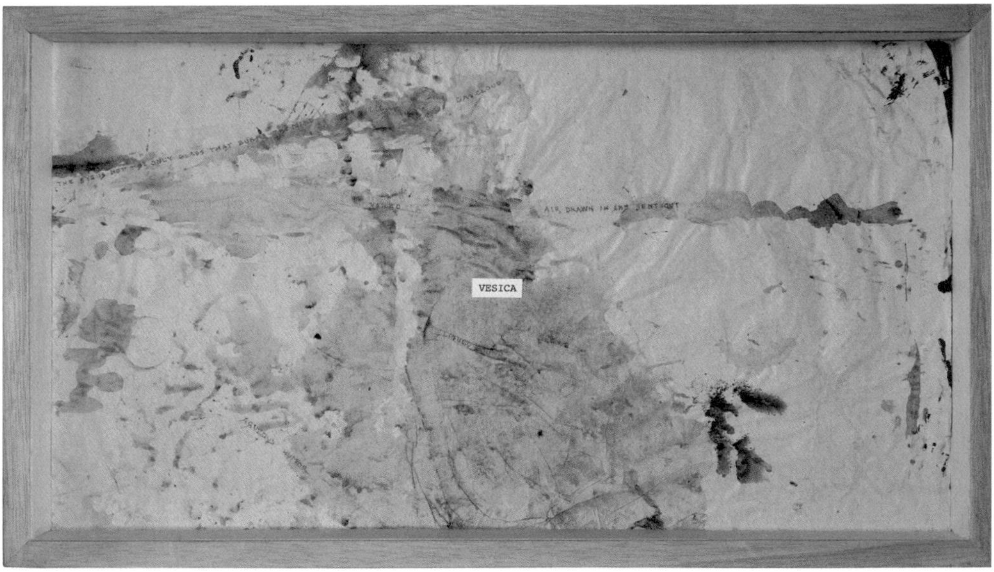

4 Terry Fox, *VESICA*, 1997, mixed media on paper, 37.7 x 70.7 cm, Kunstmuseum Bern

to the case of a musical presentation, it is the Good in life, when it is lost or when it has almost been lost, that becomes so precious."[19]

Then we rediscover, almost incidentally, our verse "THE EYE IS NOT THE ONLY GLASS THAT BURNS THE MIND" in a picture. It is positioned at the upper left of *VESICA* from 1997, gently fading as part of a "bubble" that has spilled its contents across a pictorial surface, characterized by folds and informal blackish color gradients, against which the centered capital letters of the title stand out (fig. 4). And finally, it reappears in combination with other sentences on the reverse side of a bricklayer's trowel (fig. 5). It is written along the handle in vertical black letters, in the form of pattern poetry, and intersects and connects with other sentences written horizontally in red, giving rise to a textual composition aligned to the simple geometric construction of the trowel. The other text reads:

THE EYE THAT SEES BUT
CANNOT SEE ITSELF
THE KNIFE THAT CUTS BUT
CANNOT CUT ITSELF
THE MOIST TOOTH OF THE
FLUID

With such paradoxes, which Fox really loved, and which cannot be explained using even the most advanced methods,[20] we are again inhabiting the realm of indifference, with our verse now rather becoming pictorial. The old wood of the trowel designed for the craftsmanship of smoothing and beautifying now appears verbally roughened by the mystery of a language that sets traps for thought. In the seventeenth-century, the eye in science and art was elevated to a medium

19 Robert Walser, "Ich wohnte einem Konzert bei," in *Das Beste, was ich über Musik zu sagen weiß*, ed. Roman Brotbeck and Reto Sorg (Berlin, 2012), pp. 132–35, esp. p. 134.

20 On paradox, see especially Patrick Hughes and George Brecht, *Die Scheinwelt des Paradoxes: Eine kommentierte Anthologie in Wort und Bild* (Braunschweig, 1978).

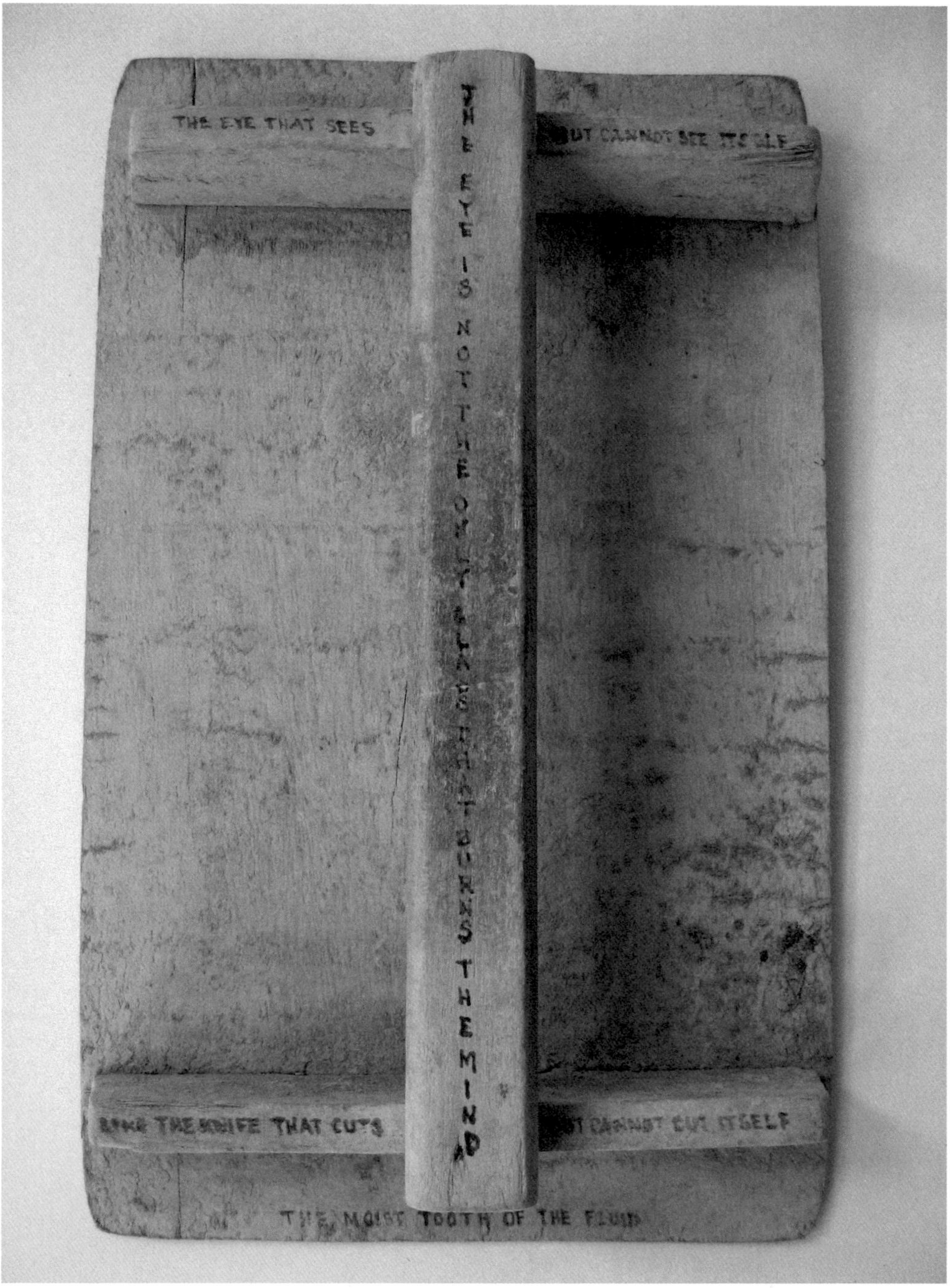

5 Terry Fox, (*Untitled*), ca. 1983, wall sculpture with text, wood, pigment felt-tip pen, 35 x 21 x 7 cm, Estate of Terry Fox, Cologne

of reflection on reflection.[21] The artist can dispel such "mirroring" when he reveals the corporeality, the material, the senses, the politics inherent to their original nature, when he celebrates the dominance of vision in favor of perception by means of subversive resonance. It was impossible for Ford to know that artists like Fox would later be creating reality instead of rendering it, and that this very Terry Fox, who was also a musician, writer, filmmaker, photographer, draftsman, scientist, philosopher, and theorist, would arrive and—with meager means and a delicate feel for sound waves of all kinds—cheerfully and politically associate vision with a culture of the time as a subversive establishment of resonant situations; indeed, it is true: "Th' *eye's* not th' *onelyGlass* that *burns the mind*." And like in a concluding demonstration, as if he wanted to affirm his very being, this sentence is "mirrored" in the last artwork by Fox, the seven-minute video *Window Tapping*, which the artist recorded with Marita Loosen-Fox (at the camera) in his studio/apartment in Cologne (fig. 6). We see the fingertips of his right hand tapping on the windowpane. A shadowy view of the back courtyard, the glass as a joining separator. The tapping is neither casual nor nervous. It is a conscious act and thus powerful, decisive. But here Fox denies the regular pattern that might easily emerge, for the comforting acquiescence of rhythm is to be avoided.

Michael Glasmeier
Ron Meyers
Carsten Seiffarth

Translated from the German
by Dawn Michelle d'Atri

21 On this, see also Michel Foucault, *The Order of Things: An Archaeology of the Human Sciences* (1970; repr., New York, 2013).

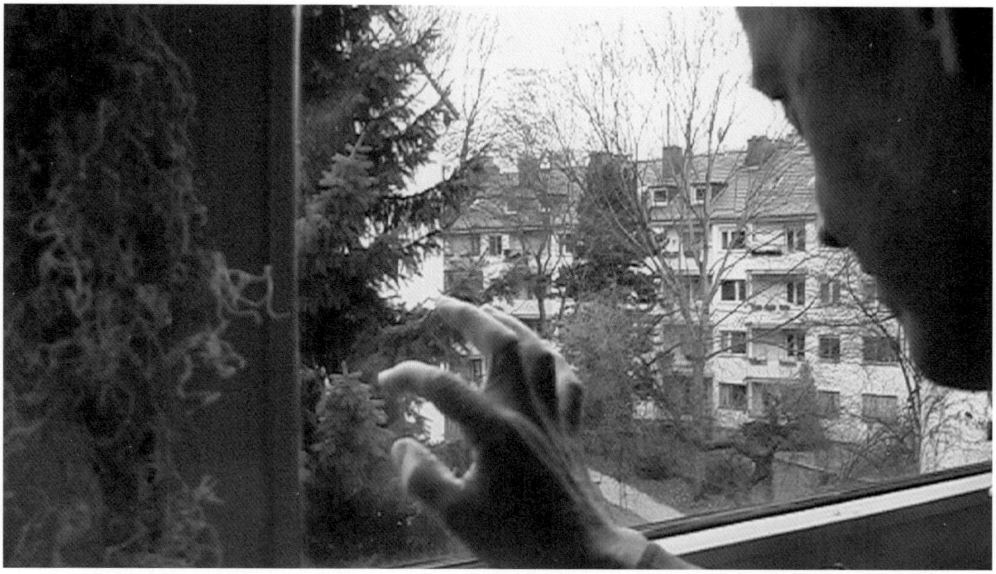

6 Terry Fox and Marita Loosen-Fox, *Window Tapping*, 2008, video, 7 min., video still, Estate of Terry Fox, Cologne

Simon Ford
The Conflagration of London.
(Epilogue):
"The Author to the Graver,"
London, 1667. (Reprint)

Conflagratio Londinensis Poetice Depicta.

THE Conflagration OF LONDON: POETICALLY DESCRIBED,

Both in

LATIN and *ENGLISH.*

Ut Pictura, Poesis. Horat. Art. Poet.

The Second Edition, with large Additions.

LONDON,
Printed for *Sa: Gellibrand*, 1667.

The AUTHOR *to the* GRAVER.

Upon occasion of a Draught *expressing* London in Flames, *designed to have been* prefixed *as a* Frontispice *to the* Poem; *but* forborn *upon* second thoughts.

Hold Graver, *hold*! In vain thou dost engage
To crowd the *Book* into the *Title-page.*
Thy *Plate* too much beneath thy *Project* falls.
For, though it shew us *Flames*, and *tottering Walls*,
If that be *all*, thy *Title* thou'lt *bely*:
None takes the *Scene* to be the *Tragedy.*
No; *Londons Flames* should so be set to *view*,
That those who *see*, in part may *feel*'em too;
And even those that *cannot see*, may find
Th' *eye*'s not th' *onely Glass* that *burns the mind.*
Say then; canst thou *express* the *shriekes* and *cryes*,
That *rent* the *Clouds*, and *pierc'd* the melting *Skies*?
Can thy *Descriptions* accent *Babels Voyces*,
Or give due *Ecchoes* to *confused Noyses*?
Canst thou express the *bawlings* of a *Croud*,
Wherein *none's heard*, 'cause *every one* is *loud*?
Or the *Extortions*, *Thefts*, and *cozening feats*
Of *Porters*, *Carters*, *Water-men*, and *Cheats*?
Canst thou describe the *sounds* of *tuneless Bells*,
Whose *awkward Musick* tolls their *Steeples Knells*?
The *cracks* of *tumbling Houses*, and the *greeting*
Of *tottering Roofs*, and *battering Cannons* meeting?
Canst thou to view present the *hissing steams*
Of *melted Metals* check'd with *cooling streams*?
Or draw the *medley* of *compounded smells*,
Forc'd, some from *fragrant*, some from *nasty Cells*?

Canst

Canst reach the *Horrors* of *distracted minds*,
Where *ghastly fear* with *woful grief* combines?
Grief, which *expression* from *amazement* borrows,
Whiles *Tears* are *stifled* by *profounder sorrows*.
Or th' *Hurrey* which *distemper'd Fancies* fills,
Where *Thought* stabs *Thought*, and *Project*, *Project* kills?
Where *what* to *save*, 's in *doubt*, till *all* be *lost*,
And *slow Resolves* by *speedy Fates* are crost?
Canst draw the *Misers Passions*, while he *lags*
In *midst* of *Flames*, hugging his *darling Bags*;
Whom, *loath to lose*, and *loath to give*, divide,
Neer *sacrific'd* to what he *deifi'd*?
Or a *just Love* 'twixt *equal Children* parted,
Where *one* must be *preferr'd*, th' *other deserted*?
Or, whiles both *Goods* and *Childrens danger* scares,
The *Mothers bowels*, and the *Fathers cares*?
Or *labouring throws*, and *Births precipitate*,
Where the *Fright's Midwife*, and the *Nurse* is *Fate*?
If *none* of these within thy *Picture* come,
Confess it *short*, and give the *Poet* room.
Poetry is an *Intellectual Mint*,
That stamps a *Picture* with a *spirit* in't;
Whose *secret Magick* Senses want supplyes,
And makes *Spectators* where it finds no *Eyes*.
Thus that *old Bard* doth in his *Iliad* draw
Battels to th' *life*, 'tis said, he *never saw*:
And makes those *Hector* and *Achilles* see,
Whose *outward Organs* are as *blind* as *He*.
'Tis *sacred Flame*, whose *subtil Influence*
Can *melt* the *Soul*, and never *scorch* the *Sense*.

'Tis

'Tis the *Minds Microscope*, that helps the *Eye*
To the *least insect-thought's Anatomy*:
That *secret'st motions* through their *symptomes* traces;
And renders *Souls* as visible as *Faces*.
This, this. can *Londons Fate* most lively shew,
That paints its *inside-Flames*, and *outside*, too.
And such an *Artist*, *London*, wish I thee;
And *next*, would *wishing* do't, *That I were He*.
Which, *Graver*, though *I'm not*, *my Draught* of *thine*
Hath th' *odds*, which *better Poems* have of *mine*.
Barr *Emulation* then, and try thy *Art*;
The *Poets Zany* is the *Graver's part*.
Thy *Preface-Lines*, I grant, may *somewhat* do
To stead the *Stationer*, and *Poem* too.
For oft the *Book*'s turn'd for the *Baby-Letter*,
And *sorry Cuts* helps *Ballads* off the better.
In *Legends* too, some say, (nor is't *deny'd*)
Some are by th' *painted Saints* best *edify'd*:
For *Lyes* in *Picture*, with their *Art delight*,
Which, told for *Truth*, the Hearers *Faith affright*.
Yea, perhaps, thou may'st *wiser Readers* draw,
To *greet* a *Muse*, till now, they *never saw*.
For 'tis the *Bush*, that leads us to the *Wine*;
And men know where the *Sight* is, by the *Sign*.
On therefore, but with my *advice* comply,
And thus thy *Scene* fit to the *Tragedy*.
Conceit *Troy*'s Flames, and those that *Nero* made,
To *symbolize* with the *sad Tune* he play'd:
Or those he caus'd, whose * *Name* did *Burning* bear,
When *Jove* and *Rome* to *Geese* obliged were.

* *Brennus*

With

With thoſe that laid *Jeruſalem* in *duſt*:
And thoſe of *Foreign Vulcans*, tan'e on *Truſt*
From *Travellers*; t' *impregnate* thy *Deſign*,
And make *thy Fancy* more *reſemble mine*.
Then from ſome *ghoſtly Father* get a *Spell*,
To view the *Cave*, they ſay, *joyns* next to *Hell*:
From that *Original* thy *Fancy* fill,
(For that's *pure Fancy*) and then *try* thy *skill*.
Or, laſtly, *antedate* the *general Fire*
In *thought*, and thy *Invention* thence *inſpire*.
Thus *arm'd*, take *Londons ſituation* right,
And *ſpread* a *Mantle* o're't of *blackeſt Night*.
Take *Lights* and *Shades* from *its Blaze*: Lookers on
Were ſatisfi'd, it might *ſupply* the *Sun*.
Next, place in*ſtead* of th' *often-changing Dame*,
A *black Cloud*, big with *ſheets* of *Oyly Flame*;
Ruffled by *Eurus*, puffing out o'th' *Eaſt*
Ætnean Vapours from's *incenſed Breaſt*.
Let them *drop melted Starres*, toſs'd up and down
To *ſcatter ruines* through the *ſcared Town*.
Out of the *Skies*, (to ſhew from *whence* it came)
Stretch out an *Hand* arm'd with a *Rod of Flame*.
Bound with a *Scrowle*, which let this *Motto* fill,
England amend, his hand is ſtretcht out ſtill.
Let *Flames*, on *march*, a *mile* in *front* appear,
Brought up with *Ruines ſmothering* in the *Rear*:
I'th' *Van*, expreſs me *Pauls*, as yet *entire*,
But let its *Roof run* from th' *approaching Fire*.
Some *dwellings charg'd* by *ſcouting Heats*, let *ſmoak*;
And *others*, ſtand *forlorn* t' expect the *ſhock*.

On

On top of *some*, thick *Crowds* with *Buckets* arm
For *Charge*; but *flying* at the *first Alarm.*
Let *ruining Hooks* others exposed *shake*;
And *gaping Chasmes* let *Warlike Engines* make.
Express me *Roofs blown up* into the *Aire*;
And *Flames* they *flye beneath* let *meet* 'em *there.*
Next, draw a *reeking Thames*, and *Barges flying*
With *singed Sayles*, and *stifled Fishes* dying.
This done, a *Jesuit* place in *view* o'th' *whole*,
At *Faux's bo-peep* in some *sneaking hole*,
Laughing in's *sleeve*: and let this be the *Mot*,
Ha! this bits better then the Powder-plot.
Then on the *top* of *Pauls* let be *exprest*,
A *melting Phœnix* in a *flaming Nest.*
Hope will *expound* the *Emblem*; though I *fear*
Few hope, 'twill *soon* be *verified there.*
Lastly, If any *nook* remain *unfill'd*,
(He's loath an *whole Page* for his *Face* be *spill'd*)
The *Poet* in a *Cypress-wreath* insert;
(The *Lawrel* is a badg of a *Desert*,
Which he *pretends not to*: besides, he *wears*
An *heart* more suiting to an *Age of Tears*:)
Pale, like the *City's Ashes*, make his *Looks*,
(Too many *wear* its *Fires*:) by, let his *Books*
(*Jeremy's Threnes*, *Salvian*, *Gildas*, and
The *Tristia* of the *banish'd Poet*) stand:
Let his *Eyes drop* into his *Ink*, and thence
Supply his *Quill*, and *mingle* with his *sense.*
But ne're ask, *Who He is*: Find *any He*
That's *such an one*, and let him *stand for Me.*

FINIS.

THe *Latin* Poem which in this is rendred in *English* with the other Poems of the same Author, relating to the *Firing* and *Ruines* of *London*, are to be Sold by *Sa. Gellibrand* at the Ball in St. P*auls*-Church-yard.

Terry Fox, Switzerland …

Contributions to the symposium *The Eye's Not The Only Glass That Burns The Mind* by the Terry Fox Association e. V., Cologne, on occasion of the exhibition *Terry Fox: Elemental Gestures*, Kunstmuseum Bern, May 5–6, 2017

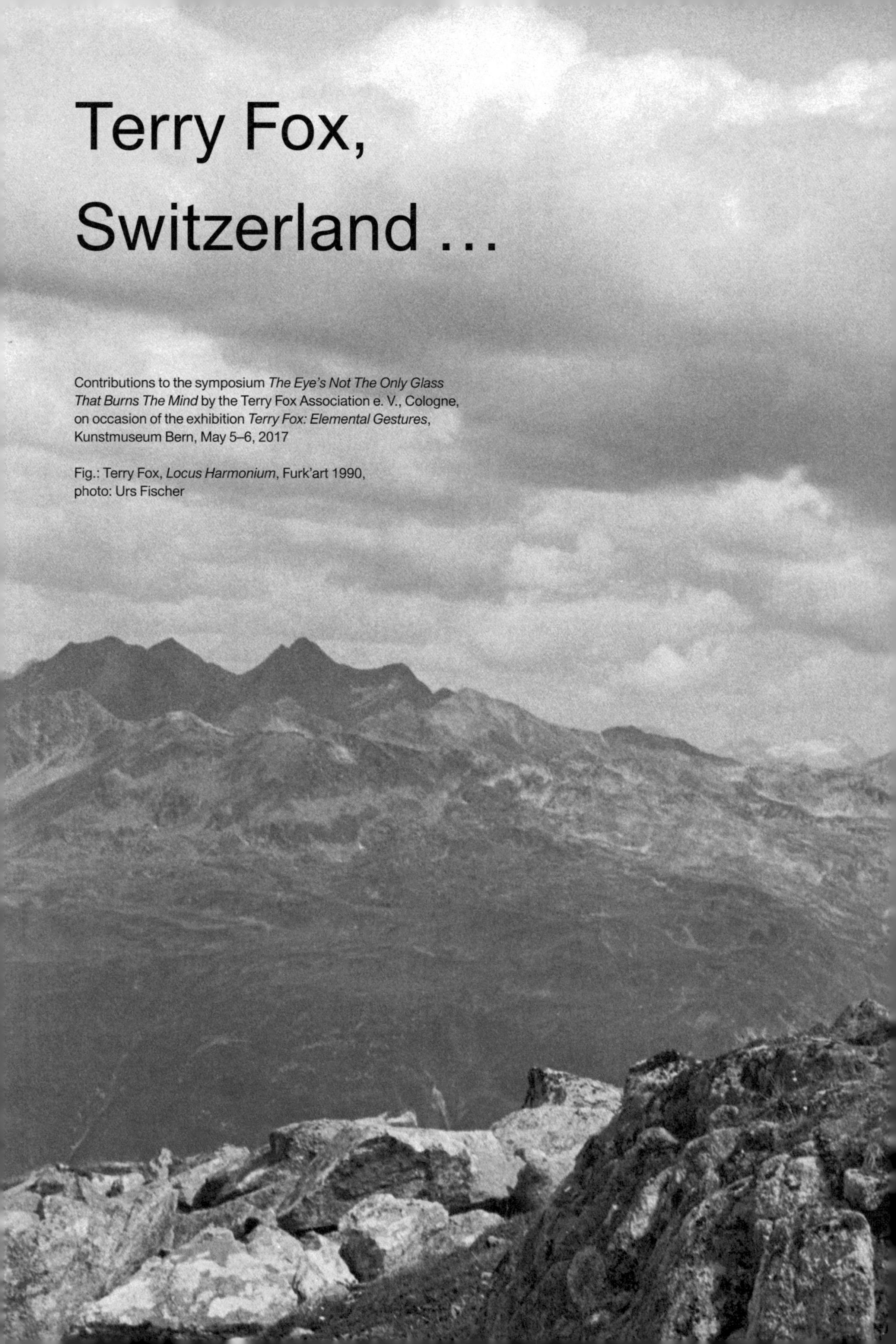

Fig.: Terry Fox, *Locus Harmonium*, Furk'art 1990, photo: Urs Fischer

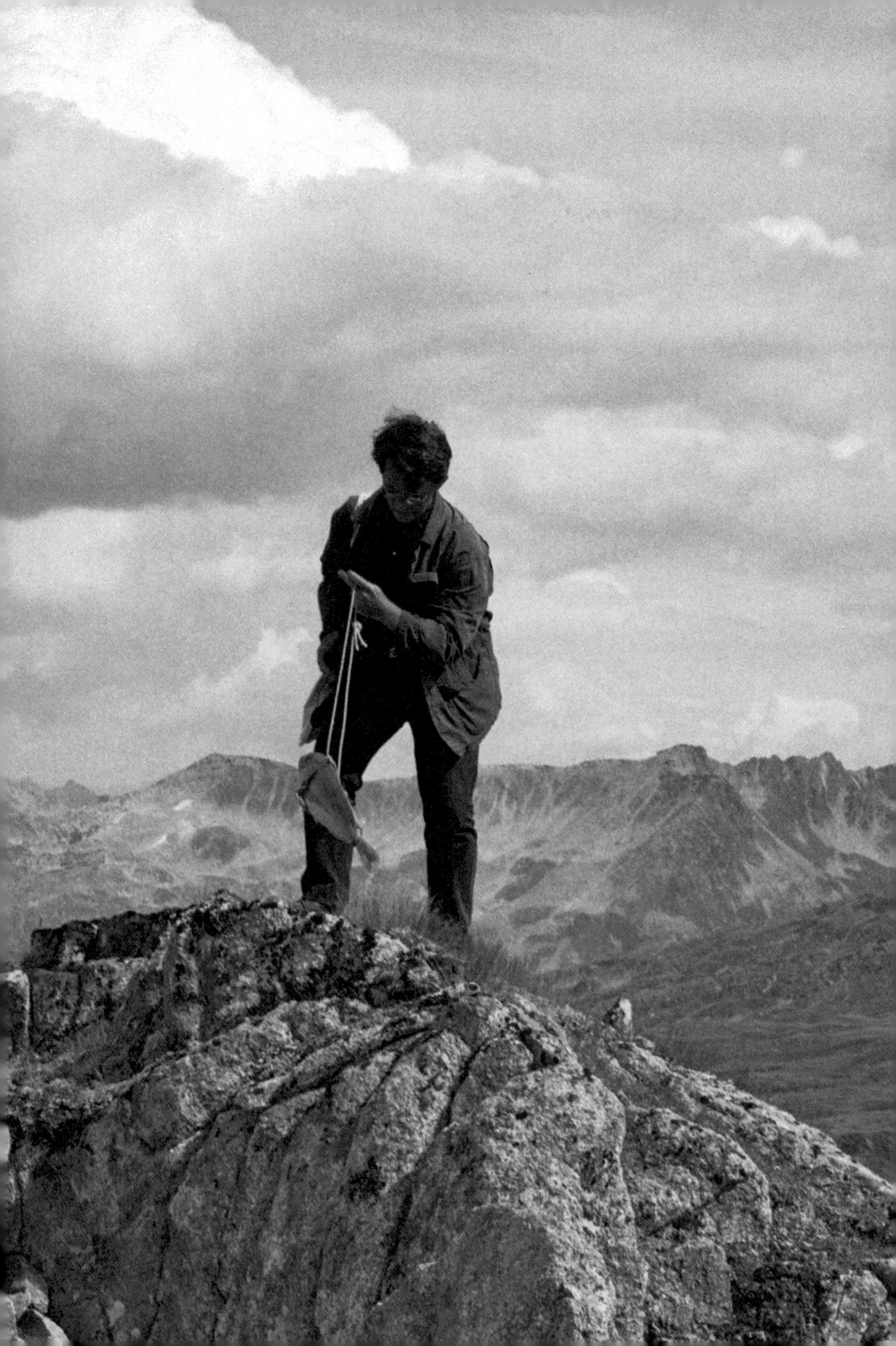

Michael Glasmeier

The Museum as a Resonating Chamber: Terry Fox and the Piano Wire

And I am merely a shadow hunched
Above the arrowy, still strings,
The maker of a thing yet to be made; . . .

Wallace Stevens

Terry Fox is the artist of the situation, of *materiale povero* and the chronotopic link between an action and the given, a quality which finds confirmation, for example, in his experiments with wires removed from pianos. By concentrating on two of his appearances in the Kunsthalle Bern, I would like to explore his use of piano wires, for Fox did not just stretch them across rooms at these events. For him they were fundamental as sculptural material and instrument at many other public events, in sound recordings, and in basic statements made by the artist from 1976 through the late nineteen-eighties. Yet to date they have rarely been the focus of consideration.

The number of documents relating to his appearances in Bern are, however, rather small.[1] The artist himself did not say much about these works, and neither reviews, photos, nor written observations exist. Since we know little, we have to speculate, in itself a lovely exercise in art history, with the incomplete and clandestine objective of securing ideas through a combination of imagination and evidence. So to start with, I would like to take a look at *A Candle for A.W.* from 1980. The initials A.W. stand for Adolf Wölfli, whose work Fox got to know when he took part in documenta 5 (curated by Szeemann) in 1972. Fox was fascinated by what he saw and became friends with Elka Spoerri, who from 1975 onward was head of the Adolf Wölfli Foundation at the Kunstmuseum Bern. Through Spoerri, Fox was able to access the archive and examine the originals.[2] Wölfli was not just a composer who wrote notes and preferred a six-line staff. With his paper trumpet—an instrument as economical as a piano wire—he was also a practicing musician (figs. 1, 2). His early drawings in particular include, as part of their elaborate geometrical ornamentation, a number of almost blank notebooks that he filled with empty staves. Taken very broadly, they symbolize music and/or sound. In 1964, Wölfli researcher Theodor Spoerri stated that he saw them as the strings of instruments.[3]

1 For more on Fox's relationship to Bern, see the following work that was also fundamental in writing this essay: Kathleen Bühler, "Performative Traces: Terry Fox in Bern," in *Elemental Gestures*, pp. 127–35.

2 For more on the relationship Fox–Wölfli, see Konrad Tobler's essay in this publication.

3 For more on Wölfli's music and this citation, see Peter Streiff and Kjell Keller, "Adolf Wölfli als Musiker," in

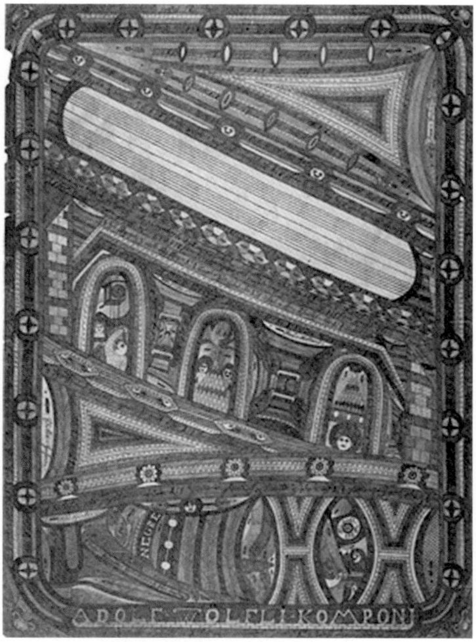

1 Adolf Wölfli (1864–1930), Negre, 1904, pencil on newsprint, 99.5 x 74.5 cm, A 9204, Adolf Wölfli-Stiftung, Kunstmuseum Bern

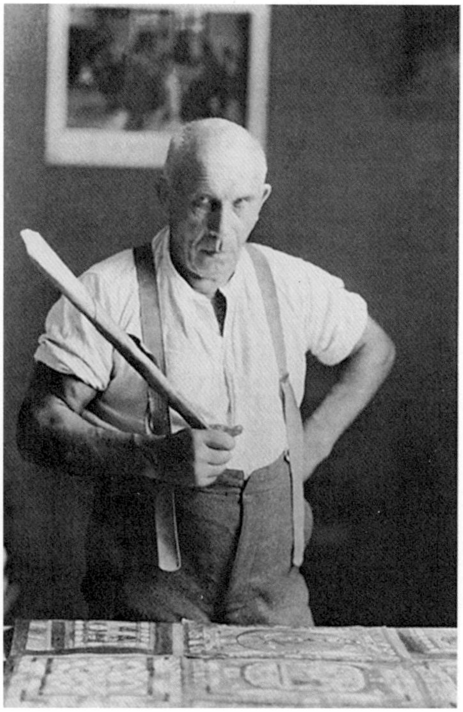

2 Adolf Wölfli with the paper trumpet, ca. 1925, Adolf Wölfli-Stiftung, Kunstmuseum Bern

We do not know for sure which room of the Kunstmuseum Bern was used for Fox's presentation or, more specifically, how the piano wire was installed there. Nor do we know exactly what his intentions were in utilizing a candle, but we can presume that in *A Candle for A.W.* it served as a (burning) measurement of time, as was also the case, for example, with *Halation* in San Francisco (1974). Ultimately, it may be assumed: Fox used a candle, because otherwise he could have continued the situation he had created indefinitely, and, occasionally at least, he wanted to set himself a time limit.[4] Of course, a candle is also a way of honoring a person's memory. In addition, some of those who witnessed the event recall Fox working with a pendulum in this piece, not unlike he did in *Circulation* (1977), where a lead ball was suspended on a piano wire hanging from the ceiling. The ball swung around a glass of water until the heavy object repeatedly brushed gently against the fragile one and they sounded resonantly (fig. 3).[5] Nevertheless, such memories contradict a short remark made by Fox as well as the sound recording of this public presentation on *LINKAGE*,[6] the LP released as an exhibi-

Adolf Wölfli, exh. cat. Kunstmuseum Bern (Basel, 1976), pp. 81–89. The reference to Spoerri can be found in note 3 of that text.

4 For more on the experience of unlimited time, see Michael Glasmeier, "Kurzfristige Anwesenheit: Terry Fox in Bremen und Worpswede," in Michael Glasmeier, *Geräusche, Ritornelle für eine Kunstgeschichte des Klangs: Von Fra Angelico und Claudio Monteverdi zu Marcel Duchamp und Terry Fox*, ed. Tania Prill and Andrea Sick (Hamburg, 2016), pp. 23–26.

5 See Konrad Tobler's essay in this publication.

6 Including audio, text, and photo documents, *LINKAGE* takes an almost didactic look at a variety of Fox's sound works and the different possibilities of working with piano wires: a longer recording from the attic of the Künstlerhaus Bethanien in Berlin from 1981, when the artist was a DAAD artist-in-residence; on the other side of the LP, five additional examples of his art that are linked and blend into one another; the second piece originated in Bern. *Terry Fox. LINKAGE.* (Acoustic Wire Sounds),

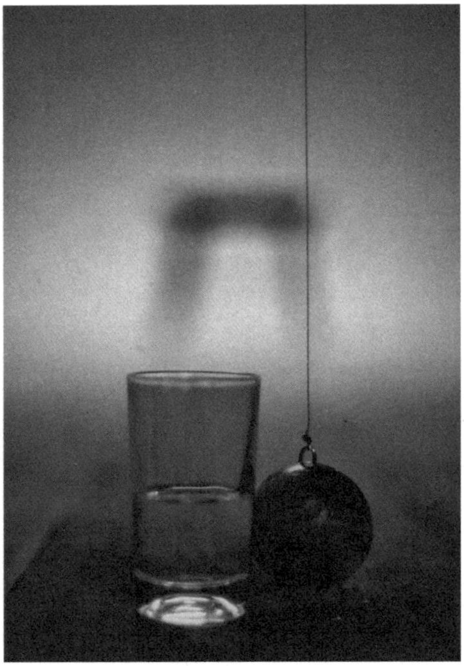

3 Terry Fox, *Circulation,* 1976, exhibition view Artist Gallery Site, 1977, photo: Alan Scarritt

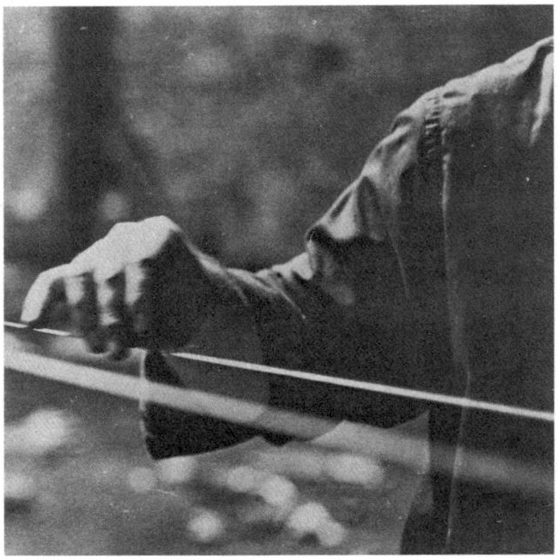

4 Terry Fox, *LINKAGE*, exhibition catalogue and LP, Kunstmuseum Luzern, 1982, cover

tion catalogue by the Kunstmuseum Luzern in 1982. In the informative booklet accompanying it, the artist speaks of the technique he employed, of "the sound of the rosined wire stroked with the bare fingers,"[7] a photo of which was featured on the album's cover (fig. 4).[8] Alongside a few other applications—to which I will return later—Fox had developed this form of action to use with stretched piano wires. It consisted primarily of walking along an object and stroking it gently. Fox also reports that in doing so he was "... using the walls as natural resonators."[9]

But then a document from the preliminary stages of *A Candle for A.W.* was discovered in the archives of the Kunstmuseum Bern. Addressed to Paul Klee specialist Jürgen Glaesemer, then curator of the Paul Klee Foundation and the museum's graphic art collection, the letter revolved around Fox's ideas for Bern.[10] He speaks of sound (not music) and how he wants to use the existing space as a "resonator" for sets of very long piano wires, strung from wall to wall. No matter how he ultimately realized the work, two things about this letter are absolutely noteworthy. In favoring the term "sound," Fox decisively rejects the term "music"—at the time, John Cage was working to overcome this separation by giving all sounds and noises equal status as music. It may be assumed that Fox associated music with concerts and the music industry and, in contrast to Alvin Lucier or Fluxus, was not interested in them, not even as objects of parody. What continued to be essential for him was the sculptural aspect of his sound experiments and not playing, satirizing, enacting, or performing them, nor virtuosity in doing so. It was about the duration of the sculptural acoustic experience: "In other words the room itself

Installation und LP, exh. cat. Kunstmuseum Luzern (1982), n.p.

7 Terry Fox, "Notes for the Record," *LINKAGE*, n.p.

8 See "Notes for the Record" for more illustrations/photos on this topic.

9 Ibid.

10 Found in the archive of the Kunstmuseum Bern.

will become an instrument." He thus refines and expands an idea that Marcel Duchamp wrote about in the *Green Box* (1934), under the heading "Musical Sculpture": "Sounds lasting and leaving from different places and forming a sounding sculpture which lasts."[11] This aspect, which connects the invisible with the visible in the situation, is essential for Duchamp's entire oeuvre. And like Duchamp, Fox recognizes that the physical event fosters artistic insight and higher aesthetics.[12]

Fox then surprises us in his letter with the lovely concept of a "resonating chamber," a room that resonates with the listener. I like this idea very much as it gives the rather ethereal notion of a resonating space a location. The space becomes smaller, more concrete, is connected more strongly with the interior and its own uniqueness—making it cozier.[13] Consequently, the sculptural idea takes on a central position, and creates a closer and more intimate relationship between the work and the audience. As Fox stated in an interview in 1993:

"I'm interested in sculpture. For me the piano wire also is a sculpture. First and foremost it's a steel sculpture.
Sound is sculpture. . . . One guy asked me if I could define sculpture, but that's the wrong question. To define it is impossible. I mean who knows what it is, anyway? Even traditional sculpture; Sir Isaac Newton called Greek statues 'stone dolls.' But sculpture is . . . well, it manifestly occupies some space, or some time."[14] This broader concept of sculpture—one which had also fascinated Joseph Beuys, with whom Fox collaborated in 1970 — expands the more common definition of sculpture as a three-dimensional physical object created by an artist, to include the categories of action, time, and surrounding space. A sculpture intervenes in a space for a specific period and establishes itself as well as those perceiving it as a situation that, with the occurrence of sculptural sound, is provoked and defined by the production of resonance. Thus sound as sculpture means creating volumes through resonance in order to promote a situation for a specific duration; in short, to produce a "resonating chamber."

As such, piano wires do not sound (fig. 5). They have to be stretched and attached to a resonator—in this case the walls. Depending on the length, density, tension, and material of the wires, they generate specific sounds, rich in overtones. In a violin, for example, such a resonator, indispensable for amplifying and making tones audible, is that marvelous and often precious wooden body with f-holes. And it is what produces the distinctive sound of each individual instrument.[15] The hollow space formed by its wooden plates is called a sounding box. The recording from the Kunstmuseum Bern is the product of a similar spatial, technical, acoustic, dynamic combination and almost sounds electronic on *LINKAGE*, which is why Fox nearly always emphasized the fact that

11 *Marcel Duchamp*, ed. Anne d'Harnoncourt and Kynaston McShine (New York and Philadelphia, 1973), p. 45. For more on Duchamp and music, see, for example, "Marcel Duchamp und eine Kunstgeschichte des Geräuschs," in Glasmeier 2016 (see note 4), pp. 55–66.

12 For the visual aspects, see, for example, Lars Blunck, *Duchamps Präzisionsmaschinen* (Munich, 2008).

13 I have also used the following terms—"hyper-auditory chamber" and "sounding chamber"—to indicate the chronotopic intimacy of the audible, in Glasmeier 2016 (see note 4), pp. 153–68.

14 Terry Fox, "Exploring the Limits: Interview by René van Peer," in *Ocular Language*, pp. 157–83, esp. p. 183.

15 See, for example, *Die Physik der Musikinstrumente: Spektrum der Wissenschaft; Verständliche Forschung* (Heidelberg, 1988).

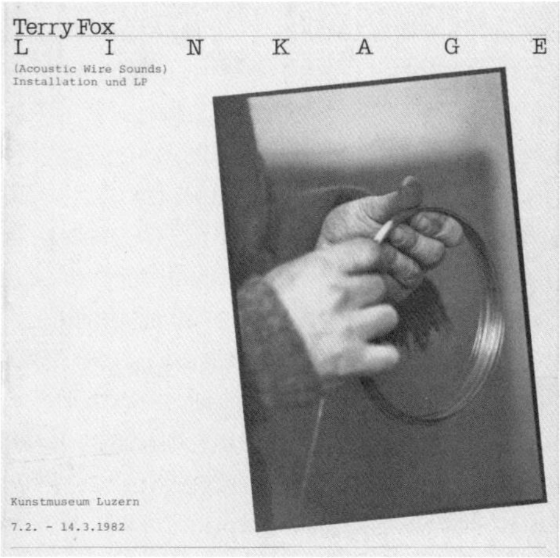

5 Terry Fox, *LINKAGE*, exhibition catalogue and LP, Kunstmuseum Luzern, 1982, inside cover

these recordings came about more or less naturally ". . . and the only electronics involved was the recording equipment."[16] These recordings introduce us over time to an essentially steady and powerful, pulsating spectrum of sounds, rich in overtones and oscillating within itself, that occasionally changes, is structured by breaks, and can vary its pitch and inherent rhythmic character. It allows the listener to imagine a space whose acoustic tension is triggered by an agent who, in stroking the piano wire, is improvising with the utmost concentration and calm, and is, above all, taking his time and so expanding the space of repetition. For as Claudio Monteverdi, who would have celebrated his 450th birthday this year, formulated it: ". . . speed and quality do not go well together."[17] The artist executing these actions in Bern is, of course, a part of the resonating chamber, part of the instrument that he has created. Like the audience, he is inside the instrument. It is important here for us to realize that by stringing the wire between the walls, the room itself becomes an instrument. The piano wires are not *played* in a *concertante* fashion. Rather the stroking of the wires is primarily a physical, acoustic measure taken to enable the perception of a specific wall sound, spatial vibration, et cetera. The room, walls, action, and audience become one for a length of time, in what we might call a situation of resonance, one in which the artist is both initiator and listener; and the listener, partner.

Moreover, by defining the walls as resonators of the museum's heterotopia, Fox has done nothing different than all artists before him have done, more or less, or after him will do: they play the walls of a museum or establish themselves in relation to them. At the same time, Fox literally transforms the museum space into what it should be: namely, a "resonating chamber," whereby I use the concept of resonance broadly, along the lines of Hartmut Rosa, and so associate it with world experience and appropriation.[18] Such modalities have traditionally developed their own forms of expression in the visual arts and particularly in museums, in order, conceivably, to create some kind of special realm with an essentially quiet atmosphere—a realm defined by how objects are hung, the color of walls, location of labels, wall texts, seating, picture height, architecture, and so on. By consciously choosing to conduct an acoustically powerful experiment and physically playing the museum walls, Fox — as a visual artist whose sculptural concept is closely tied to sound—reveals this visual resonating chamber as a genuinely corporeal, vibrating, experienceable

16 Fox (see note 7), n.p.
17 From a letter to Alessandro Striggio, January 20, 1617, in *The Letters of Claudio Monteverdi,* 1980 Cambridge, p. 131.

18 See Hartmut Rosa, *Resonanz: Eine Soziologie der Weltbeziehung* (Berlin, 2016).

sound-resonating chamber. In so doing, he not only achieves cultural resonance, but through his concentration also brings into play an element that in no way seems inappropriate for the visual side of art: the contemplative. That is, the heightened concentration gripping the player and the listener in equal measure. Fox uses the museum as an instrument, and transforms both a general and specific resonating chamber, as unique site of resonance in the here and now, for the duration of the event. As in a concert, the intensity of the forces released often leaves the audience only one means of resisting them: individual or group coughing or clearing of the throat, which one can hear the audience doing in Bern on the LP *LINKAGE*. Only, here there is no stage and the question of acoustics, which of late was almost hysterically discussed in light of the Elbphilharmonie in Hamburg, resolves itself on its own. For even if the artist uses physical-acoustic means, it is the space itself—one could almost speak of its Being[19]—that, as an instrument, makes its own individual resonance available to us for contemplation for a longer, extended, expanded time. This is wonderful and differs considerably in its intention from the primarily musical-instrumental application of monochords by Ellen Fullman or Alvin Lucier. In 1977, a year after Fox first used them, Lucier strung a piano wire across a room and connected it to electronic equipment and magnets for his composition *Music on a Long Thin Wire*. Later, in the early eighties, Paul Panhuysen and Johan Goedhart followed with their spatial wire works; and today we have William Close, an epigone through and through.

19 See Gaston Bachelard, *The Poetics of Space* (New York, 2014), Penguin Books edition.

This brings me to Fox's second presentation at the Kunstmuseum Bern in 1987: *THE EYE IS NOT THE ONLY GLASS THAT BURNS THE MIND*, a title going back to a line from the poem "The Conflagration of London" (1667) by the English author Simon Ford.[20] It took place within the scope of the exhibition *Die Gleichzeitigkeit des Anderen* (The Synchronicity of the Other), which was conceived by the aforementioned Jürgen Glaesemer. Gravely ill with AIDS at the time, this exhibition should be considered Glaesemer's "legacy."[21] He put together works by artists and writers—such as Joseph Beuys, Christian Boltanski, Paul Bowles, Jean Genet, Duane Michals, Meret Oppenheim, and Adolf Wölfli—first, to attain a collective poeticization of the arts and, second, to transform the arts into an intellectual edifice of the Other par excellence. An endeavor worthy of consideration not only in light of today's crude populism and rampant xenophobia, but most definitely also as thematic precursor of a number of Biennale or documenta exhibitions over the past twenty years. In addition, the presentation featured an opulent program of music, film, and sound events. Extremely rich in material, the accompanying catalogue with its many texts resists the urge to rely on over-theorizing, or even meta-theorizing, and ascribes to the arts, above and beyond any kind of theory, their respective effective powers.[22]

20 See additional explanations by Michael Glasmeier, Ron Meyers and Carsten Seiffarth in this publication.

21 See Bühler (see note 1), p. 128.

22 See *Die Gleichzeitigkeit des Anderen: Materialien zu einer Ausstellung*, ed. Jürgen Glaesemer, exh. cat. Kunstmuseum Bern (Stuttgart, 1987), pp. 271ff. To quote here from the afterword: "Perceptions about the Other also become accessible to us in our everyday lives. Multi-layered rituals of interpersonal communication give the encounters and dealings we have with the Other a manageable form. In Eros and sexuality, the Self and the Other touch and penetrate one another for moments; birth, life and death may be experienced as one. The Other may also become accessible to us through inward

Indeed, in this exhibition the existential demand on art was authentic and could be experienced in the artists' works. In any case, inviting Fox not only makes absolute sense in light of his presentation in 1980, but particularly because the artist, with his early experience and practice in ritualistic, political, and body-related work, appears utterly congenial in this context. And although it may seem as if Fox gradually gave up his emphasis on self-experience of the body—and after the discovery of the labyrinth in Chartres in 1972, which turned out to be so crucial for him, replaced it with a situating of spatial experience and a playing that propelled sounds to the foreground—processual and economical factors as well as perseverance and intellectual wit remained constant components of his art. And they can even be found in and behind the static character of his sculptural objects and typefaces.

So what did Fox do in Bern in 1987? At present no answer can be found to this question, as the dearth of material available here is even more catastrophic.[23] Fox, who compiled a list of his works in 1998 for the catalogue of his retrospective in Saarbrücken, had consistently noted briefly the form of action for each work. But when it comes to *THE EYE IS NOT THE ONLY GLASS THAT BURNS THE MIND*, he omitted even this information. Instead he pointed out that he created a site of resonance with Glaesemer on the harmonium: "Materials: piano wires (Fox), harmonium (Glaesemer)."[24] And so it is doubly disappointing that no sound recording exists! Exhibition curator and artist joined forces to produce resonance. But with a harmonium of all things—that peculiar, pietistic instrument whose development in the late eighteenth century was inspired by Chinese influences, and which was last heard in John Huston's *African Queen* (1951), when, in her small makeshift church, Katharine Hepburn tried, with her "hallelujah" pump organ, to encourage the black congregation to sing a few hymns! Nevertheless, the harmonium was well chosen as partner of the piano wire, as it belongs to the class of aerophones or wind instruments, instruments, which are "sounded by the so-called 'free reed'—a metal tongue that is screwed or riveted over an accurately-cut aperture in a metal frame and is caused to vibrate by air pressure supplied by the mouth [harmonica] or by bellows [harmonium, accordion]."[25] Again, the magic word here is "vibrate." For in contrast to the organ, the harmonium is not tonally pure but rich in overtones. It is the ideal partner for a joint appearance with a stretched piano wire, as it too lacks, as it were, any tonal purity. Both always vibrate sympathetically and whir around the base tone. With their respective base tones, they generate an acoustic cosmos that in the micro-range can extend itself endlessly. Of course, the harmonium does so in a more civilized fashion than the rather raw piano wire. Thus the artist and the exhibition curator synchronously transform a room in *Die Gleichzeitigkeit des*

contemplation, in meditation or trance and ecstasy, triggered by psychological or physical preconditions, through religious ideas as well as drugs. Confrontation with the Other may even lead to realms that manifest themselves in enlightenment or madness. We are confronted with this Other in the givenness of our birth and our death: in our knowledge of Non-Being;" trans. Catherine Kerkhoff-Saxon (C. K.-S.).

23 It could be that the aforementioned pendulum, which I referred to in discussing *A Candle for A.W.*, was first used here simply as the form of a ball suspended vertically on a piano wire.

24 See Terry Fox, "Katalog der Arbeiten mit Klang / Catalogue of Works with Sound," in *Works with Sound*, pp. 98–107, esp. p. 104.

25 James Howarth, "Free-Reed instruments," in *Musical Instruments through the Ages*, ed. Anthony Baines (Baltimore, 1961), pp. 318–26, esp. p. 318.

Anderen into a site of resonance, by reacting to one another with "other," quasi subversive, instruments; I imagine that here, as in 1980, long-sustained notes were produced and then accompanied by the mechanical wheezing of the harmonium. No purity, only off-the-wall instrumental energy from the belly of the instrument, the belly of the museum.

It is hardly surprising that both instruments can be traced back to prehistoric times. It has already been pointed out that the harmonium, with its kinship to the harmonica, goes back to China in, to be more concrete, about 1100 BC, prior to any form of composition, tonal purity, and demand for "civilized" harmonies. Its origin is as an instrument of direct improvisation, and obviously this is even more the case with the piano wire. It goes back to archaic prehistory, namely, to the hunting bow, which may also be made to elicit tones, as can be seen in a French cave painting from about 15000 BC. Even more interesting in this context is the "ground bow," which already at this early date functioned using resonance. A pit is dug to serve as a resonance cavity or sound bowl, and close to it a wand is stuck into the ground with a string tied to its free end. The other end of the string is knotted into a piece of bark or similar material, which is placed over the pit like a lid over a pot and is weighted down by a ring of stones or earth. The wand and lid are then adjusted to create sufficient tension to keep the string taut (fig. 6).[26] In this example from Uganda, we have all the elements of Fox's sound architecture generated with instruments. For me it is significant that this archaic relationship constantly resonated in his work and was visible in both his tendency toward an economy of means and in his approach of searching for ways to deal with sound. This subversion, with which Fox removes himself from both the art and music industries, characterizes and functions as the leitmotif of his work. It is the remote, unpretentious, consistently anarchic, and at first glance unspectacular quality that not only becomes visible in his actions with piano wires, but is found in all his work. Labeling Fox an "artist's artist" completely misreads his intention, whose subversion manifests itself in its universal and democratic receptibility. Nothing about it has the quality of a secret society, is elitist, or can be appreciated only by other artists. Everyone, absolutely everyone is a comprehending, contemplative part of, for example, a site of resonance, if they are open to it. Incidentally, since the Renaissance, every artist has made art for other artists. Otherwise there would have been no development of ideas, not to mention "pathos formulae." What is more, I have the suspicion that artists who have been labeled "artist's artists" are always those who do not supply the art market with the "necessary" fodder.

Using the simplest of means, the ancient ground bow turns our planet into an instrument. But by stringing piano wires in museums, a church, cars, a tunnel, abandoned building sites, an airplane, and his studio, Fox takes this phenomenon further. In so doing, he recurrently returns to the source of creative, improvised sound experience. This is in itself a democratic attitude, because it acts on experiences that would have to be called anthropological, and yet in the evolving processes of civilization and media have been registered only in the background or on the sidelines. More than just his public "situations," Fox's entire oeuvre is

26 Klaus P. Wachsmann, "The Primitive Musical Instruments," in ibid., pp. 23–54, esp. p. 38.

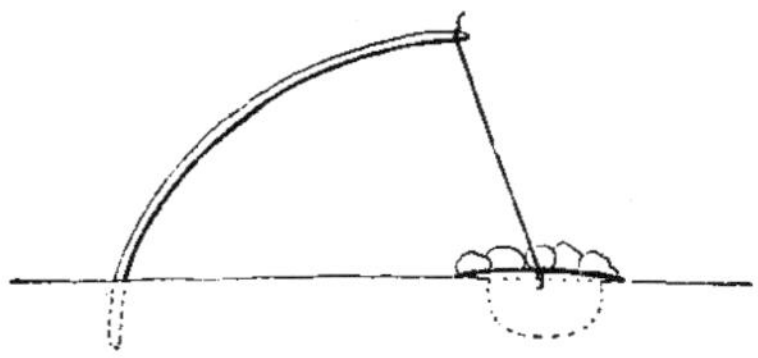

Fig. 9 Erdbogen, Uganda

6 *Erdbogen*, illustration in Anthony Baines, *Musikinstrumente: Die Geschichte ihrer Entwicklung und ihrer Formen* (Munich, 1962)

informed by, among other things, exactly such elemental experiences of media, by "elemental gestures." Fox was not interested in the stage, concerts, the big screen, or other elements of cultural spectacle. He used artistic action for physical encounters with the simplest of materials; photography, for a diary-like compilation of banal objects; video, for small, unremarkable temporal events; language, for spelling things out again; and spaces in their architectonic enclosure of emptiness. I have already alluded to Fox's concept of sound—proceeding from it, he was able to redefine each of the media he employed by falling back on what is elemental and essential. Thus he made them equally productive for himself and every viewer/listener, especially when it involved moving toward essential, fundamental experience.

Like the harmonium, the accordion, which belongs to the same family of instruments, is still considered out of place in a concert setting—at the Elbphilharmonie, for example. Categorized under "folk music," it is for the most part seen as a musical instrument made to accompany vocals. Yet Glaesemer's playing in Bern references at the same time one of Fox's very early pieces and the artist's fondness for subversive instruments. In April 1969, Fox sent out invitations to a special event on Union Street in San Francisco, titled *What Do Blind Men Dream?* There, a "beautiful blind lady was to play accordion at a huge construction pit from 5:30 p.m. until dark."[27] (fig. 7) And this is exactly what happened, for Fox had asked the street musician and her partner to perform at this specific location. Fox himself did not attend this "Public Theater," as he programmatically termed it, but photos exist, as does, allegedly, a sound recording. What has repeatedly impressed me about this piece is the freedom Fox allowed the musicians, the location, the viewers/listeners. Freedom even at the risk of the piece—which it is per definition—not being noticed by anyone or, on the other hand, by everyone who just happens to be strolling along Union Street, and consciously or unconsciously only feels the vibrations of the instrument or sees the extremely concentrated and absorbed blind musician with her partner. The site of resonance = the time of subversion. In its radicalness, this sound work, which is probably Fox's first, is comparable to the best works of Fluxus or the sculptural spaces of an artist like Michael Asher. It is more than just conceptual art. It is a part of a real time of political life, delivered by an artist who had briefly lived in Paris in 1968.

Moving on from this piece of "Public Theater," which is spun off of almost twenty years later in Bern, I would now like to start talking—in contrast to Fox in his own statement—about music. For the accordion player was, in fact, making music and not only from the perspective of her own

27 Terry Fox, "Elemental Gestures," *Arts Magazine* (May 1970), pp. 48–51, esp. p. 51. Reprinted in *Metaphorical Instruments*, pp. 12–15, esp. p. 15.

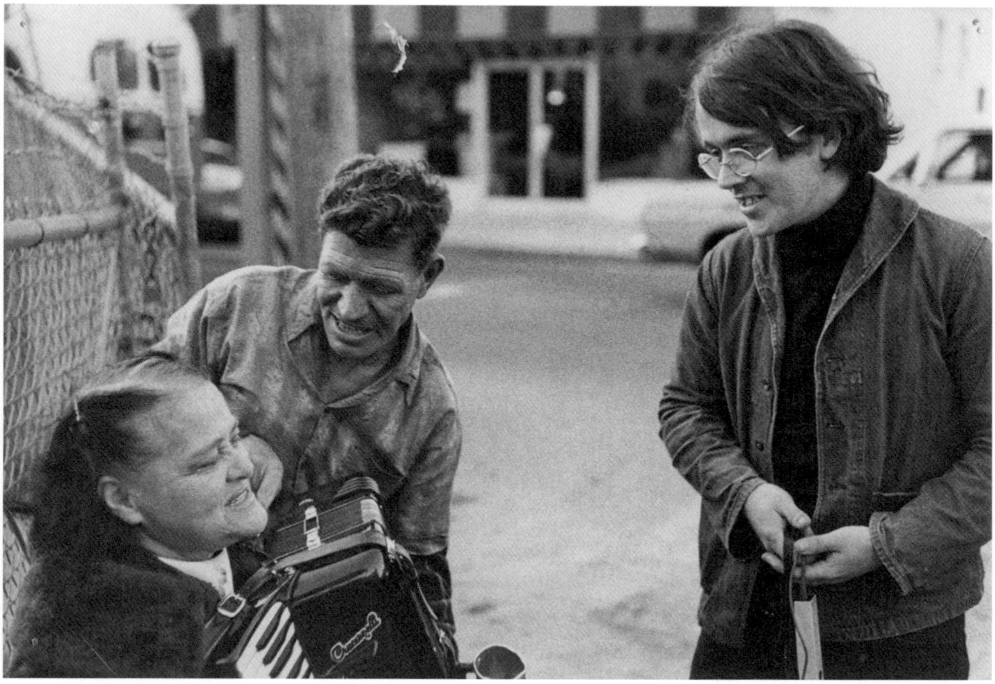

7 Terry Fox, *What Do Blind Men Dream?*, performance from the series *Public Theater*, Union Street, San Francisco, 1969, University of California, Berkeley Art Museum and Pacific Film Archive, Berkeley. photo: Barry Klinger

aspirations, but also in how sound was organized, which for Fox takes place in improvisation and the choice of instruments: an organizing that occurs in the moment of its happening. Moreover, if I listen to Fox's sound recordings today, they are not mere documentations of sound. They provide the sound of a music which was, as said, exemplified by the piano wire and resonates differently, that is, depending on the way it is played. As Adorno so aptly remarked: "To interpret language means to understand language; to interpret music means to make music."[28] The musical component in Fox's work is also substantiated by the collegial collaboration of artists whose instruments, it seems, often had little status. Fox himself reports that these interactions were important to him, "because I sensed a very direct similarity in our work and was anxious to see what would evolve by forming a 'duet'..."[29] Besides working with Beuys, as I mentioned earlier, out of 120 appearances, Fox "collaborated around 30 times with other artists and non-artists," as he himself calculated in contributing to a commemorative volume for Georg Decristel, who died in 1998.[30] Fox had kept up a great friendship with this Austrian poet, musician, and artist, who was—to complete the compendium of unorthodox instruments—a master on the Jew's harp. Again, the Jew's harp is rich in overtones and uses the mouth, like language, as a resona-

28 Theodor W. Adorno, *Essays on Music* (Berkeley, Los Angeles, and London, 2002), p. 115.

29 Eva Schmidt, "Terry Fox on Georg Decristel: An Interview," in Georg Decristel, *weg bewegen / moving away: Eine Auswahl aus seinem Werk*, ed. Sonja, Michael, and Stephan Bahn (Innsbruck, 2003), pp. 51–56, esp. p. 54.

30 Ibid., p. 55

Künstlerhaus Bethanien

Veranstaltungsreihe Performance 5. bis 20. Mai 1981

Terry Fox

A Table of Simple Sound

10. Mai 1981 21 Uhr Dachboden

unter Mitwirkung des Dichters und Maultrommlers Georg Decristel

"A Table of Simple Sound" ist eine Situation von Terry Fox und Georg Decristel. Sie ereignet sich im Dachboden des Künstlerhauses Bethanien. Die Dauer ist unbekannt. Dem Besucher wird nahegelegt, zu horchen, umherzuwandern und einfach seiner Neugier zu folgen, vielleicht sogar empfänglich zu sein für die Geräusche, die durch das Environment erzeugt werden, wie auch innerhalb und oberhalb desselben. Diese Geräusche können musikalisch sein oder auch nicht, gelegentlich sogar hörbar. Anfang und Ende sind nicht vorhersagbar. Der Besucher ist nicht verpflichtet zu bleiben oder zu gehen.

Terry Fox und Georg Decristel

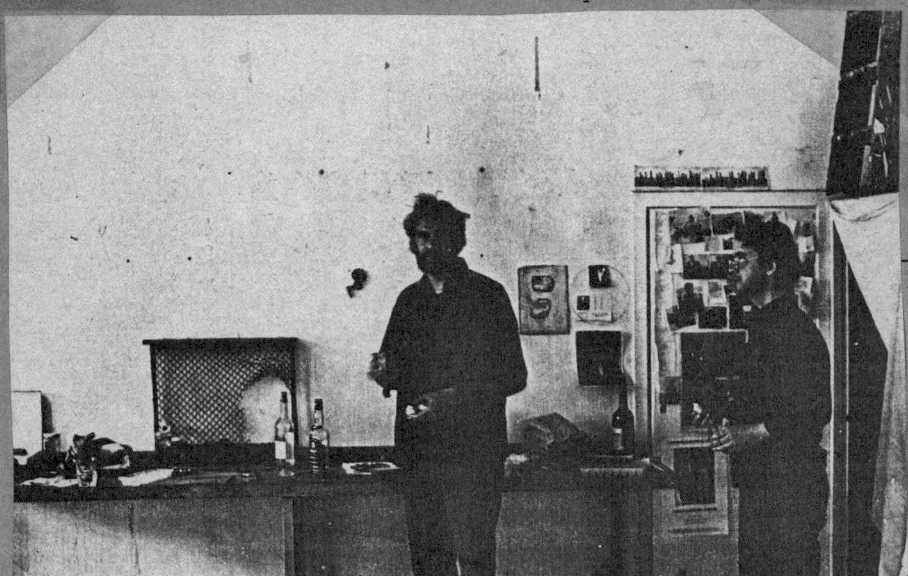

Mariannenplatz 2, 1000 Berlin 36
Telefon 6 14 80 10, Vorbestellungen 6 14 90 21
Fahrverbindungen U-Bahn Kottbusser Tor, Bus 28, 29, 41, 75

8 Terry Fox and Georg Decristel, *A Table of Simple Sound*, 1981, invitation flyer, 29.6 x 20.9 cm, Estate of Terry Fox, Cologne

ting chamber and to articulate sounds. Furthermore, it has a wire or metal tongue, which is made to vibrate by striking it (a piano wire, so to speak, in miniature). Once again, a folk instrument that can be traced directly back to the archaic ground bow. Starting in 1977, Fox often performed with Decristel, in part because their instruments complemented each other so wonderfully (fig. 8). It was a matter of mutual changes, and not just during their improvisations. Hence, to play with Glaesemer in Bern was not a one-off event, but rather an encounter sought out by Fox as part of a subversive strategy that revolved around not taking himself as a performer too seriously. Art as communication with oneself, with others, and with everyone together.

Besides stroking piano wires with his fingers, as Fox did in Bern, wires could be stretched on the floor and hit with a tiny muted hammer, as he did in *552 Steps Through 11 Pairs of Strings*. Presented in 1976 in the artist's studio, this piece was based on the structure, the number of steps, and the concept of time found in the labyrinth at Chartres Cathedral, whereby the score was formed by a string resembling a rosary with 552 knots. For the duration of the piece, which was one of Fox's first experiments with piano wires, the audience sat below the studio in a darkened room, not unlike the belly of a guitar, and listened for four-and-a-half hours to the "giant horizontal harp" above them. Here, too, the artist repeated his subversive exercise of vanishing as a performer, of remaining discreet (fig. 9).[31] Another recording had been made in his studio in 1975. In it, a wire was stretched over a long box and played with a violin bow. The sound produced there was completely different from the one during a later recording, made in Fox's Berlin studio in 1981. In it, the wire was beat with a "wooden shish kebab stick . . . using the finger to define the various notes of the wire,"[32] according to a score based on the path of the Berlin Wall.

May these examples suffice, for the time being, to illustrate the spectrum of musical possibilities and strategies. In principle, the relationship between length, thickness, and craftsmanship of piano wires can vary endlessly, as can the way they are played, whether with fingers or utensils, as can the type of resonating chambers. Also crucial in each case is the score, the realities of the space, the occasion, and the artist's intention. And of course, rhythm, change in pitch, and modulation of sound all depend on the way the wires are played. Anyone who knows how different Beethoven's sonatas sound on a Steinway than they do on an eighteenth-century pianoforte can appreciate how special each individual interaction between a piano wire and a player may be. If we take the instrument's interior, it was Erik Satie in 1914 who covered the wires of a piano with strips of paper to change the sound of this instrument, which had by then come to be considered quite bourgeois. In 1925, Henry Cowell wrote a piece that was to be played directly on the wires in a piano. And in 1940, John Cage prepared a piano with a wide assortment of materials. From then on, the piano was for Cage and other composers more than its keyboard—it was now also a percussion instrument. Eventually, in 1957, in the Six Gallery in San Francisco, after all kinds of slapstick experiments,

31 Excerpt from the sound recording on *LINKAGE* (see note 6); for the recent release of the entire recording, see Edition Telemark (Berlin, 2017).

32 Fox (see note 7), n.p.; samples of both these sound works are also on *LINKAGE* (see note 6).

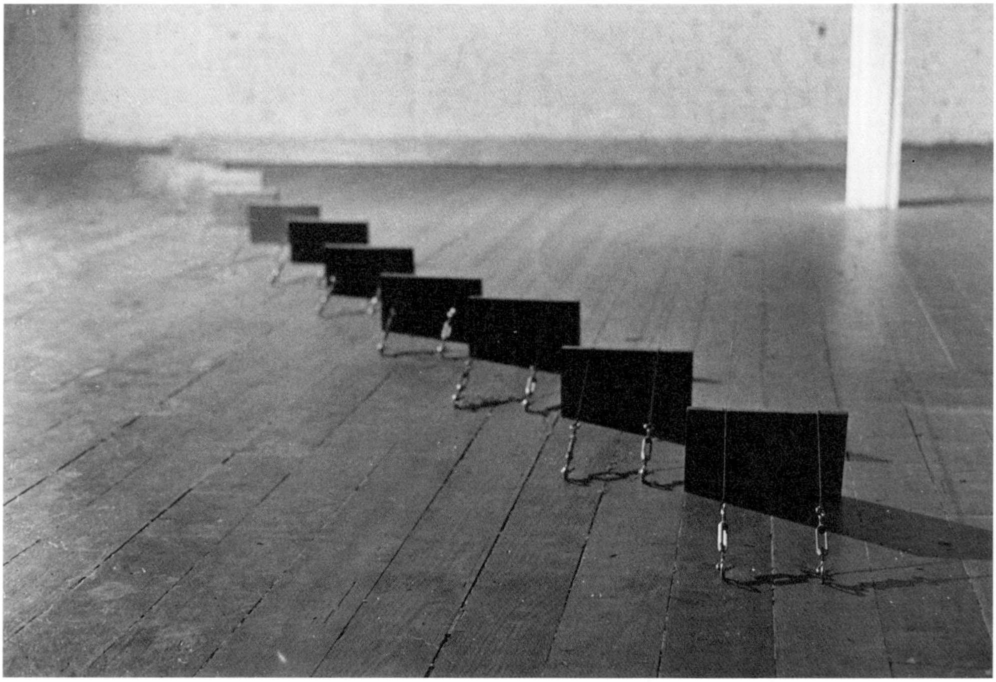

9 Terry Fox, *552 Steps Through 11 Pairs of Strings,* 1976, performance, San Francisco, photo: Terry Fox

a piano was publicly destroyed for what was probably the first time, in a legendary performance by pianist and sculptor Edward Silverstone Taylor. Among the adherents of Viennese Actionism and Fluxus, further destructions followed thick and fast. The strings, which had been attached with such effort to the piano's frame, were being set free again.[33]

However, in the visual arts, strings had been set free from instruments into a symbolic realm much earlier. Since ancient Greece, a broken string has stood for the danger of dissonance in a world attuned to harmony, where harmony embodies the spiritual, the immortal; what is broken, but still attached to the instrument, represents the corporeal, the ephemeral (fig. 10). And since the Renaissance, the broken string of a lute symbolizes tainted virtue; or in politics, an endangered alliance.[34] In any case, it is interesting to observe how such strings, set free in an era in which its artists, like Giorgione or Parmigianino, were often also outstanding musicians, have behaved in images since then. In inlays found in rooms of the Vatican (ca. 1514), broken strings form freely undulating ornamental lines. In the picture *Saint Cecilia with Saints*, painted on wood by Raphael between 1514 and 1516, musical instruments lie, in accord with legend, destroyed and scattered chaotically on the floor. The sounding box of the viola da gamba has been dented, and except for a single unruly string, the rest are missing (figs. 11, 12).
And in paintings done on canvas, tautly stretched strings have also enjoyed lives of their own, as can be seen in Caravag-

33 For more on the extensive history of piano destructions, see Gunnar Schmidt, *Klavierzerstörungen in Kunst und Popkultur* (Berlin, 2013).

34 Reinhold Hammerstein, *Von gerissenen Saiten und singenden Zikaden: Studien zur Emblematik der Musik* (Tübingen and Basel, 1994).

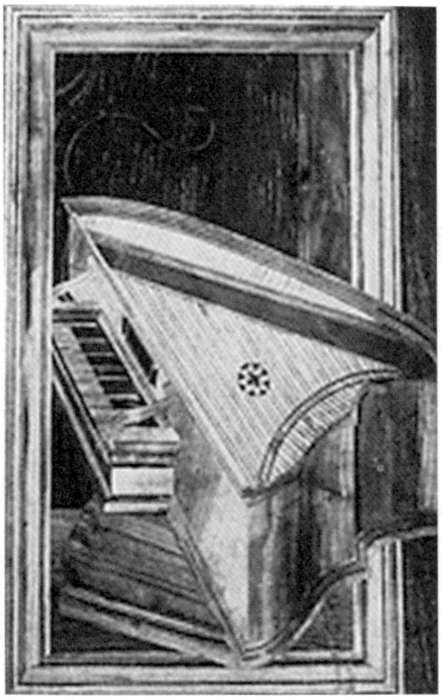

10 Giovanni da Verona, spinet with broken wire, ca. 1514, inlay, Vatican rooms, Rome

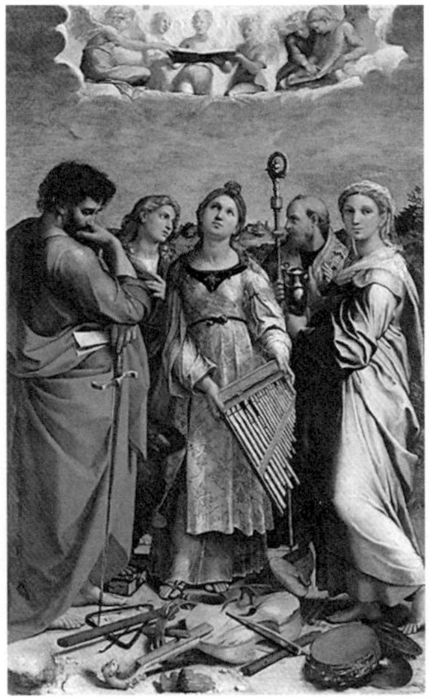

11 Raphael, *Saint Cecilia with Saints*, ca. 1514–16, wood, transferred to canvas, 238 x 150 cm, Pinacoteca Nazionale di Bologna

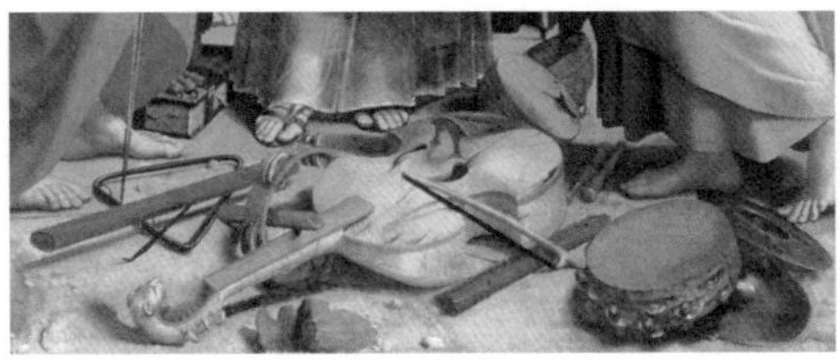

12 Raphael, *Saint Cecilia with Saints*, detail

gio's works. Here, in the lower third of the highly erotic *Amor vincit omnia* (Amor Victorious) from 1601–02, we can marvel at string instruments that are, however, no longer playable: for Amor also triumphs over music (fig. 13). Perhaps this is why the viola and the lute are now seen to have an intimate physical relationship: this is seen even in the illogical stretching of one of the lute's gut strings over the neck of the viola (fig. 14).[35]

Nevertheless, it is still a long way to the freely strung piano wire, a highly complex and varyingly strong structure, the steel of which can attain a tensile strength of up to 240 kilograms per square millimeter. Yet even Caravaggio advises us to keep in mind the visual aspect of taut strings. As Fox remarked early on: "The piano wire is a sculpture," a "steel sculpture," which means in its stroke or line-like quality, in its "almost nothingness," as Vladimir Jankélévitch would call it,[36] it turns into a kind of "drawing in space," something that has fascinated sculpture since the second decade of the last century. With it, sculpture found its own and specific form of openness in which volumes effectively approach zero. So early on we find what is for us an interesting linear tautness in space, seen for example in the works of the Constructivists Naum Gabo and Vladimir Tatlin. Through them, spaces within spaces or physical lines of perspective are created using the simplest of means; an idea taken up, varied, and expanded by Lucio Fontana, Gianni Colombo, François

35 For more on corporeality in Caravaggio, see, for example, Valeska von Rosen, *Caravaggio und die Grenzen des Darstellbaren: Ambiguität, Ironie und Performativität in der Malerei um 1600* (Berlin, 2009).

36 See Vladimir Jankélévitch, *The Forgiveness*, trans. Andrew Kelley (Chicago and London, 2005), pp. 34ff.

Morellet, and Norbert Kricke in the fifties;[37] though this was done most consistently from 1967 onward by Fred Sandback, who—born in 1943, the same year as Fox—made "drawings in space" visible using strings. Also a lone wolf and individualist, Sandback characterized his sculptures in 1998 as: ". . . diffuse interface . . . built of thin lines that left enough room to move through and around. Still sculpture, though less dense, with an ambivalence between exterior and interior. A drawing that is habitable."[38] The distance between a "lined chamber" and a "resonating chamber," and vice versa, does not seem all that far to me. Although there is this difference: Fox does not create special spaces with his wires, but rather his drawings in space tend to be constructed diagonally and thus behave similarly to lines of perspective. In other words, their hardly visible bodies provide different situational dimensions and forms of thought depending on how they are aligned.

In 1982, Martin Kunz invited Fox to stretch piano wires across the premises of the aforementioned *LINKAGE* exhibition at the Kunstmuseum Luzern. This time, however, the artist did not produce sounds on them alone or with friends but let the public join in. Moreover, the wires were clearly now to be regarded as sculptural drawings in space, as they were visually dominating, especially when no sounds were being produced on them (fig. 15). In addition, these "almost nothings" functioned as the medium guiding the way

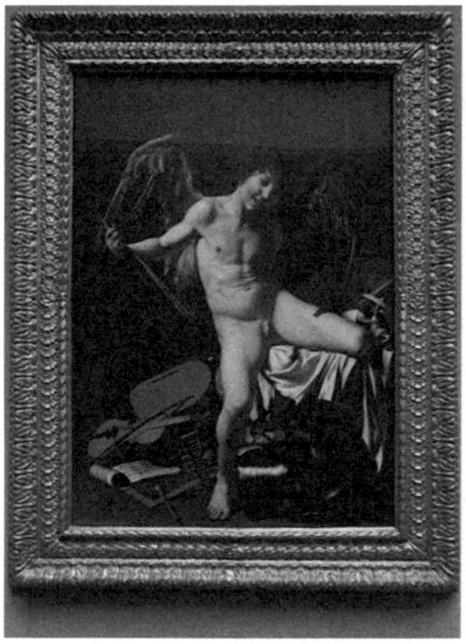

13 Caravaggio, *Amor vincit omnia*, 1601–02, oil on canvas, 156 x 113 cm, Staatliche Museen Preußischer Kulturbesitz, Gemäldegalerie, Berlin

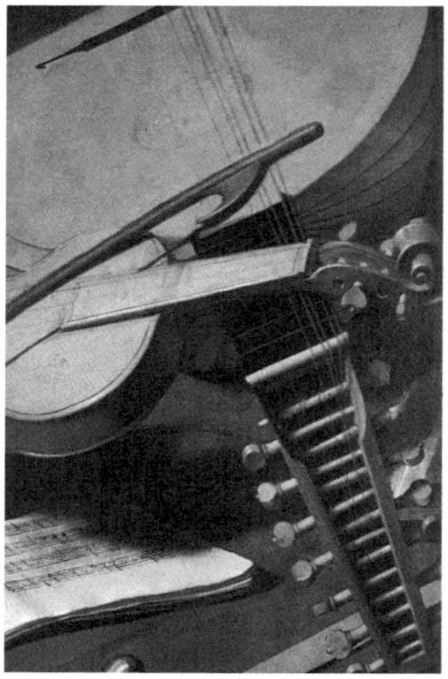

14 Caravaggio, *Amor vincit omnia*, detail

37 For more on the history of "drawing in space," see Michael Glasmeier, "Pedestrian Spaces, 1913–1945: Notes on a History of Drawing in Space," in *Spaceliner*, ed. Ilkay Baliç, exh. cat. Arter, Istanbul (Istanbul, 2015), pp. 81–108.

38 Fred Sandback, "Untitled," in *Fred Sandback*, ed. Friedemann Malsch and Christiane Meyer-Stoll, exh. cat. Kunstmuseum Liechtenstein, Vaduz, and others (Ostfildern-Ruit, 2006), p. 152.

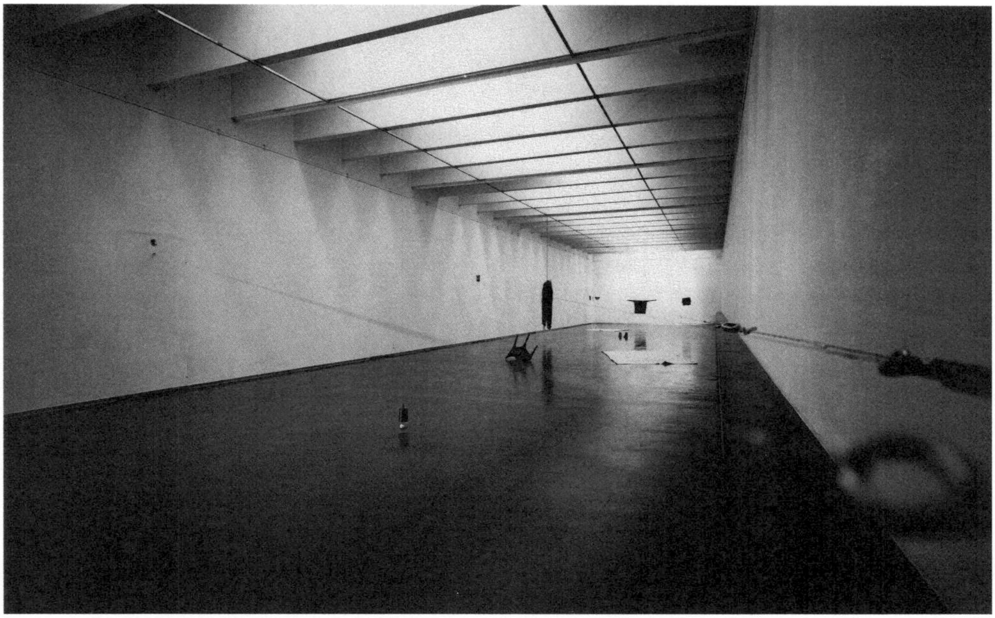

15 Terry Fox, *LINKAGE*, 1982, exhibition view, Kunstmuseum Luzern, photo: Robert Baumann

through a collection of extremely diverse and, for the most part, highly political, poetic, and acoustically motivated exhibits, labels, sketches, and objects: ranging from an overturned chair, articles of clothing, a pendulum, a plaster cast of teeth, a red telephone, the three wise monkeys, a pendulum on the verge of smashing an egg, and a sculpture of the "harmonious hammer and sickle," to the aforementioned labels and drawings. At the time, Siegmar Gassert wrote in a remarkably insightful review: ". . . in their constellation, the few objects and sketches appear like situational images in which the visitors, as players and observers, reproduce themselves in sound, while simultaneously having to make and test associations. This real sequence of action, consisting of wandering about and listening to the sound architecture of the space, unavoidably confronts the visitor with the objects in real-time processes of current political experiences and events. This, in turn, constitutes another 'linkage': in the way sound is used not as an acoustic element of, for instance, scored music, but as a body-focused transition to sensory-informed associations towards the present situation."[39]

Within this composed structure, the piano wire clearly references the visual and haptic union that aims at collective, direct communication. The players or "duets" have turned into an uncounted, unknown audience that is now free to "play" piano wires, in the absence of the artist, during specific opening hours. Their sounds, ranging from "cautious to overpowering . . . hereby directly impact the body of the player, so that it becomes a physical part of the sound installation."[40] The space is both instrument and exhibition, sculpture

39 Siegmar Gassert, "Terry Fox in Luzern: Schwingungen der Zeit," in *Basler Zeitung*, February 16, 1982, republished in *Metaphorical Instruments*, pp. 92–94, esp. p. 93; trans. C. K.-S. After reading this review, it becomes clear that the artist's emphatic political stance should today be reconsidered for its resolve, especially in light of the "simplistic" discourse surrounding Documenta 14.

40 Gassert, "Terry Fox in Luzern," p. 92; trans. C. K.-S.

and situation, in a grand agreement that goes beyond all tentative concepts. Sounding drawings in space that, in their highly complex reverberations, poeticize the visible in the audible. The subversion of vibrating energies emanates unbridled from an audience that wants to see, hear, wander, and understand its own actions in reflecting on space as a political, artistic, and bright resonating chamber.

Translated from German by
Catherine Kerkhoff-Saxon

Lisa Steib

CENTEROFATTRACTION: On *Cynosure* and Other Text Objects

Terry Fox used everyday found things and basic materials to construct complex objects and drawings that take on a reserved presence in the exhibition space. The spectrum of the text-based objects extends from various sign languages and levels of poetry and metaphor to riddles and plays on words. Sometimes the words and sentences in Fox's prints, drawings, and sculptural works are easy to decipher, and sometimes the riddles they pose defy a solution. Strung together without any punctuation, and running in unusual directions and sequences, the individual letters call upon the viewer to stop and think, to concentrate—while at the same time inducing the slow reader to move. The works ask to be circled around, both mentally and physically. Grids of letters, some of them very dense, turn this perceptual process into a challenge well beyond any everyday reading experience. Thus, the guessing and deciphering unlocks an intricate artistic universe in which individual works are connected to one another in direct or subtle ways. Basic forms and existential themes are present, as are personal and literary references. In Terry Fox's work, text and object are intimately connected. The boundaries between two-dimensional techniques and room-sized constructions are porous. Hence, works with text can also take the form of actions, editions, videos, and books. The only medium Terry Fox quickly and permanently distanced himself from, in the nineteen-sixties, was painting. He saw his art as sculpture—including the actions. Communication was the keyword throughout his work since the nineteen-seventies. The individual works also communicate among one another and enter into new constellations in each exhibition.

Terry Fox's Treatment of Object and Text
The series *Catch Phrases* consists of "27 Units" made between 1981 and 1984 in Berlin, Naples, and Minneapolis (fig. 1). Two- and three-dimensional techniques are indissolubly connected in this series, which presents a challenge not only in terms of viewing the individual works, but in their preservation and restoration. A grid of letters, a drawing, and an object made of iron join to form one of these "units." The entire series can be viewed in a book published in 1985 by the Kunstraum Munich and designed in cooperation with Terry Fox. The book includes a magnifying glass to enable the reader to focus on each individual letter close up.[1]

1 See *Terry Fox: Catch Phrases*, exh. cat. Kunstraum München e. V., 1985, unpag. The number of drawings corresponds to the twenty-six letters of the alphabet plus a title drawing. Terry Fox also used optical devices in other works, for instance mirrors (see note 22).

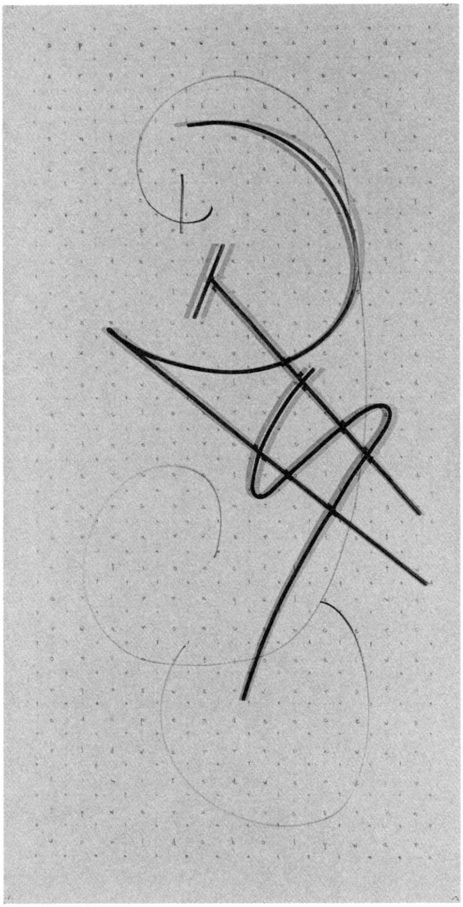

1 Terry Fox, *Catch Phrases*, title work of the 27-part series, 1984, drawing, wall object, paper, pencil, pigment felt-tip pen, steel tube, 179 x 92 cm, photo: Marilyn Westlake, Estate of Terry Fox, Cologne

In exhibition situations, where the work takes on the form of a steel sculpture, it already entices the eye from a distance; in book form, the sculptural element is presented as a two-dimensional text image. The publication also includes Terry Fox's extensive description and explanation of the series, a clear commentary on the part of the artist. It ends with a statement stressing that each drawing should be perceived on its own: "It takes a very long time to read one of these drawings from top to bottom, but it is only through this process that the content of the drawing is understood."[2] Taking his *Catch Phrases* as an example, one can observe how the transitions between drawing, sculpture, and artist's book can be overcome without resorting to ordinary techniques and categories.[3] In addition, Terry Fox had a "broad interest in materials."[4]

Individual elements of a work repeatedly turn up in new contexts, particularly texts and text fragments. What Bernd Schulz wrote concerning Terry Fox's actions also applies to many of his sculptural works and drawings: "The goal of artistic activity is less the artwork as an (unchanging) image than the form of activity connected with the objects. Characteristic is the use of simple, 'impoverished' materials, often used repeatedly in changed contexts in a kind of esthetics of continuation."[5]

Since the seventies, Terry Fox had been using a repertoire of elements in very different locations—always in response to the respective architecture and qualities of the space. This gave rise to unique situations. In 1972, Terry Fox drew a sketch in connection with his action *Pont* in the Ileana Sonnabend Gallery in Paris.[6] The dedication after the title ("for Dorothy") was to his girlfriend at the time, the artist Dorothy Reid, who had accompanied him to Paris. Integrated into the drawing is a handwritten list of the objects used, including a writing tool: chalk. At the time, the declared goal of Terry Fox's

2 Terry Fox, 1984, in his commentary on the series *Catch Phrases*. Terry Fox, *Catch Phrases*, in Munich 1985 (see note 1), unpag. (German/English).
3 On the series *Catch Phrases*, see for instance Beate Eickhoff, "Terry Fox: Text and Language Works," in *Elemental Gestures*, pp. 186–97, esp. pp. 187ff.
4 As Bernd Schulz once formulated it in a conversation with the author in Berlin about Terry Fox. Undated.
5 Bernd Schulz, "Foreword," in *Works with Sound*, pp. 7–11, esp. p. 7.
6 See the sketch in *Elemental Gestures*, p. 121; previously published in 1982 in *Metaphorical Instruments*, p. 42.

actions was to charge spaces with a certain energy. The transformation processes, which have been described multiple times, go far beyond concrete materials. Whether it was flour, water, candles, or text fragments—it was about what was dwelling within these visible elements, what they harbored in terms of energy:

"When I make a performance I usually come to the space to have an arrangement, then I see the space and the energy in the room. I make a performance trying to energize the room: that's the main point. . . . I try to make something that is poor into something that's total, rich. Rich in the sense to make alive again, strong."[7]

Asked in the same 1973 interview what the written word means for him, for instance the quotes by Antonin Artaud (1896–1948) that he frequently referenced throughout the seventies, Terry Fox responded: "The words are just to pose the words. The sentence is used in a different sense than in Artaud."[8] What was important for him was to represent the words, to "pose" them, not (or at least less importantly) to quote particular authors. Terry Fox did not randomly name-drop; on the contrary, he deliberately selected succinct text passages he'd encountered in books, without shying away from entertaining or difficult language games. He seldom used his own texts. Whenever he used a riddle or a quote by a certain author, it was one that had evidently stuck in his mind for a while, sometimes for decades. The text material that Terry Fox borrowed from various contexts takes on a meaning that is contingent to the respective situation in which we, as its audience, read it. With conspicuous frequency, an ambiguous riddle-poem turns up that clearly, in its original riddle context, asks for a solution:[9]

A Headless man had a letter to write;
'Twas read by one who lost his Sight;
The Dumb repeated it word for word,
And he was Deaf who listened and heard.[10]

This rhyme was presented multiple times in exhibitions, written in white chalk on the underside of a chair turned upside-down and lying on the floor, and always in the English original. In 1982, Terry Fox also sent out the "headless man" in the form of an invitation card to an exhibition in Bologna.[11] The same year, he integrated one of these text chairs into his solo show *Linkage* in Lucerne. In 1987, at documenta 8, the text was delivered in Morse code using four car horns that sounded it out in various languages (*Ricochet*).[12] The sheet music was preserved and shown in exhibitions after Terry Fox's death. While in the eighties the interpretations of the quatrain usually pointed in a political direction, and the content was read literally as a "statement" about the Cold War,[13] in later works, a concrete solving of the

7 "Terry Fox interviewed by Achille Bonito Oliva," in *domus* 521, Milan (April 1973), p. 45. Original interview (in English) reprinted in *Metaphorical Instruments*, p. 44.

8 Ibid.

9 See Lisa Steib, "JUMP QUICK BROWN FOX OVER THIS LAZY GOD: Dem Rätsel lauschen," in *Locus Solus*, publication accompanying the exhibition *Terry Fox—Locus Solus*, Barkenhoff / Heinrich-Vogeler Museum, Worpswede, ed. Beate C. Arnold, Barkenhoff-Stiftung (Worpswede, 2011), pp. 4–18, and Eickhoff 2015 (see note 3).

10 Quoted from a handwritten version by Terry Fox, which he sent out on an invitation card in 1982 (superimposed with a drawing) for his solo exhibition *3 scimmie* in the Fernando Pellegrino Gallery in Bologna. Reprint of the front of the card in *Metaphorical Instruments*, p. 88.

11 See *Metaphorical Instruments* and Worpswede 2011 (see note 9).

12 See Terry Fox's description of his action in *Works with Sound*, p. 85.

13 See *Metaphorical Instruments*, pp. 88–89.

riddle was key, and accepted.[14] Terry Fox skillfully steered these various interpretations through precise staging of the respective exhibition situations. Viewers were still guessing in his first posthumous solo show, *Terry Fox — Locus Solus*, which took place in Worpswede in 2011. Earlier, in 1998 in Saarbrücken, the same enigmatic poetic sentence was printed on strips of thick paper hung on the window overlooking a table where a bowl of nuts sat next to a nutcracker. The riddle was even hidden in the wall-sized drawing series in the collection of the Folkwang Museum in Essen.[15] In a catalogue essay from 1999, which was the first to examine the works with language and text, Eva Schmidt describes two different levels to the riddle: Terry Fox constructs textuality, creating riddles and encoding. The works, correspondingly and in inner consistence, are conceived as closed in upon themselves. He provides us with something to read that we have to decipher. Then, behind the first layer of deciphering, appear the great riddles that can never be solved.[16]

Exhibition Situations and References

In 1990, Terry Fox, in cooperation with the Galerie Löhrl in Mönchengladbach, showed several text objects in the Syndikat Halle in Bonn (*Terry Fox: Installation, Objects, Drawings*, August 29 to October 7, 1990). Among the works shown was a piece titled *Cynosure*, which has been in the collection of the Kunstmuseum Bern since 1991 (fig. 2). This wagon object was closely connected to an installation consisting of text on white wooden slats perched on glass bottles that wound its way through the space and took on the role of a musical score: during an action titled *Lesung* (Reading),[17] which took place on August 29, 1990 in the context of the exhibition, Terry Fox moved along this work toward the wagon object, which functioned as a kind of point of attraction (fig. 3-5). Prior to this, visitors were able to have a look around the exhibition space for about three-quarters of an hour. Terry Fox began his action near the entrance. It lasted nearly thirty minutes and was described in the local press as follows:

"Bent over, concentrated, he read every single letter, repeated the word they formed, and drew the bow of a string instrument across a short, thin steel pipe tied to wood. The sound is almost impossible to describe. It issued forth into the space with an unbelievable intensity, its continuously modulating pitch went through the startled visitors and made their eardrums vibrate palpably. The overpowering sound permeated head and body and left little room for thought. Because Fox played the instrument at a measured pace at first, sound-sensitive visitors had a chance to leave before he began intoning the individual letters in an ongoing rhythm. Only very few left, in fact, while others held their hands over their ears, but most gave in to the unusual experience and allowed themselves to be haunted by the sound, albeit with mixed feelings. In the end, only very few visitors took the arduous task upon themselves to decipher 'Running Text' step by step, following the artist's example."[18]

14 See Siegmar Gassert, "Terry Fox in Luzern: Schwingungen der Zeit," *Basler Zeitung*, February 16, 1982, quoted from ibid., pp. 93–94 (reprint of the original article) and Steib 2011 (see note 9).

15 Terry Fox found inspiration for his works with riddles and plays on words in C. C. [Charles Carroll] Bombaugh, *Oddities and Curiosities of Words and Literature (Gleanings for the Curious)*, ed. Martin Gardner (New York and London, 1961), esp. p. 299.

16 Eva Schmidt, "Text Bodies, Text Labyrinths," in *Works with Sound*, pp. 46–52, esp. p. 52.

17 In the exhibition catalogue of 1990, the action is translated as *reading*. See *TERRY FOX: OBJECTS (TEXTS) / DRAWINGS (TEXTS)*, exh. cat. Mönchengladbach 1990, pp. 7 and 25.

18 Christiane Fricke, "TERRY FOX–READING: Syndikat

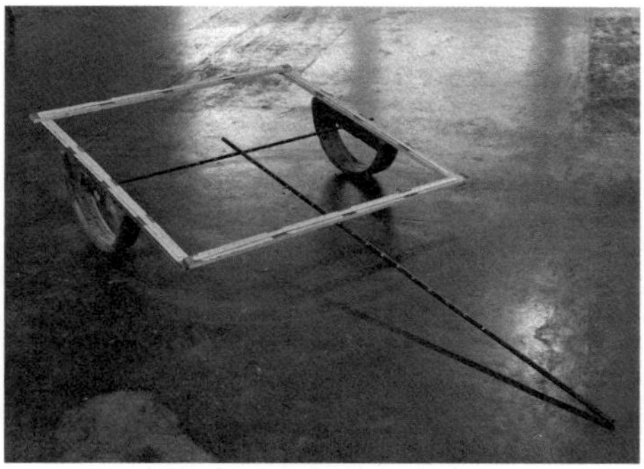

2 Terry Fox, *Cynosure*, 1990, exhibition view, Syndikat Halle, Bonn, 1990, sculpture with text, wood, iron, oil paint, ink on paper, 310 x 149 x 35.5 cm, Kunstmuseum Bern. Photo: Galerie Löhrl

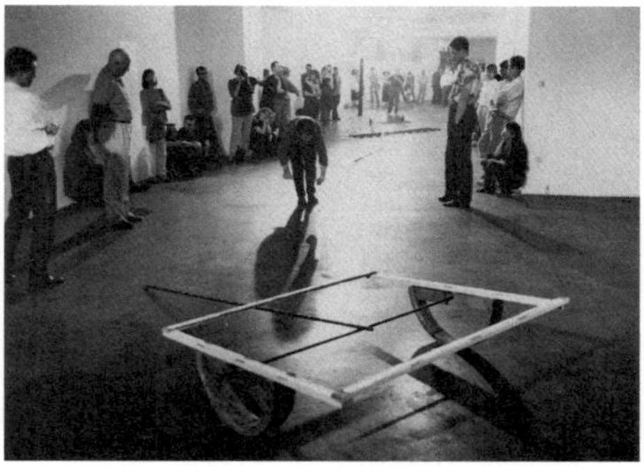

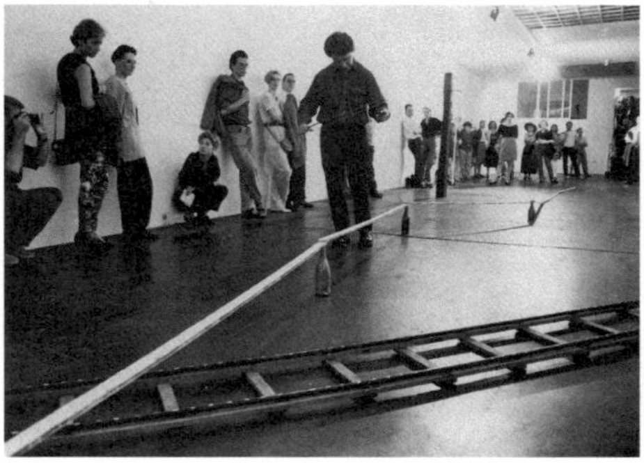

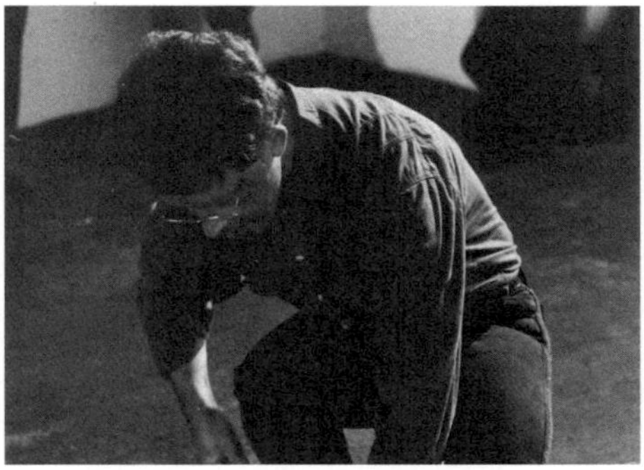

3–5 Terry Fox, *Lesung*, performance, 1990, Syndikat Halle, Bonn. Photo: Franz Fischer

The work that Terry Fox read out loud in the exhibition situation was titled *Running Text*, according to this report from 1990. One year later, in 1991, it was shown in Mönchengladbach, this time titled *Delineation*. It's clear that Terry Fox presented his works in a flexible way, not merely in terms of the title: in some exhibitions, the individual wooden slats were shown as an autonomous work leaning against the wall next to one another, or once again in an interplay with *Cynosure*.[19] The text in *Delineation* arose during a time that Terry Fox was living in New York City. It is an associative description of the emotions and movements of passersby on the street that he observed from his studio there.

In the exhibition catalogue of 1991, sketches and texts were printed in large format to allow the writing on the objects to be read. The status of these drawings is not always clear. For example, compared to the installation, the text in a sketch for *Delineation* reads in the opposite direction: from up to down. In another sketch published in the catalogue, the wagon object is still labeled "WAGON." In the frame work of the accompanying exhibition, however, it had the title *Wagon (Target) Text*. It was only at a later point that Terry Fox determined the final title *Cynosure*. The first association is that of a handcart. War, escape, agriculture, baggage transport: in certain situations, two-whee-

Halle, Bonn, August 29, 1990," in ibid., p. 25. Modified version of an article in the *Bonner General-Anzeiger*, September 1–2, 1990.

19 Views of alternative installations of *Delineation* can be found in *(RE/DE) CONSTRUCTIONS &c. terry fox*, exh. cat. Kunsthalle Fridericianum (Kassel, 2003), p. 43, and in *Elemental Gestures*, p. 131.

led carts are a simple and easy means to transport materials, goods, or personal belongings. Neither pack animal nor motor are needed; people pull or push their loads themselves. In the catalogue to a 1992 solo exhibition in the US, a reproduction of a photograph was published that shows Terry Fox as a young man in Italy, standing before a market wagon in 1962 (fig. 6).[20] In comparing these images, one quickly realizes that his wagon object would never have been able to function in this way. The wheels have no spokes, and are no more than semicircles. They might be parts of some machine's flywheel that Terry Fox discovered and used as found objects in his work. In other works, he also altered everyday objects and materials that he'd randomly come across: for instance the mirror[21] in *Dal cielo del fuoco (for Joseph Beuys)* (1986, Kunstmuseum Bern) and a stuffed fox with an oversized bottle from the *"Lauschenden" Fuchs* ("Listening" Fox, 1998).[22] With its little note and its seemingly everyday content, a small edition from 1992 seems innocuous at first: a cassette

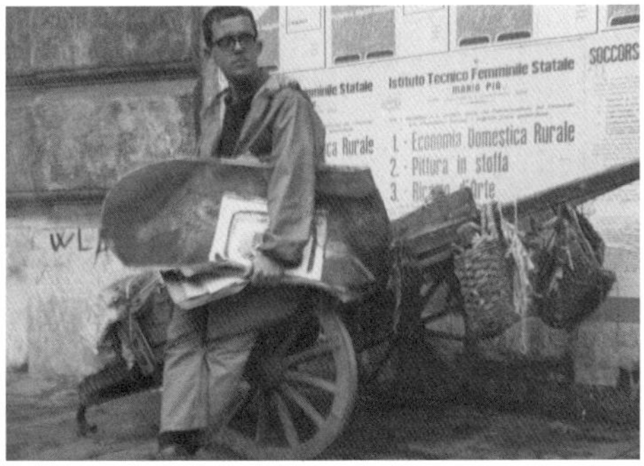

6 Terry Fox in Rome, 1962

case contains a small iron spring, inside of which is a tiny branch of thyme, a stone, and two blank keys. Inside a slip of paper was the solution for a rebus for anyone who couldn't come up with a solution, even after a fair attempt at solving the puzzle. It's an edition object that was issued at Christmastime 1992. The written instructions on the note with the solution were: "OPEN IN FEBRUARY."[23]

A second look at *Cynosure* reveals that the wagon's movement is only possible in fantasy. It's about associations here, and these add additional dimensions to the puzzle. Of the curators and critics who have commented on the work, it's usually the wheel's lack of function they emphasize.[24] Whether the static wagon is perceived as being at a standstill, or just broken, remains an open question. Terry Fox's works often harbor ambivalence. They feel raw and alluring at the

20 *TERRY FOX: Articulations (Labyrinth/Text Works)*, exh. cat. Goldie Paley Gallery, Levy Gallery for the Arts in Philadelphia, Moore College of Art and Design, Philadelphia; University Art Museum, University of California, Berkeley; Otis Gallery, Otis School of Art and Design, Los Angeles; Santa Monica Museum of Art, Santa Monica (Philadelphia, 1992), frontispiece.

21 Terry Fox used mirrors in several works, for instance in the video *The Rake's Progress* (1971, 30 min., University of California, Berkeley Art Museum, and Pacific Film Archive), which was only rediscovered a few years ago. According to Steve Seid, it's not a final version: "Not a finished work but a rehearsal tape, it finds Fox first establishing a camera setup through which he will eventually be shot performing before a freestanding pane of glass. . . ." See Steve Seid, "Thinking Inside the Box: Conceptual Video in the Seventies," in *radical LIGHT: Alternative Film & Video in the San Francisco Bay Area, 1945–2000*, ed. Steve Anker, Kathy Greitz, and Steve Seid, exh. cat. University of California, Berkeley Art Museum, and Pacific Film Archive (Berkeley, Los Angeles, and London, 2010), pp. 165–70, esp. p. 168.

22 It's a game with language and object: on the glass bottle, an imprint of a brand named "TERRY" can be read. The title refers to the original installation of the fox in the context of the exhibition *ATARAXIA* in the Stadtgalerie Saarbrücken, 1998. See *Works with Sound*, p. 13 (ill.). Other objects from the rebus series are also constructed from simple, everyday materials and found objects.

23 *REBUS*, 1992. After eight weeks of unsuccessful guessing, the owner could open the piece and finally place the objects in proper relation to one another: "Springtime in the Rockies" was the solution to the riddle (spring, thyme, rock, keys). The edition was made in collaboration with Ronald Feldman Fine Arts, New York.

24 Kathleen Bühler was the first to examine the text in *Cynosure*. See Kathleen Bühler, "Performative Traces: Terry Fox in Bern," in *Elemental Gestures*, pp. 127–35, esp. pp. 131–32.

same time, while the sounds they generate can be perceived as both stimulating and repulsive, as the review of his action *Lesung* showed. At the same time, the many layers that go to make up the straightforward-seeming text objects transform them into highly compressed constructs. The wagon itself is also characterized by this kind of complex simplicity.

Traveling

Constance Lewallen summarized the works in the Bonn exhibition thus: "Taken together, the objects and drawings in the show were metaphors for a rail journey."[25] On the floor lay a work that was reminiscent of railroad ties (*Ferrovia*, 1990) (fig. 7); on the ceiling was a construction made of wire that brought cables running between electricity poles to mind, and hence observations one might make while looking out the window during a train journey [*Wire (Rail) Text*]. In both cases, one was able to read individual words in the works. After a glance at the ceiling, the visitor could decipher the words "MIND," "WOUND," "COMMON," "MOUND," "SOUND," and "SOON" from the wire object.[26]

Being on the road is a theme that also marked Terry Fox's personal biography. As a young man he traveled to Europe for the first time, to Italy. This trip was followed by many others, some of them for long periods, some for a short time. Among other places, he lived in Rome, Paris, Amsterdam, Naples, and Berlin. San Francisco was also a place that left its mark on him, where he lived for several years in the nineteen-seventies and which always drew him back. Before Terry Fox moved to Cologne in the mid-nineties, he'd been living in Liège, Belgium, which Arnold Dreyblatt interprets as follows:

"His decision to move to Liège, Belgium from Florence in the 1980s reflected a desire to have the best of both worlds: a site near the cultural centers of Northern Europe and the chance to remain invisible in a marginal working-class city (with a large Italian population) and most importantly, to be left alone."[27]

For his form of art, Terry Fox found far more support in Europe than in the United States, even though two galleries there represented him.[28] Regarding a sojourn in Switzerland, he wrote a postcard to his friend and artist colleague Tom Marioni: "Hey Tom! You are going to like BERN!!!! I have never been treated so well in my life—beautiful people, space, accommodations."[29]

Some of the concentrated works Fox made in Belgium came together in the exhibition *Terry Fox: Elemental Gestures* (2015–17) (fig. 8). A work titled *Exposition* (1990) (fig. 9) was also made in Liège. In this drawing and collage, elements of

25 The author adds in parentheses: "(Fox formulates much of his work while traveling by train through Europe.)" Constance Lewallen, "Terry Fox," in Philadelphia 1992 (see note 20), pp. 6–35, esp. p. 31.

26 See Fricke 1990 (see note 18), p. 24.

27 Arnold Dreyblatt, "A 'Material Community' of Things," in *Elemental Gestures*, pp. 19–23, esp. p. 21.

28 Ronald Feldman Fine Arts, New York, and Gallery Paule Anglim, San Francisco (renamed Anglim Gilbert Gallery after the gallerist's death in 2015).

29 Presumably sent on May 4, 1989 (the year in the postal stamp has not been clearly made out to date). The postcard is in the Archive of the Museum of Conceptual Art (MOCA), located in the University of California, Berkeley Art Museum, and Pacific Film Archive. Transcribed by the author and quoted from private research material. A clear comparison with materials in the data bank of the BAM/PFA not yet digitized at the time of the research has not yet been possible. See https://webapps.cspace.berkeley.edu/bampfa/search/search/# (all URLs accessed in October 2017).

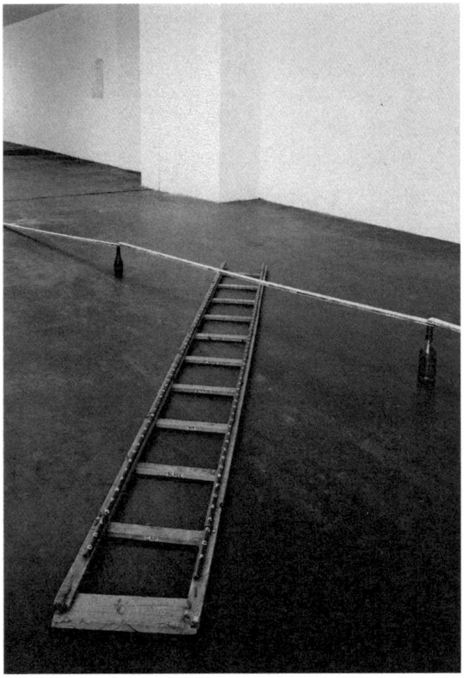

7 Terry Fox, *Ferrovia*, exhibition view, Syndikat Halle, Bonn, 1990, installation, sculpture with text, iron, wood, oil paint, ink on paper, 318 x 36 x 6 cm, private collection. Photo: Galerie Löhrl

Cynosure and *Delineation* are superimposed and complement one another.[30] Once again, the links between the works seem close, the various planes of text important, and the materials plain: adhesive strips, paper, pencil. Many objects are both drawing and sculpture, and ignore the differentiation between two- and three-dimensionality. They are "multilayered" in both form and content.

Astronomical Allusions

The final title of the wagon object, *Cynosure*, means both the center of attraction and the North Star of the constellation Ursa Minor (known in German as the "Little Wagon"). This allusion between title and object is only directly accessible to native English speakers, which makes many of the works particularly tricky for Europeans. The constellation is also called "Little Bear." Throughout various epochs and cultures, different myths, animals, and objects were associated with star clusters. On a map of the stars comprising the Little Bear (1603) by Johann Bayer (1572–1625), the bear is standing on its head. In his *Uranometria*, a first atlas of the stars, Bayer set out with the greatest possible precision to represent the night sky in fifty-one such maps.[31] With the publication of *Coelum stellatum christianum* in 1627, the Augustinian monk Julius Schiller (?–1627) attempted to transform the variations common until that time into Christian versions (that did not, however, prevail in the long term).[32] The English word *Cynosure* comes from the Ancient Greek,[33] which opens up an additional path into mythology, one I will not, however, pursue further. The Latin term for the Little Bear (*Ursa minor*) can be translated more directly and almost literally.[34] One could spend ample time just with the titles of Terry Fox's works. An investigation into the entire oeuvre—the abundance of references, hints, allusions, and plays on words—reveals a bottomless pit. The text objects in particular can lead the viewer far afield from his or her spontaneous reactions and

30 See the large-scale reproduction of *Exposition*, 1990, in Mönchengladbach 1990 (see note 17), p. 14.

31 In 2010, a reprint was published: Johann Bayer, *Uranometria*, facsimile (Gerchsheim, 2010). See the digitally published version of the historical maps of "Ursa minor (Little Bear)" by the Heidelberg University Library, http://digi.ub.uni-heidelberg.de/diglit/bayer1648/0010?sid=dd6b29fce4bfe7d71c3fcc-ba8610c112.

32 Via the library of the ETH Zürich, a PDF can be viewed that offers an idea of the forty-nine copper plates from Julius Schiller et al., *Coelum stellatum christianum* (Augsburg, 1627). Johann Bayer also contributed to t his atlas. See http://www.e-rara.ch/doi/10.3931/e-rara-8720.

33 (Ancient Greek) = "the dog's tail."

34 *Ursa minor* (Lat.) = translated literally means "smaller female bear." As a term for the stellar constellation, the masculine form "the bear" (*ursus*) is not used in Latin.

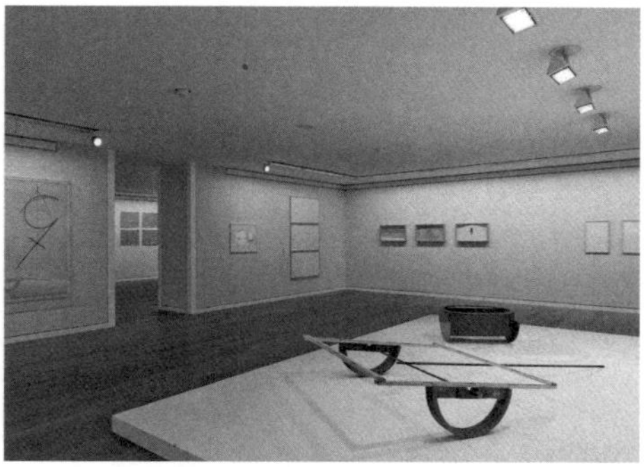

8 Terry Fox, exhibition view of *Elemental Gestures*, Von der Heydt-Museum, Wuppertal 2016–17. Photo: Antje Zeis-Loi

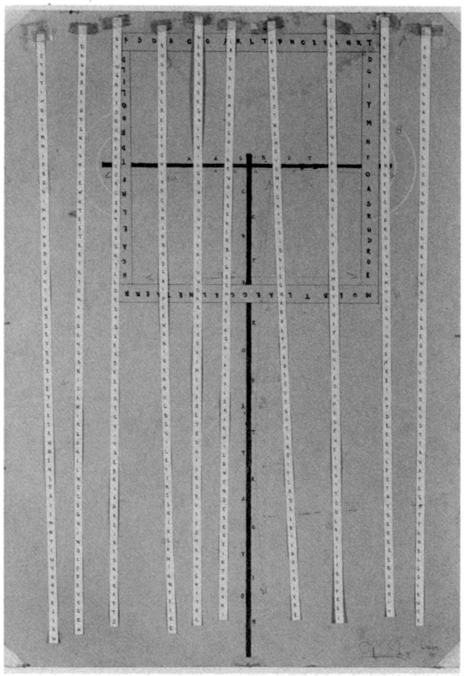

9 Terry Fox, *Exposition*, 1990, drawing, collage, acrylic, pencil, ink, paper, and adhesive tape on cardboard, 73 x 52 cm, Kunstmuseum Bern. Photo: Galerie Löhrl

thoughts; in the case of *Cynosure*, all the way to astronomy.

In a 2015 exhibition, the Research Library in Gotha attempted to make astronomical phenomena clearly understandable: “More than most scientific disciplines, astronomy knows how to catch the eye—this goes both for the phenomena that can be observed in the sky and the representations in manuscripts and prints of what has been seen. At the same time, astronomy revolutionized seeing by using astronomical and optical apparatuses that, as ‘extensions’ of the eye, made things previously unseen visible, which called for a new way of looking at the world that went beyond the obvious.”[35] Terry Fox’s works seduce the viewer into peering beyond the evident presented in the exhibition space—and to think it a step further. Both in its external form and through its title, *Cynosure* refers to a particularly compelling star whose name is now “Polaris.”[36] Transposed onto the construction of the “wagon,” the Pole Star would be at the tip of the shaft resting on the ground, a rather unassuming position. Additional parallels lead away from the external appearance to more general processes of human perception: “We don’t merely recognize the ‘Little Wagon’ in the form of the object. The way in which we connect points in the sky to form a familiar shape is also akin to a reading process and is reflected in the act of perceiving this work.”[37]

35 This explanation continues: “For this reason, the numerous illustrations in the astronomic works of the early modern period were not merely of a specialized and aesthetic nature. They also fulfilled a clear pedagogical purpose, namely to school people in this new way of seeing.” http://himmelsspektakel.uni-erfurt.de/sektion-8/.

36 See the websites of the Working Group on Star Names (WGSN) of the International Astronomical Union (IAU), https://www.iau.org/science/scientific_bodies/working_groups/280/.

37 Wall text in the Kunstmuseum Bern, exh. *Terry Fox: Elemental Gestures*, 2017.

I would like to thank Seraina Renz for her cooperation and inspired exchange over Terry Fox’s work.

On the Text

Terry Fox's wagon lures us into examining details, reading what's written on it, moving around it slowly.[38] Anyone who takes a closer look discovers letters equidistant to one another, aligned in rows. Each of these letters is carefully applied to the ground: Terry Fox used white oil paint to write the letters on the dark, crisscrossing iron rods. He used ink to apply the rest of the "characters" onto paper strips, which were then affixed to the wagon's wooden frame. The texts oscillate between handwriting and drawing; on the one hand, they are legible, and on the other legibility is just what they precisely resist. It requires a good deal of patience and concentration to glean meaning from them. A word's spelling usually dictates the way it is written. Unusually, Terry Fox spells words practically, by giving the same formal attention to each individual letter. He is uninterested in capital or small letters, punctuation, or other peripheral matters. His artistic conversion of an ordinary language system into various artistic formats usually remains as unpretentious as the works themselves (handwriting, typewriter, printing process).

Anyone who takes a little time will probably decipher the two phrases "M A G N E T" and, (on the wagon's shaft), "C E N T E R O F A T T R A C T I O N." The text on the frame is also comparatively easy to read, once the viewer discovers that the reading principle involves skipping over a letter: highlighted in color, every second letter provides a kind of reading cue. The process is simple, but it requires a considerable feat of attention on the part of the viewer, provided he or she becomes active. Suddenly, reading is no longer a self-evident thing. The texts on Terry Fox's works demonstrate what a person fluent in a language easily forgets: that it's difficult to learn a (foreign) language, to practice fluid reading, to acquire the skills to write—handicraft in the truest sense of the word. In the first step, each text is literally a "manuscript" written by hand in a concrete sense. But when the use of writing utensils and paper demands effort, the meaning, purpose, grace, and poetry of a language often remain elusive.[39]

Terry Fox had a keen interest in various language and sign systems: Morse code, Braille, sign language, political graffiti, sheet music, and not least the sign he developed himself, which unites all the letters of the Latin alphabet—all of these appear in different guises in some of the works. Transformation processes can be found here and in his actions: Morse codes are presented as (acoustically silent) drawings, while Braille, meant to be touched, is paradoxically presented as a system that is only visually legible. This confronts the senses with things they are not used to and challenges perception and thinking on a constant basis.

Terry Fox clearly expected us to decipher the texts, even if the grids of letters in certain works pose a challenge to the reader. In many cases, Fox wanted us to discover his tracks. The drawings, which oscillate between construction and documentation and were published for the first time in 2015 in the exhibition catalogue *Terry Fox: Elemental Gestures*,

38 Depending on the installation, it's no longer possible to walk around the works. For this reason, the texts can only be followed physically as far as the museum presentation and/or the objects' protection allows.

39 Terry Fox was forced by illness to adapt his technique to his physical abilities: some phases of the illness gave rise to shaky drawings and prints that for the most part were made without the artist's hand. Typewriter and index cards were also faithful companions.

also make this clear. In a sketch for *Cynosure* using blue and red, the principle of alternating colors in the individual letters is explained through demonstration (fig. 10). What can be deciphered through this manner of reading, whether it be on an object or in the catalogue? "S H O R T," "N E A R," "D I M," "F A R," "D O U B L E," "C L E A R," "H A L F," "D U L L."[40] These prefixes that can be attached to the word "sighted" run through the lines of text in the frame. Terry Fox leaves it for us to decide if someone is "shortsighted" in a physical or mental sense, and whether or not sight is good or bad. Here, too, political interpretations are possible—as in the aforementioned *Catch Phrases*, which express skepticism toward euphemistic (largely military) terms and exaggerated formulations (yellow press).

When one views the overall work of Terry Fox, it is no surprise that the terms joined together in *Cynosure* circle around the notions of seeing and focusing. It could, however, come as a surprise to viewers who had primarily considered him a sound artist. Furthermore, he plays a game with synonyms which all circle around a central "focal point." Another term that can be found on the wagon is "centroid." Quoting the artist, Constance Lewallen writes about the group of works to which *Cynosure* belongs: "Fox has described the works as 'all about centering.'"[41] Terry Fox took this theme of circling around a center and expressed it in concrete terms in works with pendulums that he made in the course of his investigations of the floor labyrinth in Chartres Cathedral. The print *Pendulum Spit Bite* (1977) was made using a special pendulum device, and published in California by Crown Point Press (fig. 11). The work is an aquatint resembling a view of the universe, among other possible associations, that Terry Fox signed on all four sides. Astronomical constellations were also important orienting tools for sea travel. It's interesting that Terry Fox integrated a term from shipbuilding into *Cynosure*, namely, "M E T A C E N T E R."[42]

Balance

One last aspect that *Cynosure* calls attention to is something that can easily be overlooked in the exhibition, but is certainly very present for restorers and for anyone who has already been involved in setting up an exhibition of Fox's work. People who have had access to his notebooks and sketchbooks could find in them the statement: "EVERYTHING HELD TOGETHER BY BALANCE."[43] The work is kept in place without screws or nails, through the equilibrium of the material alone, which is in a permanent balancing act. It would be easy to bring the wagon into an unstable position if it were to leave its metaphoric state

40 Kathleen Bühler writes: "The combination of the many different allusions, evoking both seeing and understanding in general, creates the right frame of mind for perceiving this 'Little Wagon' as a celestial phenomenon. For Terry Fox, the viewers' participatory approach should be so intense that it allows them to undergo a similar experience in reading the words as he himself had when he wrote them. In his view, the external appearance of the work is only a bridge enabling the viewer to access the experiences described in the text." Bühler 2015 (see note 24), p. 132.

41 Lewallen 1992 (see note 25), p. 32.

42 In physical terms, it seems to be about the ship being constructed in such a way that it lies in the water in the most stable possible manner. "The term 'meta' (Greek: apparent) suggests that this intersection is not a true center, and hence is not a fixed point," writes Prof. Dr.-Ing. Stefan Krüger in *Hydrostatik von Schiffen*, Institut für Entwerfen von Schiffen und Schiffssicherheit, Technical University Hamburg-Harburg, August 2008, http://www.ssi.tu-harburg.de/doc/webseiten_dokumente/ssi/vorlesungsunterlagen/Hydrostatik_Skript.pdf.

43 See the double-page color illustration of the sketches for *Consonant* and *Cynosure* in the sketchbook *Beuys Mirror, Bern* (undated) in *Elemental Gestures*, pp. 160–61.

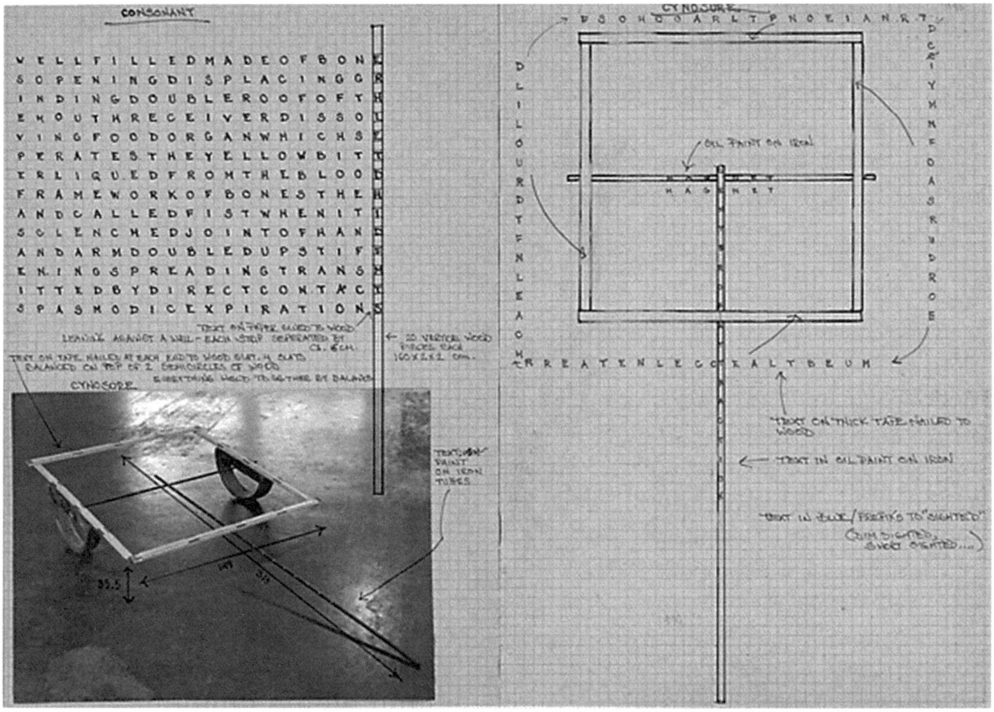

10 Terry Fox, (*Untitled*), from the sketchbook *Beuys Mirror, Bern,* undated, mixed media on paper, double-page spread, 29.8 x 21 cm, Estate of Terry Fox, Cologne

and begin to move. The construction is fragile, and thus the opposite of useful and efficient—ultimately, it's a symbol for human existence.[44]

The large number of associations and dimensions contained in *Cynosure* resist any one interpretation. The strength of Terry Fox's work lies in the ambiguity of his objects and actions. He has not made a strategy of any particular theme or medium; he's always remained open to influence and inspiration, without losing his autonomy:

"In numerous objects and installations, Terry Fox uses his own or found poetic texts that force the reader to follow the deciphering of a given spatial structure, which makes the 'reader' himself a performer in a space that interlocks real space with the space of consciousness."[45] This mental space that Bernd Schulz describes is especially apparent in Fox's (artist's) books. For this reason, his publications are also to be understood as centers of attraction. The reading experience that can arise calls for both concentration and patience, and hence calls for a very quiet situation that goes beyond the possibilities and conditions of an exhibition visit.

View TEXTUM (WEB)

The artist's book *TEXTUM (WEB),*[46] one that hasn't been the subject of much

44 See Lewallen 1992 (see note 25), p. 32.

45 *Works with Sound*, p. 10.

46 Terry Fox, *TEXTUM (WEB)*, ed. Het Apollohuis (Eindhoven, 1989). Edition: 1000. Facsimile of a "Notebook" by Terry Fox with a two-page "Decoding card."

attention to date, is laid out as a notebook, a school notebook (see fig. VII-IX in plate section). It was published in 1989, in cooperation with Het Apollohuis in Eindhoven. In this publication, which on the outside seems so reserved and unassuming, a variety of languages and signs merge: carrying across the page are typewritten sentence fragments similar to the *Catch Phrases* that Fox collected from European and American news reports and tabloid headlines; Italian graffiti and medieval carpenters' signs (which marked the wood for subsequent steps in the working process) are on top, while Braille writing runs throughout the notebook (from up and down and from page to page, transformed into red dots); Morse code has an almost painterly quality and is spread out over every page; when the book is leafed through, Fox's alphabet sign jumps playfully across the pages.[47] Included with the publication is a double page of card stock with keys for deciphering and reading the Braille and Morse code. But the reader may also need paper and pencil to solve the puzzle, because the lettering is stylized and not easy to make out, and the language systems first need to be decoded. Notebook pages that are confusing at first glance turn out to be completely simple: one word that can be decoded, for example, is "simple." Yet, as Constance Lewallen succinctly observes: "But the underlying text of all the *Textum* drawings illustrates the subversion of language—exaggeration, euphemism, military doublespeak. If these require an attentive reader to decode them, one could say the same of all of Fox's work. None of it comes easy."[48]

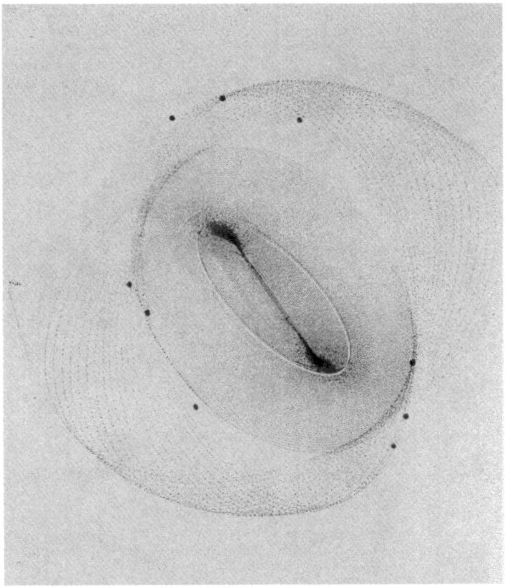

11 Terry Fox, *Pendulum Spit Bite*, 1977, graphic reproduction (edition of 25 published by Crown Point Press, San Francisco), aquatint etching on paper, 101.4 x 124.3 cm. Photo: Crown Point Press

On the level of the letters of the alphabet, meaning in *TEXTUM (WEB)* can be gleaned directly and easily throughout the book's fifty-four pages by putting together individual letters. The hidden message exists without odor, color, taste, form, and thoughts—and leaves the last word to silence: "O D O R L E S S C O L O R L E S S T A S T E L E S S F O R M L E S S T H O U G H T L E S S A N D S I L E N T." Which

47 Constance Lewallen writes about *TEXTUM (WEB)*: "As in *Catch Phrases*, each drawing is multilayered and has as its base a typewritten text on graph paper. Half the drawings list phrases Fox collected from the American news media in Europe; the other half reproduce headlines from the *Weekly World News*, a tabloid published in Florida that specializes in sensationalist and bizarre stories ('Children Sucked from a Damaged Jet,' 'Granny 73 Dumps Her Hubby Because He Was No Don Juan,' 'Siamese Twins To Face Firing Squad,' 'Jealous Computer Kills Top Scientist.' Fox overlayed Italian graffiti signs on the first group and medieval household signs over the second. The household signs are simple, abstract arrangements of horizontal and vertical lines. They were instructions marked on planks of wood to tell carpenters what the wood would be used for—a cradle, a chair, or cabinets. All of the drawings include a line of Braille, a column of Morse code, and a circular sign Fox invented that combines all the letters of the alphabet, all of which can be read from the first to the last page. Each drawing, then, comprises five languages that, if not decipherable to everyone, have meaning for certain groups of people." Lewallen 1992 (see note 25), p. 30.

48 Ibid., pp. 30–31.

in turn opens a path to a sculptural text object embodying these very same ideas: *Ovum Anguinum* (fig. 12).[49]

Silence is a theme that runs throughout Terry Fox's work. He was a bibliophilic sculptor who liked to use sound, and yet did perfectly well without it. In the truest sense, words are spelled out and entire language systems dissected. The text objects testify to a talent for observing the content and form of language(s) in a precise and critical way. They can neither be read nor deciphered if perused quickly or spoken hastily. They demand and require a conscious, concentrated quietude: silence.[50] In 1990, Christiane Fricke summarized it in her review: "Artists who are able to bring our fantasy, thoughts and senses into vibration are rare. Terry Fox is one of these."[51]

Translated from the German
by Andrea Scrima

49 See *Ovum Anguinum*, 1990, Von der Heydt-Museum, Wuppertal (ill.), in *Elemental Gestures*, p. 168.

50 Along with the term "silentium" for silence, the Latin language also has the word "tranquillitas" which means both "still air" and "tranquility."

51 Fricke 1990 (see note 18), p. 25.

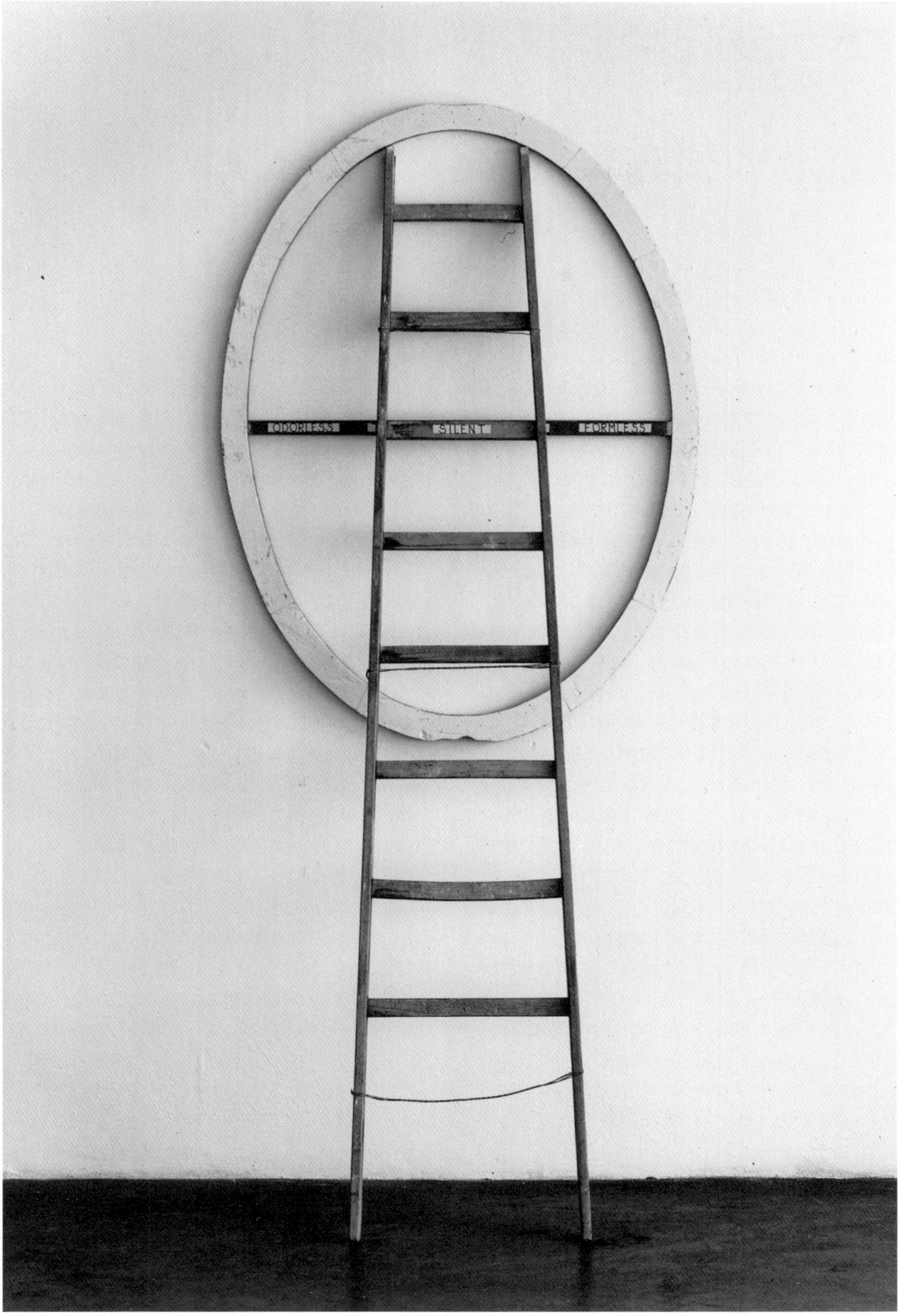

12 Terry Fox, *Ovum Anguinum*, 1990, wall sculpture with text, ink on paper, oil paint, wood, 240 x 110 cm, Von der Heydt-Museum, Wuppertal. Photo: Antje Zeis-Loi

Konrad Tobler

Adolf Wölfli, Terry Fox, Labyrinth

There's a saying: "Where the fox and hare say good night to one another, the wolf isn't far off." Fox and hare, Fox and Beuys—and then Wölfli, Wölfli Adolf. While the relationship between Terry Fox and Beuys is well documented, his relationship to Wölfli, although it's more than just speculation, can only be grasped sporadically. One instance is the action or performance Fox put on in the Kunstmuseum Bern in 1980: *A Candle for A.W.*, a work all traces of which have since vanished, a work that only exists as a rumor, as it were. I spoke with numerous possible witnesses from the time, but no one, not even Gerhard Johann Lischka, can remember. Thomas Pfister, former director of cinema in the Kunstmuseum Bern and a walking encyclopedia in many respects, is the only one with a vague memory of a swinging pendulum and a bottle, which the pendulum circled around in a steadily diminishing radius—until it tipped over? And was the bottle a kind of candlestick, so that the candle fell over too, and went out? This ephemeral action has remained ephemeral, which presumably touches upon the core of Terry Fox's work concept [see commentary, p. 25].

Whatever the case: Fox became acquainted with Wölfli's work at Documenta 5 in 1972, in which he also took part, in the section "Individual Mythologies." At the time, Fox remarked succinctly that the overall exhibition was fairly negative, but that the work of the mental patients—he used the word "insane"[1]—was pure exaltation and the only thing in the exhibition that really moved him.[2] However: this is also where Fox met Theodor and Elka Spoerri. Theodor Spoerri was responsible for the "Art of the Insane" department in Kassel, while Elka Spoerri was the scholar who deciphered Wölfli's writings, revealing the literary dimension of his work in addition to the visual. The truth is, just as A. W.'s works would never have enjoyed the understanding and reception they did without Walter Morgenthaler and his 1921 monograph *Ein Geisteskranker als Künstler* (published many years later in translation as *Madness and Art: The Life and Works of Adolf Wolfli*), without Elka Spoerri, the power and range of A. W.'s art would never have been noticed to such a degree that artists such as Fox—and many more, including an amazing number of composers—referred to A. W. in their work. According to credible sources, Elka Spoerri gave Terry Fox access to works by Wölfli that were nearly inaccessible at the time, in

1 See "Insania pingens" (1961) and Harald Szeemann and Jean Dubuffet, *Bildnerei der Geisteskranken = l'art brut = insania pingens: Kunsthalle Bern, 8/24–9/15/1963*, Kunsthalle Bern (Bern, 1963), unpaginated.

2 *Elemental Gestures*, p. 50.

1972. And as chance would have it, I am writing these words in the very same room in the historic city center in which Elka Spoerri researched Adolf Wölfli's works. Thus Fox, albeit indirectly, is perhaps—or hopefully—very present here as spiritus rector. It should be added that an authoritative catalogue was published on the occasion of the major Wölfli exhibition in the Kunstmuseum Bern, in which various aspects of the research were brought together systematically for the first time: the relationship between Wölfli's actual biography and medical history and his imaginary life story; the formal vocabulary and investigations into the musical work, to name but a few thematic areas. It can be assumed that Fox, through Elka Spoerri, had access to this catalogue, another presence.

Yet this presence does not free me of certain methodological difficulties. Traces of Wölfli are barely perceptible in Fox's work. This provides space for the creation of legends. Added to this is the random fact that an anthology of texts by Robert Walser was lying on Fox's desk when he died, with a work by Wölfli on its cover. What does this thematic/formal statement mean, exactly? Walser and Wölfli, both from Bern, both patients in Waldau? Or is it more than that? I'd like to escape fixations by emphasizing that I'm merely formulating hypotheses that can only be based on potential coincidences. In order not to relegate these to a system by means of a supposedly coherent theory, I've decided to arrange the presumable, presumed, and possible aspects that connected Fox with Wölfli in an encyclopedic manner. Thus, there is no hierarchy of terms—and no claim to completeness or closure. The result is a kind of labyrinth of links that seems fitting to me, particularly because the labyrinth is a conceptual and representational element that plays an important role in the works of both Wölfli and Fox.

First of all, and slightly out of alphabetical order:

A. W.: In 1980, as stated above, Fox referred in a performance to Adolf Wölfli. Fox could not have known that Ad. W. was the very abbreviation the news sheet of the city of Bern used on December 22, 1890, to make public Wölfli's first conviction on a charge of child molestation.

Note: In an e-mail from July 15, 2017, Marita Loosen-Fox called my attention to the description of a pendulum installation in connection to the Labyrinth of Chartres: "Pendulums, which resemble the movement and rhythm of a labyrinth, figure throughout the series. In one work, a lead ball hangs on a string from the ceiling, barely touching a half-filled glass of water on the floor. When the viewer swings the pendulum, it rotates closer and closer to the glass, and, as it runs down, gently hits the glass with a bell-like tone. Hugging the glass, it then switches directions over and over again in reversing arcs, like the Chartres labyrinth." Catalogue: *TERRY FOX: Articulations*, Goldie Paley Gallery (Philadelphia, 1992), p. 20.

Action Performance

Algebra Measuring the world as Fox pursued it in his exploration of the labyrinth, searching for the sound of space—both of these themes find their counterparts in Wölfli's work, for instance in his ode to algebra:
"Allgebrah!
¿ Yes what!! What is it suppossed to mean! Oh, how fine! It's the foehn. Answer.
Allgebrah is music! Oh, is it! Absolutely! And this goes for every instumenntt. Everything that's visible to the Human Eye, or invisible! With a finely developed sense for people, goud will, hard work, and appropriate available Materiahl, it can be turned into Music= Songs=Text, in fact from the smallest to the largest object, or non-object."[3]
For Wölfli, "Allgebrah" is bliss and hatred, love and happiness, music and God, "gix" and light, father and "a,=stray."
"Allgebrah now is, Summer Allgebrah
You're Sick!
My name was Trrans=Pom'rania! That's why I'm sending him, yarn!
Full of wounds pain and, Hits! On the hard Sick=Bed.
God certainly is full'o drives! Thatt's whiy He won't get fat to-day."
Finally, Allgebrah is also rolling thunder.[4]

Alphabet A game or conceptual work with letters is central to Fox's work. Many of Wölfli's works contain elaborately drawn capital letters in a wide variety of designs, which Markus Raetz traced for the catalogue in 1976. And in his overall writings, Wölfli developed his own écriture, though for Wölfli, writing is always doing, a performative act. Language is sound, rhythm. Onomatopoeic elements regularly emerge, practically according to the laws of an automatism. Thus, a special kind of synaesthesia ensues. At one point he writes that he's staging a "control Of the female Christian=names, from the alphabet, from the letter O": "Respectfully, Doufi. Bern. Orantika! Ohandja! Opheelia! Olga! Otilia! Oreelia! Okulia! Orsiera! Olanttera! Orchida! Odessa! Odaliske! Ormara! Omaha! Oliifia! Obadia! ONaventtura! Oxantta! Ozega! Olianda! Ocidenttia! Odenttia! Oja! Ondura! Omeelia! Oporta! Ortona! Onttaria! Otorantta! Owanda! Ozareena! Ozitta! Ozohna! Olittta! Odoolia! Oternitta! Offenttura! Oogen. Ebjä!! Summa, 40 beautiful Women's=Names, not to be scoffed at in any whey"— ingenious in their malapropisms, where both Wölfli's erudition comes across (Odaliske, Ophelia), and his desire or urge to transform things in order to appropriate them: Offenttura (Ofentüre, oven doors), or Odolia (Odol, a mouthwash).

Architecture In Wölfli's works, both narrative and -> **Image** solidify into a methodical architecture. He depicts buildings, such as Waldau and the Felsenau spinning mill; he draws city maps of Bern (whether created from memory or from source material remains open). Medical history: "To reward the decorations he made on the -> **Museum's** cupboards, Wölfli went to the city today [Bern] with Mr. and Mrs. Dr. Forel and their assistant—for the first time in 25 years. He still knew his way around the city. 'Here is the Amthausgasse, there the Gurtengasse. I lived in that buil-ding, as an indentured child laborer.' He recognized the Altenberg. In vain, he searched for the Sankt Adolf Grand Hotel in this area, and was amazed not to find it. From Bundesterrasse, he pointed to a brick building standing in Kirchenfeld; 'That's St. Adolfs Elysium, also called the Coin.' Wölfli was extremely self-confident. He brandished his cane in the air and several times he hit passersby in the face with it; he didn't get along well with the bustle of the city; he often had terrible trouble when he, in his self-confident self-satisfaction, had to make way for the streetcar. They visited: the Kornhauskeller, the Bundeshaus, the Weltpostdenkmal, the cathedral. They climbed one third of the tower. They also visited the Bircher bookstore, where the recently

3 Adolf Wölfli, *Von der Wiege bis zum Graab, Oder, Durch arbeiten und schwitzen, leiden, und Drangsal bettend zum Fluch: Schriften 1908–1912*, 2 vols., ed. Dieter Schwarz and Elka Spoerri (Frankfurt am Main, 1985), vol. 1, p. 16.
4 Ibid., pp. 16–17.

published work by Dr. Morgenthaler on Wölfli lay open. He was made aware of the book, and de-monstrated the natural behavior of the undisputed -> **Artist**. In the end, they took repose in the Schänzli (café)" [Patient report from April 7, 1921].
With Fox's work, both architecture and landscape are constitutive, particularly in the -> **Labyrinth**. Both evince an inclination to -> **Ornamentation**, which in turn is to be understood as an architectonic structure and includes -> **Symmetries**.
And: the architectures of Wölfli and Fox are sound-bodies, all the way to Fox's labyrinth cat song.

Art Brut

Artist The fact that Fox saw himself as an artist in his own broad concept of the term requires no further justification.
Being an artist becomes more problematic for those who are classified within Art Brut. To what extent are they impacted by the artist's social function, what do they know, how do they see themselves and their work? It's clear that Dubuffet expanded the concept of the artist. And it's a given that Walter Morgenthaler had already blazed this trail in 1921 with his Wölfli monograph *Ein Geisteskranker als Künstler*. Apparently this also had an effect on Wölfli's image of himself, because given his background and level of education, Wölfli could hardly have known what an artist was. His own later descriptions of his profession, howe-ver, leave no doubt that he saw himself as an artist: "St. Adolf II, Allgebrahtor, Supreme Command-Er and / Music Direktohr, Great- Theaat'r- / Direktohr, Allmighty-Great- / Steamship-Capitaain, and / Dr. of Art and Science, / Direktohr of Allgebrah and Geography Staple-Manufatture / and Hunter-General."
Truly: an expanded concept of art!
Indexes of works that Wölfli made also indicate his artist's sense of identity.
His medical record testifies to this, as well: "Drawing busily in his cell, doesn't want to go into the garden, he doesn't have any time for that, he has to finish his life's work, which is of the greatest importance. Since the publication of Morgenthaler's book, pat. is even more confident, even more reinforced in his delusions of grandeur, one often hears him say that he is the greatest artist, and anyone who doesn't agree understands nothing about art; squabbles with other patients here and there who don't know how to appreciate him in keeping with his achievements" [PR April 26, 1921].
In his "Schüpfen letter" of 1922, Wölfli plans an exhibition of ten drawings, "African views" in the "Ballroom" of the Bären Tavern in Schüpfen. To this purpose, he writes a "portrait table" with titles and prices, instructions for framing the pictures, a transcription of the entire text on the backs of the ten portraits ("gesammten Täxt auf den 10 Portrait-Rükseiten"), and adds a short final chapter about himself ("kleinen Schlusskapitel über meine Wenigkeit").
As early as 1912, he planned a publication in fictitious collaboration with the Wiss printing house on Gurtengasse in Bern [Catalogue 1976 (see note 7), p. 120].
There are many more big-big-book projects in Wölfli's writings, and they all point to a well-developed sense of artistic identity.

Bern

Beuys

Biography Wölfli's work is biography, real and fictitious.
Fox's work includes his own life.
-> **Illness**

Candle Did Fox's reflection on the candle in reference to the *Children's Tapes* also apply to his action *A Candle for A.W.*? "Phenomena and their worlds. Like all the different shapes the candle can assume, all the kinds of things you can do with it, things that happen to it. Like with the flame, you can skin the flame, take away all its color and make it invisible with a fork. There were constant variations of those objects together—the fork and the candle, or the candle and the water, or the water and the bowl . . ."[5]

5 *Elemental Gestures*, p. 137.

Christ The topos of the artist as martyr persisted at least into the nineteen-eighties. The topos is usually used in connection to St. Sebastian, and often connotes homosexuality. The Christ topos as artistic self-identification is clearly older. Christ as the Crucified is a recurrent motif in Wölfli's drawings, and Christ's head, usually masked, can often be interpreted as Wölfli's self-portrait. Beuys also played with allusions to Christ in certain rituals, in drawings, and in a small sculpture made of bottles of blood. In the mid-seventies, Beuys created the installation *Show Your Wound*. Harald Szeemann never tired of speaking (rather uncritically, and hence emphatically) of Beuys's similarity to Christ, which Fox presumably took note of. It's no accident that Fox's complex homage to Beuys, *Dal cielo del fuoco*, connects the cross with the labyrinth. To sum it up: in its ritualized action, in its incorporation of blood (the Lord's and Fox's blood), and in its reference to medieval practices, Fox's action *Levitation* from 1970 can be understood as an attempt at a brief resurrection. As with Wölfli, the (albeit indirect) reference to Christ in Fox's work is also a reference to the -> **Cross** and to -> **Illness**.

City

Collage "Pat. drew all over his cell, made it very nice, but unfortunately he pasted postcards and pictures from magazines into some of his drawings, and thinks they look better that way. He'd like to order a rug for his cell, made from a drawing of his. He has enough money, he told me, and we should definitely order it in Constantinople" [Patient report, November 3, 1921]. -> **Concepts**

Concepts Much can be projected onto Wölfli's work. This includes his -> **Collage** technique, which he used without being in a position to know that collage was one of the most important techniques for the Cubists and Dadaists, who were his contemporaries.
The projection of concepts onto Wölfli's art is comparable — although there is ample indication that he very well knew which arcs of tension he wanted to construct, and to what degree he made room for improvisation within his strict rules.
This can be seen in the genesis of the *Trauermarsch*.
"He's quite busy with the funeral march he's now begun to compose & he doesn't allow himself even a minute of rest" [PR, December 5, 1928].
"He works much, draws uninterruptedly, sitting at his table, and whenever I order him to stop working, he tells me that he doesn't have the time to stop working, he has to draw so and so many pages of his funeral march, he becomes rude, and then nothing can be done with him" [PR, December 22, 1929].
In the Inselspital, he "didn't cause any problems at all; at the operating table, I had to promise to water his plants once a week, to reserve his cell for him and to bring him paper, pencils, and an eraser so that he could work after the operation & as soon as he's back in the NB [new building at Waldau], he wanted to finish the composition of his funeral march" [PR, March 18, 1930].
"Thin, his face pale, straining with the last of his energy, the pat. sits at his table and writes. He has to finish the funeral march, he has to, he says irritably. He says that anyone who knows anything about music will be able to play the march, it will be printed & bring in several hundred thousand Fr" [PR, September 6, 1930].
"Pat. very weak, cannot even sit up, he informed me today, with tears in his eyes, that he can't draw anymore, he no longer has the strength, if he could only die! He has terrible pains, and he'd so hoped to be able to finish his funeral march by Christmas" [KG, November 2, 1930].
Wölfli died on November 6.

Cosmos Starting in 1913, Wölfli created his own cosmos in his geographical notebooks, in which he is God the Father and God the Son in one (-> **Christ**). As is so often the case, fragments of an astonishing erudition flash up:
"Creation God of the Allmighty Fathr. Anno 3671 before the buhrth of Christ,

Eeternity! Anno 1.
Arisen from a pyure, absolute, Nothing, a gigantic number of allmight-y spirits hoover through the maygestic space of endless and bowndless eeternity, toward all conceivable Cardinal=-Points, fnd nothing to hold onto and no support anywhere and, God the Holy Spirit, The Allmighty, All Powerfull, All Mercifull, All Benevolent, All Just, All Knowing, All Wise and All Prevailing, Goddess, Holy Santta Maria, was in High Pregnancy. Heere spoke the greatest and most powerful of these spirits, the God, Orpheus, let there be a staar on which wee can All fnd tolerable shelter and lodging and, as He commanded, There it was. A planet, calld Eearth! Desert, raw and emptee! And it was drk as far as their eeyes couhld see! And, all spirits floated above the water . . .
And now the holy, allmighty and all-powerfull goddess, Santta Maria, bore, in one of these resplendent Gigantic=Palaces, the sweetest, highly intelligent and charming little boy, which she called, God, the allmighty father . . . . Everything was God the allmighty father, through his maygestic Allpowerfull=Word, Let there be, commanded and ord red, giving rise to true-to-life, highly elegantt, practical and comfortable, magnificent and wonderful maygestic Informattion, in the moment and, not a syngle, goohd or evil being in the realm of the endless Creation and Eternity is able to successfully defy or resist his godly will and command. Of the above statements, I am, the finalunddersignned, as a result of cowntless and, to the greatest degree of variation, highly individual experiences, really, truly, and completely convinced. At this hour I am a horrible, bitter Miss=fortt=une, befohr my very own, favorite child, befohr God, the Hol. Spirit, unable in any whay to savve and to absolve from this calamit-ouss, full of damn=ation, eearthly Human=Power and eearthly Art! Even less, myself. But God, the allmighty Fatther, shallt not forget his dear Child, the Hol. St. Adolf and faithfully fulfill his erstwhile beautiful promise for me, resurrection of the Deahd. Therefoore Praise, Honor, Prize and Thanks, to God the Allmighty Father, Lord and Creator of all Woorlds, together with everytthing that's on and in them, from Eeternity too Eeternity, Amen, amen. It shall be. Respectfully undersigned, the Hol. St. Adolf."

Cross -> **Christ**

Death

Délire Delirium. As a verb: to be crazy, talk nonsense. In a phonetic interpretation: *entlesen*, *zerlesen*, *WEGLESEN* [words with the common root meaning "to read": select, wear out through reading, remove a thing by reading]. An important exhibition in 2004 at the Musée de l'Art Brut in Lausanne, Écriture en délire, played with this.
The question is whether writing written in delirium is legible, or withdraws from legibility. And what meaning can be deciphered. And: can meaning be equated with clarity, cogency? How is it when the meaning of a text is to be read in the withdrawal of meaning? -> **Walser**

Documenta

Duration 120 hours for Fox's action *Lunar Rambles*.
Wölfli labors for years on his works, for which he presumably had an idea or even a -> **Concept**, at least his *Trauermarsch* suggests this. But did he previously determine this idea, without sketches, following his intuition and improvisation in the execution?

Écriture

Everything

Eye "The eye is not the only glass that burns the mind" (Fox).
To burn, to scorch, inner burning: this connects Fox to Wölfli.
With Wölfli, the eye is ubiquitous. Masks can be seen in his works that are clearly self-portraits. Wölfli's eye burns and ignites—into the past, real or fictitious. His inner eye sees things that no one else sees.

Fish

Folio Wölfli bound his works together into regular folios, the work *Von der Wiege bis zum Graab* alone consists of forty-four volumes.
Fox possessed a facsimile of the folio *De laudibus sanctae crucis* (The Praise of the Holy Cross), Hrabanus Maurus (ca. 780–856).

Gesture -> **Action**

Glaesemer, Jürgen *Gleichzeitigkeit des Anderen* (The Simultaneity of the Other) was the title of the 1988 exhibition in the Kunstmuseum Bern, where works by Wölfli and Fox were seen, this time in a much closer context than at Documenta 5.

Illegibility

Illness "My name was Trans=Pom'rania! That's why I'm sending him, yarn!
Full of wounds pain and, Hits! On the hard Sick=Bed."
Fox's life was marked by illness. There are numerous cross-references between his illness (that is, his biography) and the labyrinth.

Immediacy As much as Wölfli's work is marked by a certain immediacy, one that tends to fascinate viewers of the works of -> **Art Brut**, he follows -> **Systems** all the more, for instance the music in the 60-cm-thick notebook No. 15 (1918) or in the *Trauermarsch*. -> **Concept**, -> **Artist**

Instrument Wölfli played his musical scores on paper trumpets.
Fox left behind trumpetshaped objects that had no opening. The sound remained inside the instrument, which thus became an instrument of silence.

Labyrinth Daedalus was the exemplary artistic worker. An inventor, architect, technician, and artist. In Ovid's *Metamorphoses*, one reads that King Minos received a magnificent silvery white bull from Poseidon as a sign that his prayers had been heard. This pleased the king so much that he ignored his vow to sacrifice the animal to the god of the sea. Poseidon's revenge for this neglect was insidious: when Minos married Pasiphae, a daughter of the sun god Helios, Poseidon made sure that the young bride fell immediately in love with the bull. Pasiphae enlisted Daedalus's help in constructing a wooden dummy of a cow in which she could hide in order to perform the sexual act with the bull. The fruit of this union was the Minotaur, a hybrid creature, half human and half bull—an important motif for Picasso. Daedalus was ordered by the king to construct a labyrinth to imprison this dangerous and rabid monster. This labyrinth was so carefully devised that Daedalus himself nearly didn't find his way out after he finished building it.

Wölfli creates a labyrinth to shut away his own monster, his constant feelings of guilt. The structure of his pictures is labyrinthine, the structure of his stories is labyrinthine, and finally his fictitious cities are labyrinthine.
Terry Fox: "I discovered a metaphor for my physical being—not my body, but the labyrinth. I worked for years with the labyrinth. Everything I did, I placed in relation to it. Actually, my work was entirely based on it, in an almost scientific way."

Language

Legends

Letters -> **Alphabet**

Life

Lines In some of Wölfli's pictures, one can make out a musical staff, but without the notes, in other words, empty systems of lines.
In reference to this, Theodor Spoerri wrote in 1964 in his book *Die Bilderwelt Adolf Wölflis* that these lines resembled the strings of an instrument.[6] To add to this: they resemble the strings of a zither that Wölfli speaks of in his *Trauermarsch*: "Nimm D'Zittere mit!" These lines would then be imaginary potential sounds on the mute page.
Starting in 1976, Fox made room-sized sound installations using musical

6 Th. Spoerri; Adolf Wölfli, *Die Bilderwelt Adolf Wölflis* (Basel, 1964).

strings (piano wires) that in turn frame a connection to the labyrinth.
-> **Strings**

Magic

Measurement

Music In 1976, Kjell Keller and Peter Streiff attempted to transfer Wölfli's notations into music. They state that a definite translation into actual music is impossible. Thus, the notations are like a concept that might possibly sound as though Wölfli had folk music on his mind. And would have been able to write the notes to it.
Wölfli's music includes the rhythm and sound of his language, the alliteration and stage directions in texts such as: "Beat or Turn / Repeat."

Musical score

Myth

Narrative

Notations

Novalis I would be astonished to learn that Fox hadn't studied German Romanticism. In any case, a poem by Novalis fits nicely with the decidedly Beuysian impulse that I believe I have detected in Fox's work. Whether or not Wölfli knew the Novalis poem *When numbers and figures are no longer* must also remain an open question. But, though he had little formal schooling, there is much he can be credited with. Why shouldn't he also have taken note of Novalis, if his work already contains parodic paraphrases from Schiller's *William Tell*, paraphrases that almost sound like -> **Walserian irony?**

When numbers and figures are
no longer key to all creatures
when those who sing and kiss
know more than men of deep science,
when the world returns to the world
and to life in freedom,
when light and shadow join in true clarity,
and stories and poems are
discovered true stories of the world,
then, with a secret word
will go flying the altered self

Numerals

Ornament -> **Architecture**

Performance

Person / Mask

Photography It's clear that photography as documentation of the transitory is central to Fox's work. The fact that Wölfli liked to pose while having his picture taken is an integral part of the image we have of him: Wölfli in his cell, filled with works, Wölfli with a paper trumpet.
The fact that Wölfli thought about photography is less known. His fictitious travel agency is located in Madrid and is in partnership with King Alfonso VII. It's a matter of a wedding and a commission for a certain Jacob to take a picture of two chapels. Then, the "Maijestät!" says: "Indeed. If you wehre a pro oPer photographer, then the enttire thing whould be in no time, correct. Welll, but: Think I that you weren't finished a half hour ago. ¿ You know what, Jacob! I will buy you a photographic apparatus This Evvening so that you can, without much trouble, get on quickly and surely in the future. Settled! It's a deal. Bravo, Maygesty!" Shortly afterwards, a brief dialogue: "Ahahh! The photographer=factory owner's apprenthice. Holy Moses! Really! A magnificent specimen. ¿ How good and solllid it is. That it is Maygesty! For every genree! And this photographers=apparathus costs, paid in cash, 480 Fr. Maygesty! Sessa! Here's your money in silver and gold and 10 Fr. tip for the courier=due."[7]

Plan

Pose

Presence

Reassurance

Reference Fox is not the only one to refer to Wölfli. It is well known that Paul Klee had already taken an interest in Morgenthaler's book on Wölfli, as

7 Wölfli 1985 (see note 3), pp. 120–21.

did Rilke and the Surrealists. In 1948, Dubuffet exhibited 120 of Wölfli's drawings in the Compagnie de l'Art Brut in Paris. A Wölfli drawing hung in the living room of the Bern artist Rolf Iseli; this last was in the late sixties, and my first encounter with Wölfli.

Repetition Repetition marks the works of both Wölfli and Fox. But repetition is not to be understood as a perpetuation of the ever-same. Rather, repetition, according to a reflection of Kierkegaard's, is a "recollection forward": "Repetition is a crucial expression for what recollection was to the Greeks. Just as they taught that all knowing is a recollecting, modern philosophy will teach that all life is a repetition. . . . Repetition and recollection are the same movement, except in quite opposite directions, for what is recollected has been, is repeated backward, whereas genuine repetition is recollected forward. One never grows weary of the old, and when one has that, one is happy. He alone is truly happy who is not deluded into thinking that the repetition should be something new, for then one grows weary of it."[8]

Thus, repetition (Wieder-Holen) is an act of taking again, an -> **Action**, a transformation, as innocuous as it might seem to be. Repetition is a concept that includes time, includes -> **Duration**, as in Fox's 120-hour (or five-day) performance *Lunar Rambles* of 1976. On the other hand, in Wölfli's work, the writings *Von der Wiege bis zum Graab* took years to complete, from 1908 to 1912, and contained both anticipations and regresses, in other words, repetitions.

Ritual

Self

Self-reflection

Self-representation

8 Søren Kierkegaard, *Fear and Trembling / Repetition, 1843*, trans. Howard V. Hong and Edna H. Hong (Princeton, 1983), p. 381.

Sequence

Set pieces In Wölfli's work the -> **Collages**, in Fox's the headlines from the tabloid press.

Snake

Sound Soundsoundsound. Important to both. When I read Wölfli's texts closely for the first time, they seemed mute. The eccentric orthography resisted an easier read. It was only when I read and at the same time listened inwardly that the texts became fantastically dramatic, grammatically perfect reading passages, dramas, novels, poems, dramacles [a neologism: combination of drama and spectacle. A pupil of mine used the expression in an essay in which he described an accident that was a close call].
And so the meaning arises out of the sound, that of the inner voice.

Space / Cosmos In imagery and in words, Wölfli created a nearly endless -> **Cosmos**.

Spoerri

Strategies

Strings

Systems

Szeemann

Time

Tone

Vault In Fox's work, the vault and -> **Cellar** are recurring locations for his actions.
In Wölfli's view of the world, in his detailed world voyage, there are many beautiful descriptions of underground -> **Cellars**. "Yes!!! ¿ And now the Huge=Cellur! Ebyen! Theyre they come, in a row as follows. Signed Adolf Wölfli, Naturahlist.
The Seelenfels Cellur in China, Ching Provinze. 54,872,000,000, cubic meters air space.
The Seelenfels Cellur-Titi, the largest column on Eearth, supports the vault

in the middle and has a height of 1,900 meters. A Diametern of 158 feet, made of lotts of marble, zephyr, and jasper, resplendent in the widest array of colors and ornaments and, erected fully, costts the enormous sum of around 283,000,000 Fr."[9]
Isn't Fox's sculpture *A Metaphor* (1976) also a kind of column, which, with the drawing of the labyrinth in the middle, metaphorically alludes to a cosmic connection between above and below, Heaven and Earth? But, in contrast to Wölfli, the materials are extremely *brut*: two stools.

Word/image

Wound
-> **Christ**, **Cross**, **Illness**, **Labyrinth**

Writing

Translated from the German
by Andrea Scrima

9 Wölfli 1985 (see note 3), p. 365.

Max Wechsler

Terry Fox at *Furk'art*

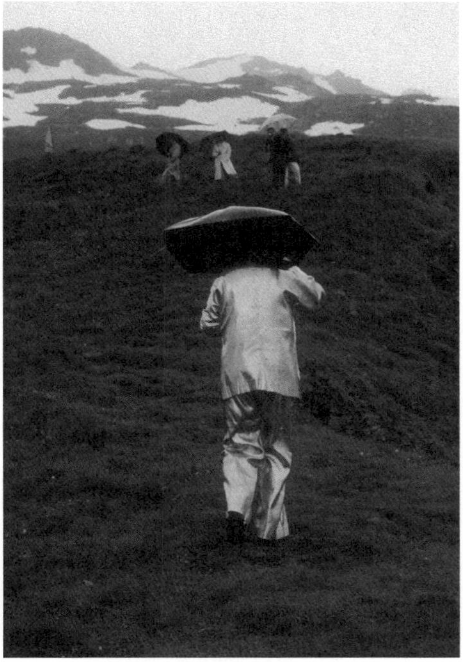

1 James Lee Byars shortly after his action, photo: Max Wechsler

So as to justly honor Terry Fox's contribution to *Furk'art*, it is first necessary to introduce *Furk'art* itself, before delving into two interventions by Terry Fox on the Furka in 1990. And in that context we would also like to discuss a performance by the Japanese artist Yutaka Matsuzawa, who staged a thematically related work in 1984.

On July 24, 1983, James Lee Byars celebrated *A Drop of Black Perfume* on the Furka Pass in the Swiss Alps. Dressed in a golden suit and patent leather shoes, a top hat on his head and his face shrouded in a black silk scarf, the artist offered the Alps drops of "black perfume" that the storm-whipped weather blew away in an instant, along with their silkily exclusive fragrance (fig. 1). Byars's dramatically loaded actionist gesture, made in the context of his exhibition at Marc Hostettler's gallery in Neuchâtel, was a poetic act situated between intimacy and grandiosity that entranced the audience and moved Hostettler, as spiritus rector of the enterprise, to create a unique "cultural laboratory" on Furka (fig. 2). Neither an extension of his gallery at 2,431 meters above sea level, nor just one more summertime art event outdoors, it was a workshop in the actual sense of the term: an open forum for doing and viewing art that allowed for concentrated artistic work under the special conditions of its remote location, far from the usual hustle and bustle of the art market.

The Furka Pass had long since forfeited its significance as a central traffic artery. The formerly chic Hotel Furkablick and its annexes were still shakily standing, but anyone who might have lost their way there was either an Alpinist or a motorized day-tripper or a dogged biker, if not doing service in the Swiss Army. The famous

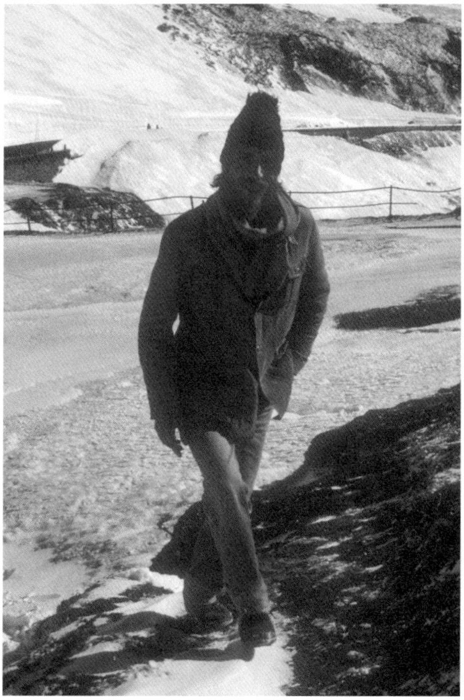

2 Marc Hostettler, photo: Max Wechsler

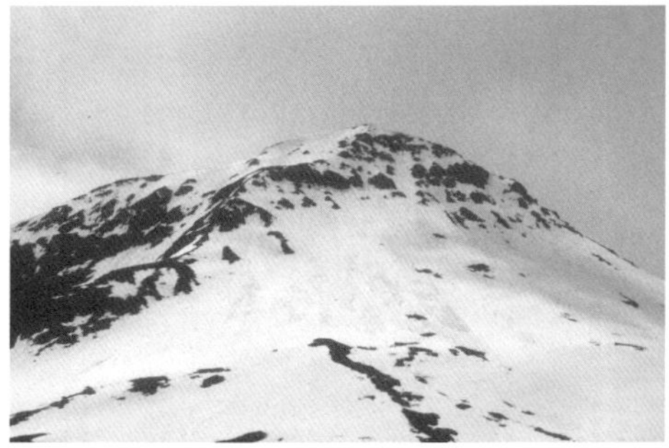

3 View of Blauberg (Blue mountain), photo: Max Wechsler

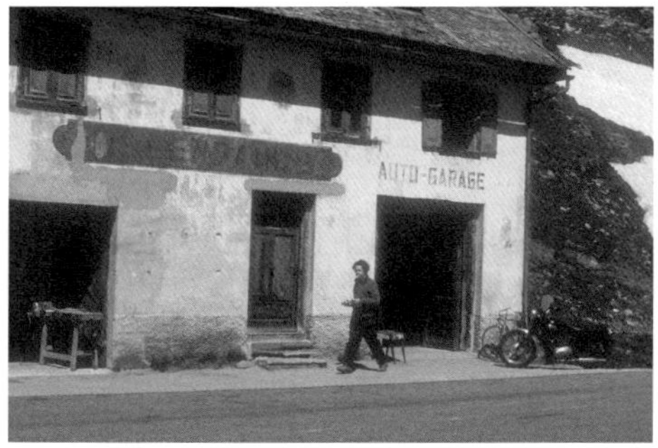

4 Panamarenko in front of his garage workshop, photo: Max Wechsler

pass in those days was not only a raw region at the weather's mercy but was a desolate place. The archaic aspect of the omnipresent natural drama came all the more to the fore: the genius loci of the Alps as a place of sublimity that arouses a euphoric effect in human beings, one that oscillates between reverent astonishment and capricious high spirits. In short: the Alps as a place of heightened perception.

The first year of the actual *Furk'art* enterprise began on June 24, 1984, with the *Introduction of the Sages to the Alps*, a mysterious action by Joseph Beuys and James Lee Byars. This heavily symbolic walking of the blue mountain introduced a new myth to the already mythically burdened Alps: the figure of the "sage," perhaps the myth of the artist on an eternal search for form, meaning, and perfection (fig. 3). The audience huddled on the pass while two figures barely discernable in the distance—one in a golden costume and the other in fur—trudged through the snow until they gradually vanished from view. On the following Monday morning it was Yutaka Matsuzawa's turn, soon to be described. In addition, in the hotel's garage, the Belgian artist Panamarenko set up a branch of his workshop for flying machines—which he kept in operation for many years—in order to work on the project *Flugrucksack* (Flight Backpack, fig. 4). The first year concluded with the 78th day of the *Nightsea Crossing* performance by Marina Abramović and Ulay on September 22 (fig. 5). The two of them sat down opposite each other—as they had previously done in so many places around the world—in the former dining room of the Hotel Furkablick. During seven hours of unmoving silence, conditions outside the room on the other side of the window

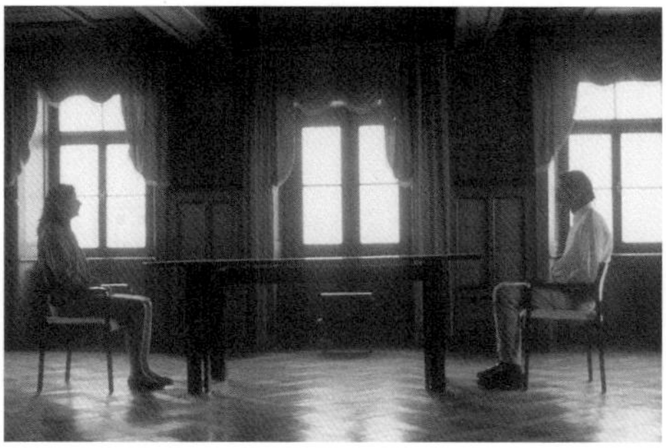

5 Marina Abramović and Ulay, *Nightsea Crossing*, photo: Max Wechsler

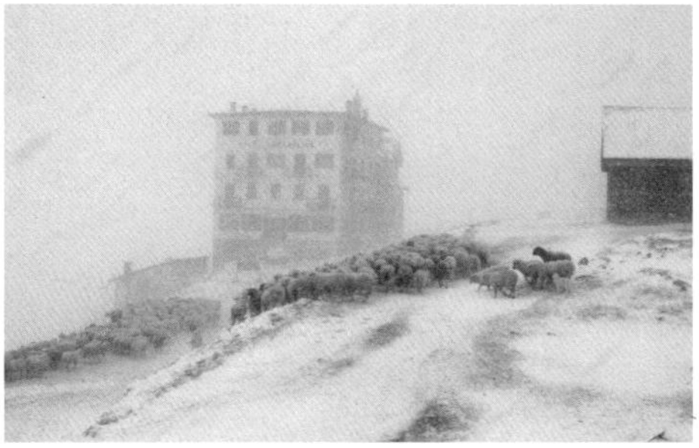

6 Sudden temperature drop during the performance, photo: Max Wechsler

were mirrored on the surface of the table between them. The wild stormy weather could be perceived as gradations between a dim and a bright sheen, a snowstorm that brewed and howled and shrouded everything in silence—and sent the sheep fleeing hastily into the valley with shepherd and dog (fig. 6).

Obviously, the entire *Furk'art* project did not remain under the romantic sign of sublimity, as in that first year. Although it was always sustained by a prevailing existential mood, over the years more than sixty artists articulated the most disparate concepts, their contributions being forms and types of art that almost always had a relationship to the place, but not necessarily a direct thematic relationship to the Alps. For instance, I would like to mention Rémy Zaugg, who for a long time pursued his explorations in painting in the

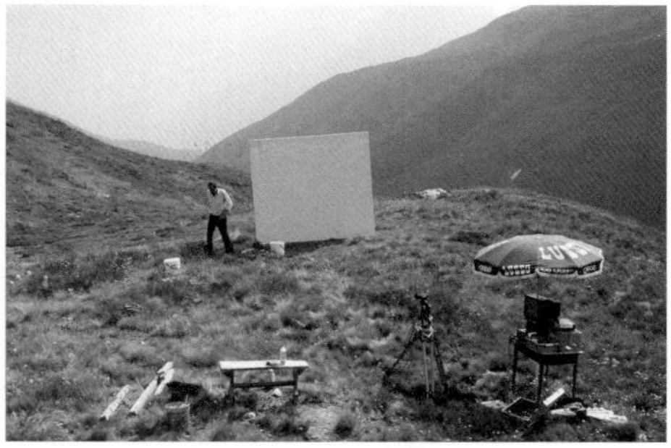

7 Rémy Zaugg paints *sur le motif*, photo: Max Wechsler

realm of pleinairism (fig. 7). Or Ian Hamilton Finlay's famous *Proposal for the Furka Pass*, which consisted of having Ferdinand Hodler's signature carved in stone and placed on the site (fig. 8). In subsequent years, Marc Hostettler was able to acquire the Hotel Furkablick for the whole summer. This also provided the opportunity to house artists and art pilgrims and to bring them into a dialogue. As of 1986, the activities really began to gain momentum and were sustained with various degrees of intensity until 1999. Also remarkable was the project to renovate and convert the building, which Rem Koolhaas and OMA concluded in 1991. In 2004, after a phase of inactivity, the Furkablick complex, together with all the art that remained on site and in the building, was acquired by the Alfred Richterich Foundation. What has emerged is the Institut Furkablick maintained by Janis Osolin, which is concerned with preserving the old collection but also deals with new approaches and a more wide-ranging perspective for the "Furka Zone."

This is not the occasion to pay tribute to the *Furk'art* project as a whole. However, the selective points just mentioned show how broad the arc of endeavors was and how intensive was the work that emerged. Last, though not least, *Furk'art* was an important locus of exchange, not only for

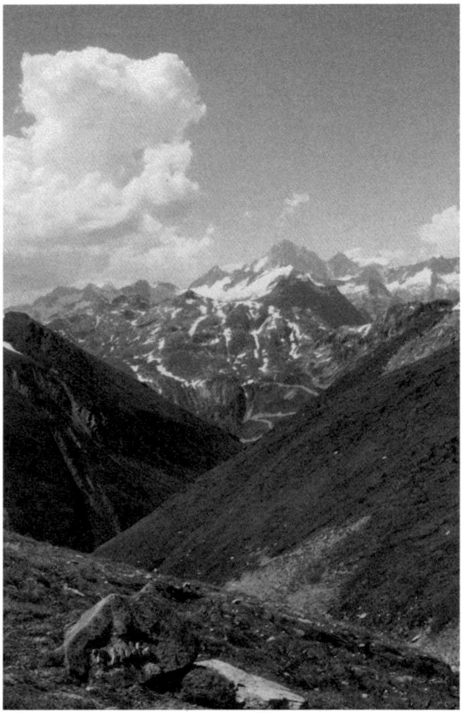

8 Ian Hamilton Finlay, *Proposal for the Furka Pass*, photo: Max Wechsler

artists to enter into conversation with each other, but also for an interested audience to get a taste of artistic motivations. The beginnings of *Furk'art* now already lie almost thirty-five years in the past, and yet the adventuresome history of this "cultural laboratory" has scarcely undergone critical interpretation and has only recently become an object of scholarly attention. Here I mention only the commendable dissertation by Jürgen Grath, published under the title *Furk'art: Spuren des Ephemeren* (Traces of the Ephemeral).[1] It represents the first serious attempt to assemble materials and create order. But much is still located in the deceptive, yet all the more intensive, arena of memory and thus, above all, in a realm of stories and speculations. And perhaps that's also good, since the thing was set up as a living field of experimentation. Therefore, it's important to pay attention to the fact that no sacrosanct statements can be made about the events, since most of the reports come from individual eyewitnesses—and that opens up a broad range of fact and fiction.

But now, finally, to Terry Fox and his project *Locus Harmonium*, as his work was titled. In order to describe this event, I am relying on my own memories as a participant in the action as well as on those of other eyewitnesses, on the existing photographic material, and, above all, on the video of the action made with the artist's agreement by Aufdi Aufdermauer. At the invitation of Marc Hostettler, Fox spent five days on the Furka and stayed at Hotel Furkablick. I believe he had traveled from Hamburg, which would fit in well with the frozen fish he brought with him. But in a later commentary on *Locus Harmonium*, first published in 2000, Fox wrote: "I decided to do an action with a fish [on the Furka], and so I bought a large sea bass in Basel on the way there."[2] I had assumed—as my fish cookbook suggested—that it was quite probably a red bream. At any rate, it was a strapping—albeit dead—deep-frozen ocean fish with a reddish tinge, whatever it might have been called. The action primarily dealt with the fact that a fish had been pulled from the sea in order to be carried up to an Alpine glacier to then be buried in the glacial ice, so that it would decompose there and end up once again in the sea. In the concrete instance of the *Furk'art* project, the fish's grave was located in the lowermost snout of the Sidelen glacier, whence the fish decomposing in the waters

1 Jürgen Grath, *Furk'art: Spuren des Ephemeren* (Munich, 2012).

2 *Ocular Language*, p. 219.

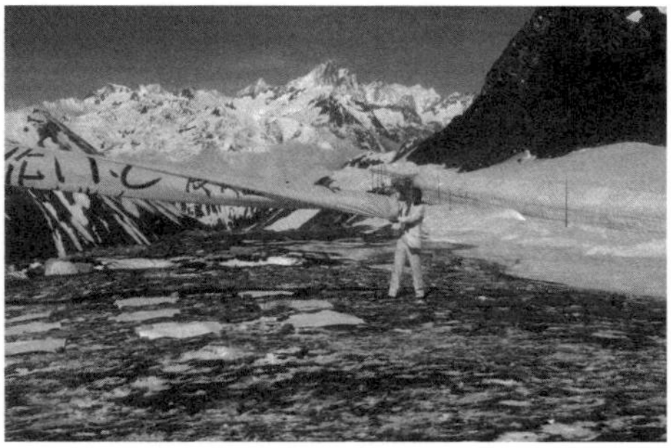

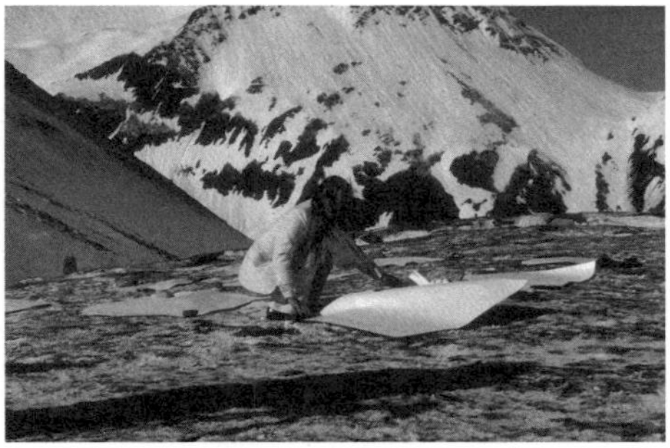

9–10 Yutaka Matsuzawa, *On the Ground of Several Places*, photos: Max Wechsler

of the Sidelen brook flowed down to the valley and into the Furkareuss. It in turn flowed into the Reuss, which flowed into the Aare, which flowed into the Rhein. And then away, back to the North Sea.

As mentioned before, the Japanese artist Yutaka Matsuzawa also made such an eternal cycle his theme in 1984. His performance titled *On the Ground of Several Places* took place on a beautiful Monday morning on the small stony plateau across from the old annex — at the border between the cantons Uri and Wallis. Matsuzawa began to spread white sheets of paper with red inscriptions on the ground, each of their four corners weighted down with a stone so that the strong wind would not blow them away. He then declaimed the contents of the inscriptions in Japanese and English and, next to the white field, continued his work with red sheets inscribed with white characters. Finally, after declaiming the white inscriptions, and standing now behind the inscribed sheets spread out among the scree, he unrolled a long pink ribbon of script which, with the beauty of Japanese characters, completed his message about the transitory nature of all things (figs. 9–10). He concluded with a graceful bow before his work and with individual words to each participant, thanking them for their participation in the action: a gesture in which proverbial Japanese politeness was expressed, but which beyond that imbued the event with a solemn, binding nature. Freely translated, the ribbon of characters proclaimed: "All you human beings, pass on, pass on, let us dwindle away." And he evoked this sense of yearning by reminding us, with this work, that this piece of earth had lain at the bottom of the sea countless years ago, and that in the foreseeable future, these sheets of paper would also end up at the bottom of the sea.

Back again to Terry Fox who, when he arrived, put the fish away in the hotel freezer and set off to explore the new environment. "I began to make many all-day hikes in the mountains searching for a place to deposit the fish during the upcoming performance."[3] It was a matter of finding the place where the fish would have its grave. One day before the action, he went alone, with a borrowed video camera, up to the Sidelen glacier and filmed a small ice cave, which apparently emitted a delicate music due to the constant dripping of thawing ice. It seemed to him, as he later commented, like "a beautiful dripping sound in the absolute silence of the surrounding environment."[4] And so he had found the burial chamber for his fish.

3 Ibid., p. 219.
4 Ibid., p. 219.

That was one aspect. Another was that Fox discovered, somewhat below the hotel, the small, old disused generator shed: a superbly disordered space with lots of wrecked machines, control panels, tools lying around, and all kinds of stuff—and it reeked quite bewitchingly of machine oils and fats. There, with no audience present, he set up a complex rebus which one could actually enter by intentionally integrating objects of all sorts—found material, banal objects, signs, and various things—into what already was a seemingly messy chaotic ambience. Especially conspicuous were the somewhat puzzling inscriptions in his typical handwritten capital letters on bottles, on pipes, and on the wall (figs. 11–13). But there were also texts that could be interpreted, such as the one on the object *Speculum*, a kind of inverted funnel whose curve bore the inscription "das auge ist nicht das einzige glas das den geist brennt" (the eye is not the only glass that burns the mind); and also playful fragments of text such as "ggabisggöpfe ggaufen gefälligst" in Swiss German dialect ("Kabis-Köpfe kaufen gefälligst" or "buy white cabbage"), which seems like simple wordplay. In this rundown transformer shed, Terry Fox had created a *situation*,[5] as he liked to call it. Then he told Aufdi Aufdermauer to go into the dark room with a headlamp and to film with the video camera everything that appeared to him to be an artistic intervention. What it all was supposed to mean remained, in the end, Terry Fox's secret. He watched the film attentively together with Aufdi and had a few prints made of it, but he expressed no judgment, nor any kind of comments that might have led further, nor did he speak about this episode in the transformer shed in the above-mentioned comments on *Locus Harmonium*. By the way, his friend Arnold Dreyblatt, who for a time was his neighbor in Lüttich, also describes similar puzzling situations: "Terry would create ensembles of found objects, collected from the abundant flea markets . . . . The items would be arranged as in a rebus, as pseudo-relics, or as optical puzzles. I would notice them in the corners of the kitchen or in his library—yet they always disappeared when I visited the following day. I would prod him about the whereabouts of a no longer visible work . . . only to be answered with indifference and annoyance. I once pushed him a bit harder, and he answered: 'Oh, yes, that one — I made that only for myself.'"[6]

The works in and around the transformer shed unfolded the evening before and the morning of the great *Locus Harmonium* action, which was set for Saturday, August 11, 1990. In the hotel kitchen before it started, Terry Fox hung the carefully bundled fish on his back and grabbed his shoulder bag, which contained, among other things, a violin bow. Then he set off along the red-white-red marked hiking path in the direction of the Sidelen hut. He crossed the street of the pass in front of the hotel, went past the Furka Pass Refuge, and soon he was on the ascending path, followed by a group of some thirty or more persons, who had traveled from all over to be present at this event. Two playful dogs were also present, a black one and a white one, and had their own very enjoyable time all the way up. The group of participants moved along the narrow, continually ascending path in a fairly lengthy formation, so that Terry Fox did in fact lead people to the Sidelen glacier in

5 See Nikola Doll, "Situations," in *Elemental Gestures*, pp. 117ff.

6 *Elemental Gestures*, p. 21.

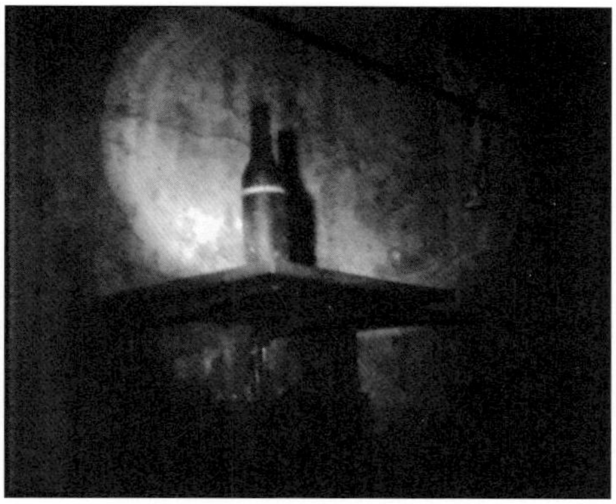

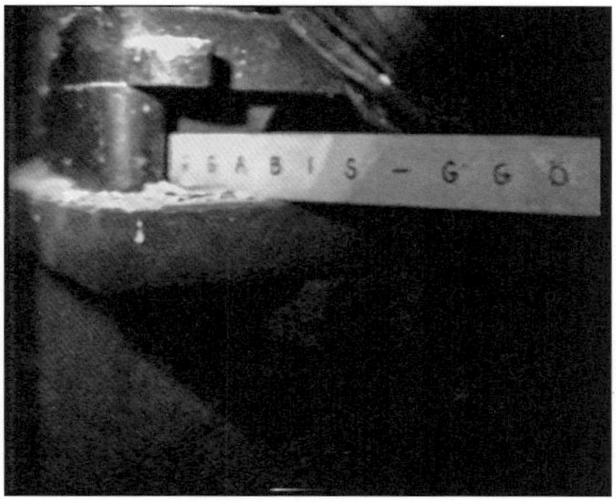

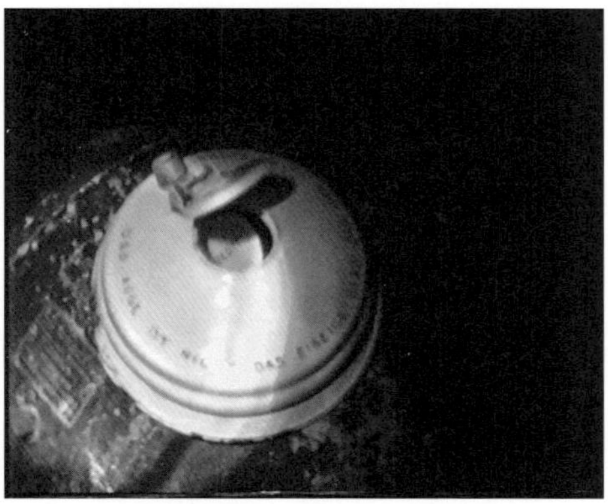

11–13 Terry Fox, *Locus Harmonium*, installation in the generator shed, Video stills from the documentation (1990) by Aufdi Aufdermauer.

"single file,"[7] as he describes it in his commentary. The hike, the final third of which led through rough terrain of loose scree, was interrupted several times by brief pauses in which the pilgrims, if they may be called that, could refresh themselves. Each time, the fish was respectfully set down: once in the icy waters of the Sidelen brook, once in a little field of snow along the way, and once on a jutting rock. Two or three times, Terry Fox made music with the sounding balls he had brought with him—the singing sounds were for the most part submerged in the rush of the wind. However, his own memory differs from my description, since as he put it: "During the walk up the mountain, we stopped two times where I played a resonant solid metal rod with a violin bow" (figs. 14–26).[8]

After about ninety minutes, the 270 or so meters had been surmounted and the group arrived at the cave that Terry Fox had discovered the previous day, in which his fish would be laid to rest. Holding the fish in front of him, with his back to the group, he gazed for a brief moment at the glacier like Caspar David Friedrich's *Wanderer über dem Nebelmeer* (Wanderer above the Sea of Fog). Then he went down to the ice, jumped over a small crevasse, and laid the fish in the chosen hollow. He then carefully closed the burial chamber with chunks of stone that were lying around and returned to us. In a relaxed atmosphere, little groups formed here and there, and the whole party gradually made their way back again to Hotel Furkablick on their own individual paths.

As indicated here, *Locus Harmonium* can be interpreted as a visual staging of the eternal cycle of life; a Christian interpretation might even be constructed in view of the obvious fish symbolism. However,

7 *Ocular Language*, p. 219.

8 Ibid.

the inherent existential subtlety of this radical action can only really be comprehended against the background of some of Terry Fox's artwork from the early seventies, when he had worked in various ways with fish. This was a time, moreover, in which Fox himself was in very poor health. I will mention *Pisces*, for instance, a two-part performance from 1971, to which I can give only cursory attention here (fig. 27). For *Pisces*, an action at the Museum of Conceptual Art in San Francisco, the artist bought two fish in a Chinatown market on February 2, 1971. The fish were laid on the ground and their tail fins connected with strings to the tongue and the penis of the artist, who was lying next to them. The shudders of the dying fish that he sensed were said to have "created in his mind an extremely graphic image of death."[9] Then the dead fish were wrapped in white cloth, tied up with string, and brought to the University of Santa Clara some sixty miles to the south, where they were laid on the floor, in a small gallery area demarcated by white cloth, next to two flashlights whose beams shined at each other. Terry Fox lay down at some distance from this arrangement—this time connected to the fish via a tooth and his hair—and attempted to dream about the death throes of the fish during a several-hours-long nap (see fig. p. 100).[10]

In closing, allow me to bring into play Gustave Courbet's *Forelle* (Trout) from 1871, now at Kunsthaus Zurich (fig. 28). It is an oppressive painting from difficult times when, after the destruction of the Paris Commune, the artist had been convicted and imprisoned for toppling the Vendôme Column. Greatly dispirited, he then withdrew to his hometown in

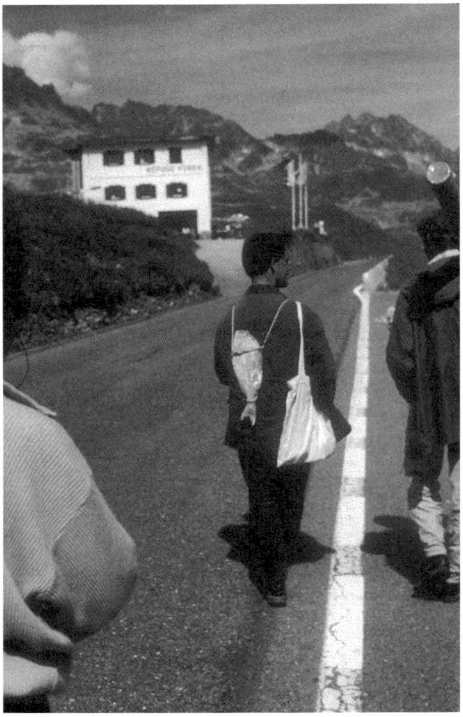

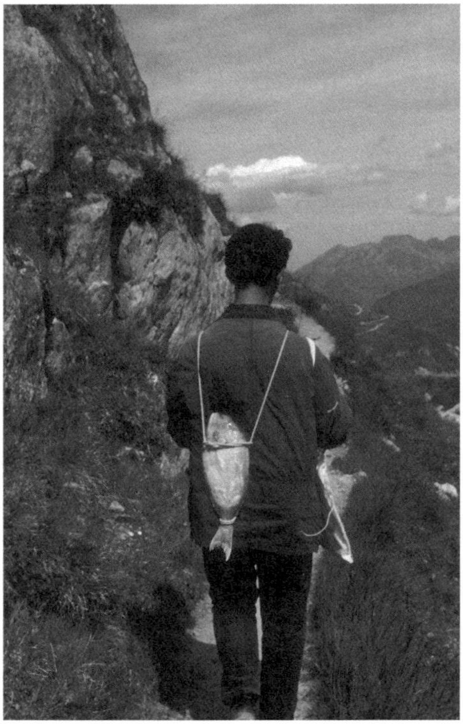

9 *Metaphorical Instruments*, p. 34.
10 See the essay by Seraina Renz in this publication.

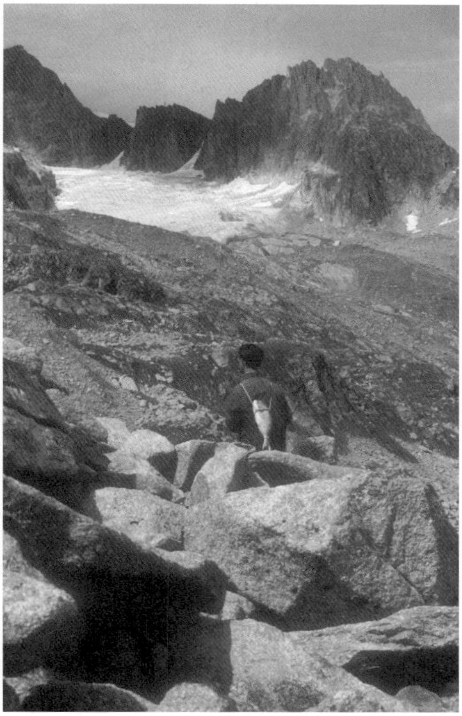

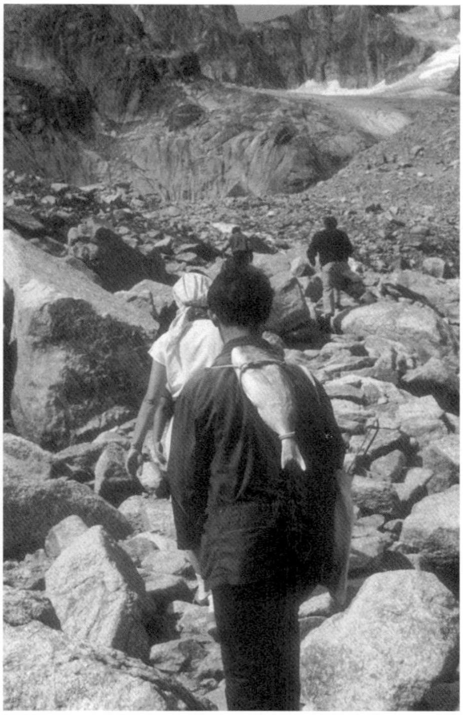

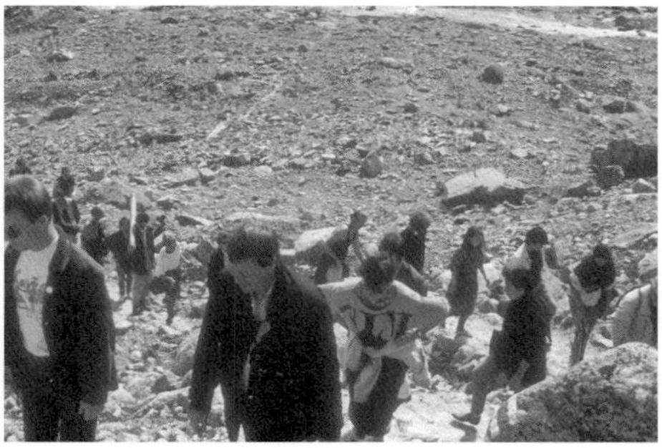

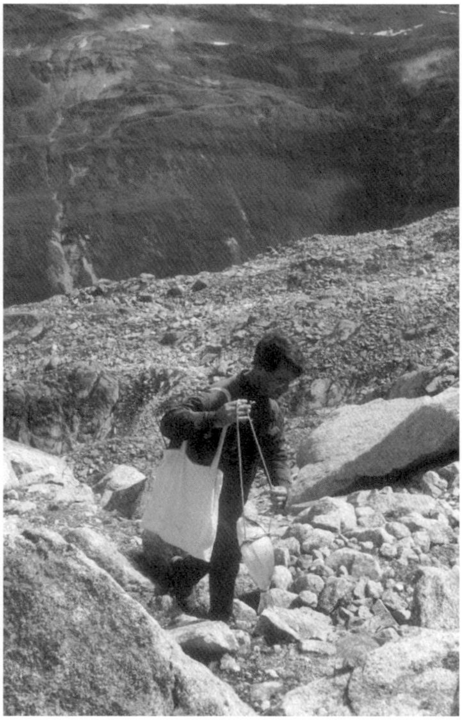

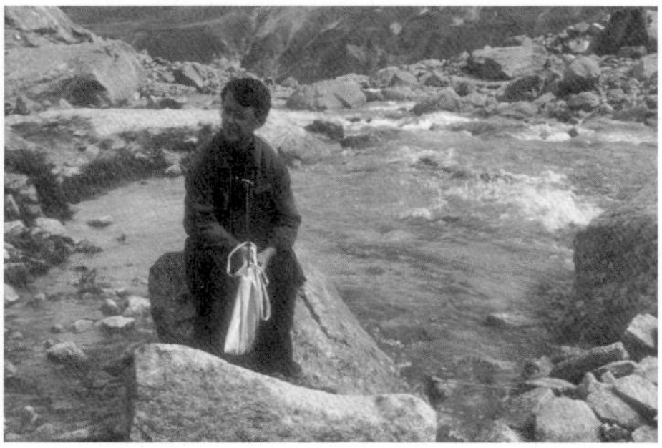

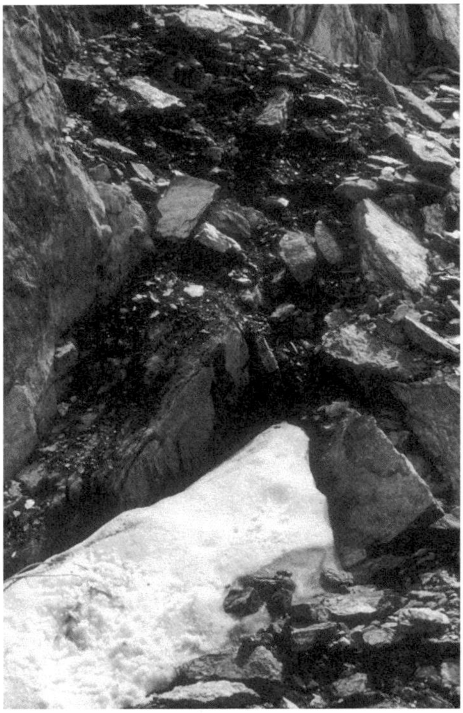
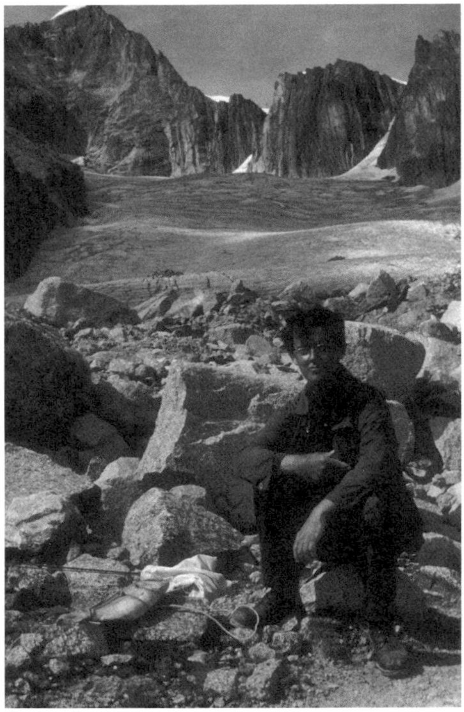
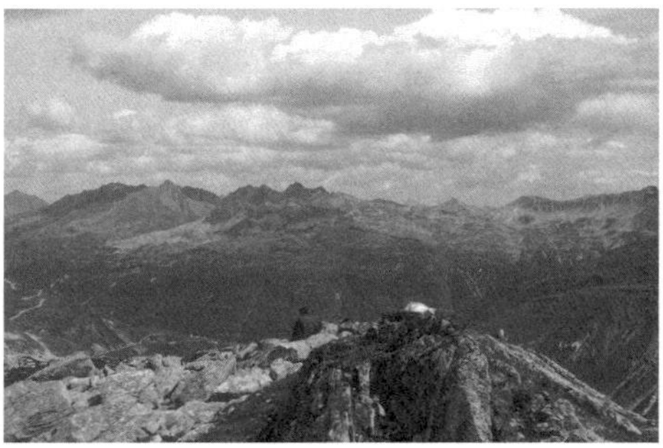
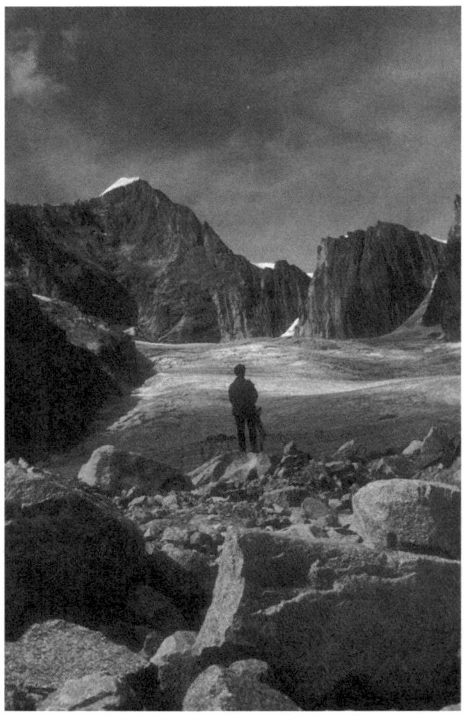
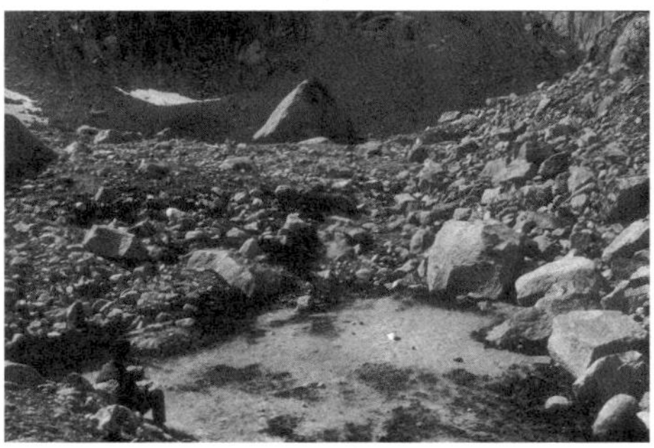

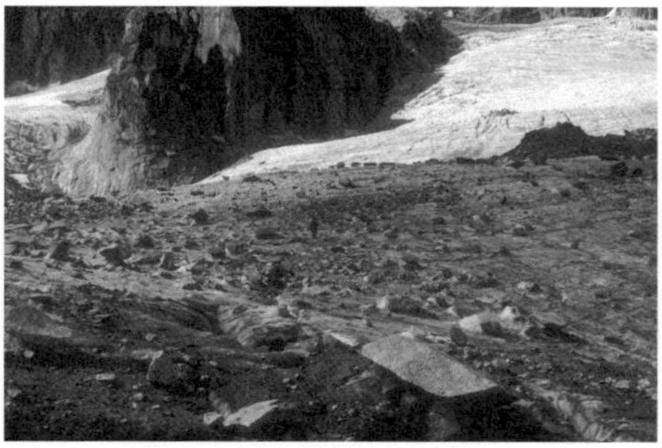

14–26 Terry Fox, *Locus Harmonium*, hike to the Sidelen glacier, photos: Max Wechsler

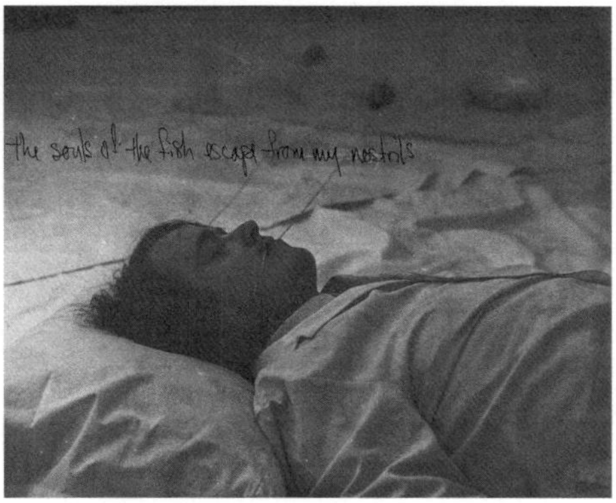

27 Terry Fox, *Pisces*, 1971, action, part 2, De Saisset Art Gallery and Museum, Santa Clara University, California, photo: Joel Glassman

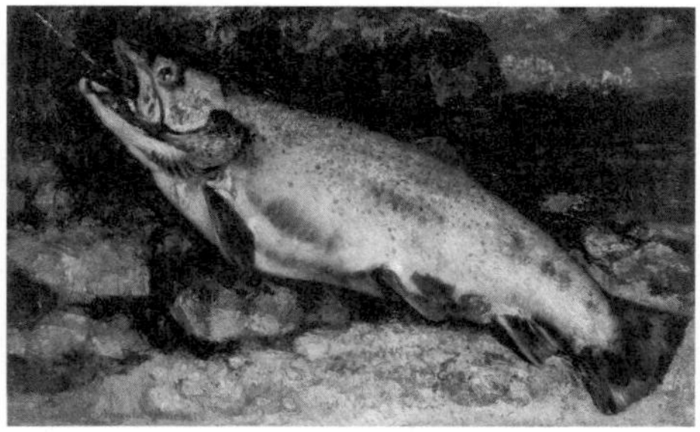

28 Gustave Courbet, *Forelle*, 1872, oil on canvas, 55 x 89 cm, Kunsthaus Zürich

Ornans, only to flee around 1873—after another accusation—into exile in La-Tour-de-Peilz, Switzerland. The painting, one of several related trout paintings, depicts a trout hanging on a hook in its death throes. Under his signature, Courbet set the inscription *in vinculis faciebat* (painted in captivity), which naturally contributed to bringing the trout's fate into connection with his own.

Translated from the German
by Andrea Lerner

René Pulfer, Käthe Walser

The Intervention of Video and Sound in an Artificial Landscape

Workshop by Terry Fox during the Video Weeks in Wenkenpark, Riehen/ Basel, 1986[1]

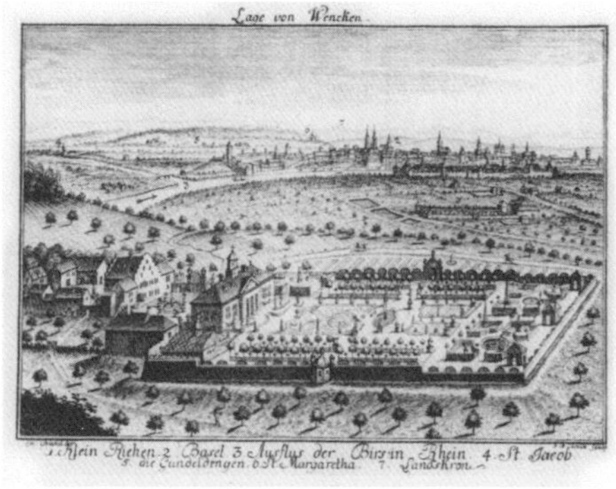

1 Emanuel Büchel, location of Wencken, 1737, copperplate, 13 x 18.5 cm

Wenken, located near Basel, is first mentioned as an estate in the year 751. The Wenkenhof estate villa and an impressive Baroque garden, modeled on French summer houses and gardens, were constructed in 1735.

In 1805, the garden's original stringently geometric order was relaxed by garden architecture in the English style, which appealed to the prevailing zeitgeist.

In 1916, the new owners Fanny and Alexander Clavel enlarged and expanded the estate with a generously proportioned English landscape park. They also used plans from 1737 to restore the French garden, bringing it into harmony with the original historical structures. From then on, this ambience—with park, garden, and villa—was a socially preferred meeting place for artists, writers, and politicians.

In 1954, the couple's interest in art history led them to found the Alexander Clavel Foundation with the intent that, after their passing, the magic and uniqueness of Wenkenpark would continue to serve as a center nurturing intellectual, cultural, and artistic life.

The prize awarded by the Alexander Clavel Foundation since 1983, which focuses explicitly on not yet established or novel art forms, may be understood in this sense as well. For the initiates of the 1984, 1986, and 1988 Video Weeks in Wenkenpark, it provided both an opportunity and a challenge to work on experimental artistic conceptions about how to teach, produce, present, and communicate about art and media.

1 Video Weeks in Wenkenpark, 1986. Workshops with Dara Birnbaum, Terry Fox, and Michael Smith. Seminar and video installation: Dan Graham. Video presentations: Bruce Nauman, Herzog & de Meuron, Imi Knoebel, Nan Hoover, Rémy Zaugg, General Idea, and others. Video productions: Roos Theuws, Helmut Mark, Hanspeter Ammann, Anna Winteler. Video interviews: Chris Dercon with Dara Birnbaum, Terry Fox, Dan Graham, Bruce Nauman, and Michael Smith.

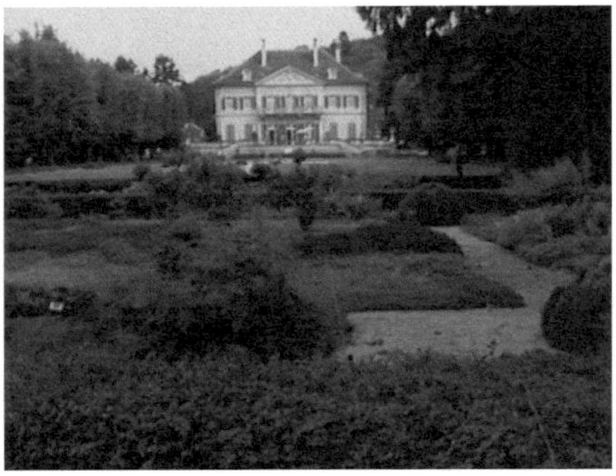

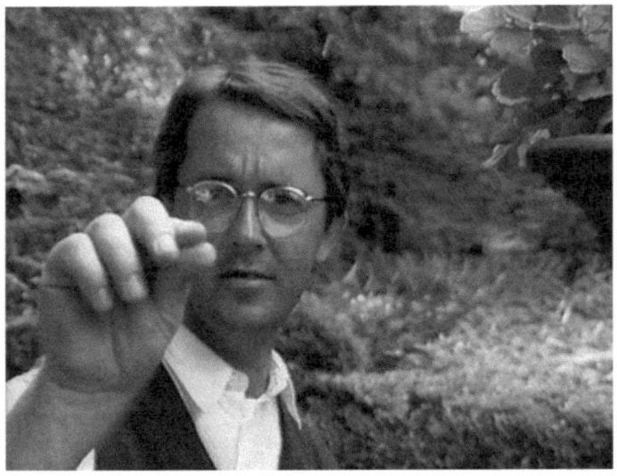

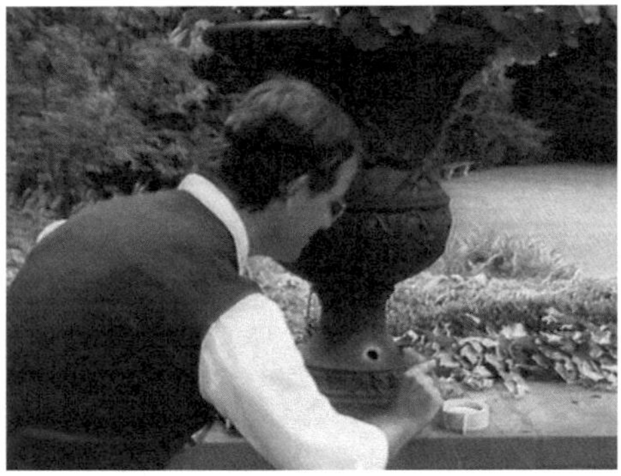

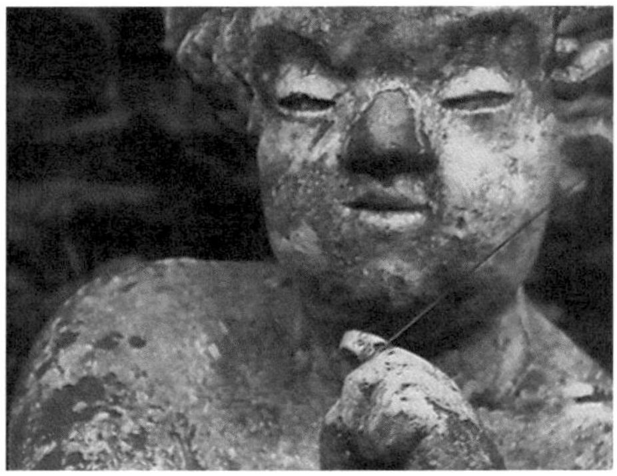

1. *Video Documentation of the workshop The Intervention of Video and Sound in an Artificial Landscape by Terry Fox*[2]

The French garden and villa in Wenkenpark constituted the historical and architectural framework for the three-day outdoor workshop on experiments and interventions with video and sound.

The video documentation on DVD[3] contains raw material from individual projects, and documentary sequences illustrating various phases of the workshop with Terry Fox.

2–5 Video stills from the documentation of the workshop by Terry Fox:

French garden and villa / Terry Fox / sculpture with piano wire.

Video recording: Reinhard Manz, *Video Weeks in Wenkenpark*, 1986

2 Video Documentation Workshop Terry Fox, July 1986, in the French Garden in Wenkenpark. Camera and editing: Reinhard Manz. *Videowochen im Wenkenpark*, 1986, 9:13 min., video, color, sound. Production: Reinhard Manz and René Pulfer.

3 *Video Rewind*, publication with DVD, Video Weeks in Wenkenpark, 1984 / 1986 / 1988. Editors: Reinhard Manz and René Pulfer, 2013, Christoph Merian Verlag, ISBN 978-3-85616-616-8. The publication is one result of the digital remastering of all the video productions realized in Wenkenpark from 1984, 1986, and 1988 by memoriav (Association for the Preservation of the Audiovisual Cultural Assets of Switzerland), memoriav.ch/projects/videowochen-wenkenpark/.

2. *Conversation between René Pulfer, Workshop Initiator, and Käthe Walser, Active Workshop Participant and Eyewitness*

René Pulfer: We've agreed to share recollections and our individual experiences related to the events that transpired at the 1986 workshop in Wenkenpark. You decided to participate in Terry Fox's workshop as a young art student. What reasons and considerations led you to that decision?

Käthe Walser: I was familiar with the LP *Linkage* that recorded performances with piano wire strung across spaces, with the publication *Hobo Signs*, and with a text about his performance *Defoliation,* which took place in the garden of the University of California in 1970. With a flamethrower, he burned a triangle in five-year-old jasmine bushes that were supposed to bloom for the first time two years later. This was a political action made at the time of the Vietnam War that impressed me and also challenged me personally.

Another reason for the decision was that the equipment at our disposal consisted of surplus surveillance cameras and monitors, probably from the chemical industry. The opportunity to use this equipment in a park excited me, for I had worked in such park settings in my previous profession as an employee at a tree nursery and as a gardener. The equipment offered me an opportunity to take the situation I had previously been familiar with professionally and turn it upside down.

René: An important element in the workshop was the intervention of suspending a piano wire, more than a hundred meters long, through the garden across its long axis. Can you describe how you reacted as a group? And what was Terry Fox's role in this process?

Käthe: I believe we all were initially somewhat at a loss on that Monday morning. Terry Fox didn't push himself to the forefront, and we really had to force him a bit and convince him to begin putting up the piano wire. At that moment, we couldn't imagine it would be possible to

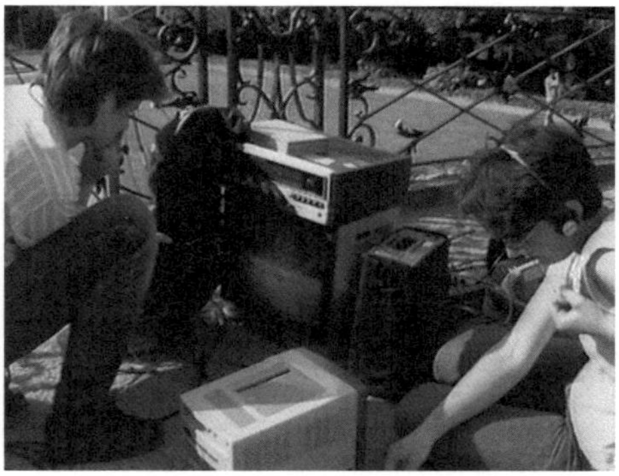

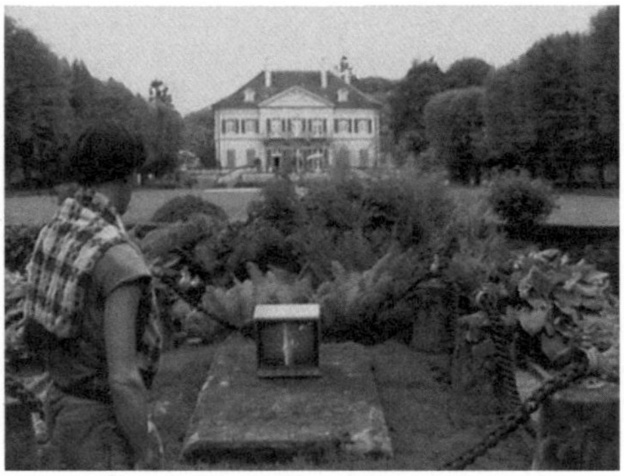

6–7 Video stills from the workshop: Video tech: Johannes Gfeller and Käthe Walser. Video installation on the gravestone of Fanny Clavel, with Omi Scheiderbauer.
Video recording: Reinhard Manz, *Video Weeks in Wenkenpark*, 1986

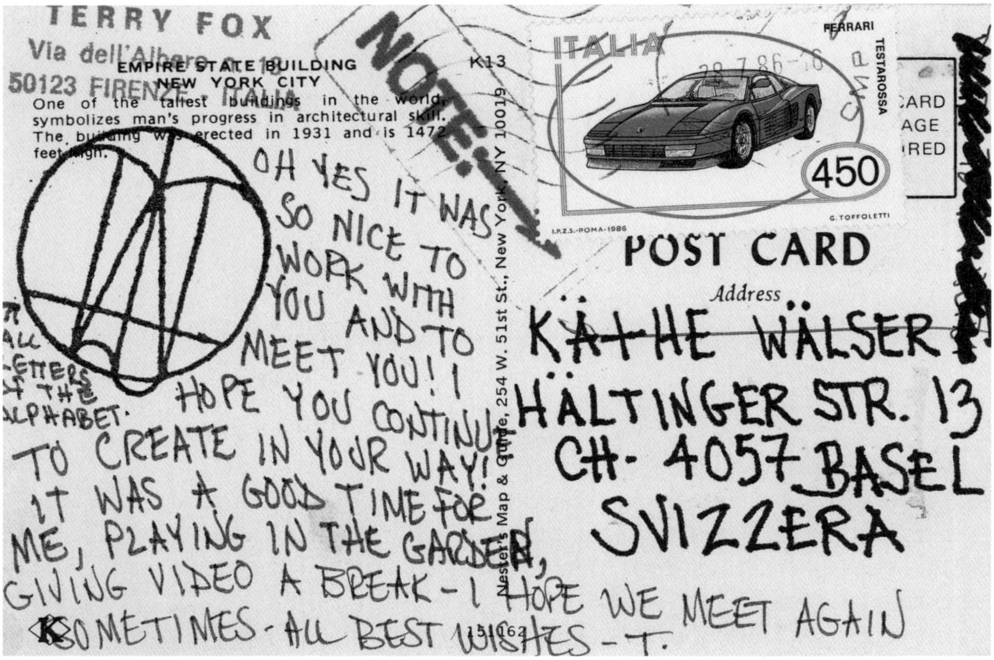

8 Terry Fox, postcard to Käthe Walser, 1986, verso

generate audible sounds with a piano wire on an open site. Of course it seemed appropriate to react to the architecture of the French park with the villa and to have the piano wire span the long axis between the villa and the end of the garden. We would have loved to attach the wire directly to the villa, since we certainly were thinking somewhat destructively and wanted to try and see if the building could be made to collapse with the help of the vibrations.

René: I have some memories and images associated with the workshop, ones like the creative atmosphere, with discussions going on about individual and collective processes, and the collaborative interaction of all forces up until the closing presentation, when all the works could be entered into and experienced during an evening program in the French garden.

Käthe: It was a collaborative working situation with the instruments that were available to us. I went on a search through the park and naturally wanted to know where the gardeners were. In a small greenhouse I found a rake and a sprinkler. I made these objects my instruments and combined them with the surveillance equipment. We helped each other, sometimes doing this or that together or alone, thought things over, and tried out many things.

The immediacy of the closed-circuit situation, which was also made audible and visible for visitors on the evening of the presentation, was very important. The sound of the piano wire was audible, the monitors stood near the objects in the park and were linked with the surveillance cameras. We were certainly also concerned with taking back autonomy from the industrial surveillance system: the monitor was not inside the villa's security room, but outdoors, visible to everyone.

René: You've been able to recall some important events in your comments. In what way did these workshop experiences have an effect on your subsequent artistic work?

Käthe: Naturally they made a very strong impression. After the workshop I continued to work with surveillance cameras for a long time. Maybe it's an overstatement to trace it back to this workshop alone, since after all, this was the start of my training and naturally quite a lot of impulses were converging. But the workshop, and the opportunity to work with Terry Fox, was certainly a very important experience.

René: One of Terry Fox's few responses to the workshop is found on a personal postcard sent to Käthe Walser:

"It was a good time for me, playing in the garden, giving video a break," as Terry Fox recalls the playful process of discovery—an important element that significantly influenced the entire workshop, creating a surprisingly unique experiment.

Translated from the German
by Andrea Lerner

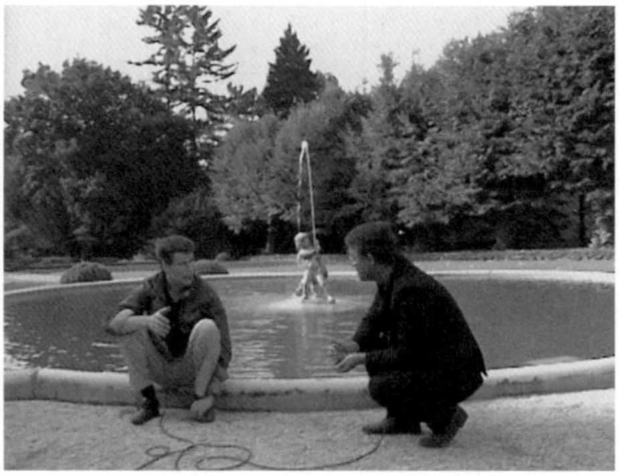

9 Terry Fox, interviewed by Chris Dercon, 1986, French Garden in Wenkenpark, video still, camera: Reinhard Manz

3. *Video: Excerpts from the Interview with Terry Fox by Chris Dercon in the French Garden of the Wenkenpark, 1986*[4]

Chris Dercon: Terry Fox, you've worked here at this spot. What is the interest in spanning a more than 100-meter piano wire across a garden as beautiful as this, and why do you want to interact with this space?

Terry Fox: I was invited to come here to do a video workshop, and I've never worked in a garden like this before, I've never worked outside, and I've never worked with people in this way, and I haven't done a workshop, so, all these things were very interesting for me. They gave me a plan of the garden and, from where I live, I worked on the plan thinking about the garden and aspects.

Chris Dercon: What kind of aspects?

Terry Fox: Of how does video relate to this, and maybe it doesn't relate at all?

4 Video interview with Terry Fox by Chris Dercon, July 1986, in the French Garden in Wenkenpark. Camera and editing: Reinhard Manz. Sound: Johannes Gfeller. *Video Weeks in Wenkenpark*, 1986, 30:30 min., video, color, sound (language: English). Production: Reinhard Manz and René Pulfer.

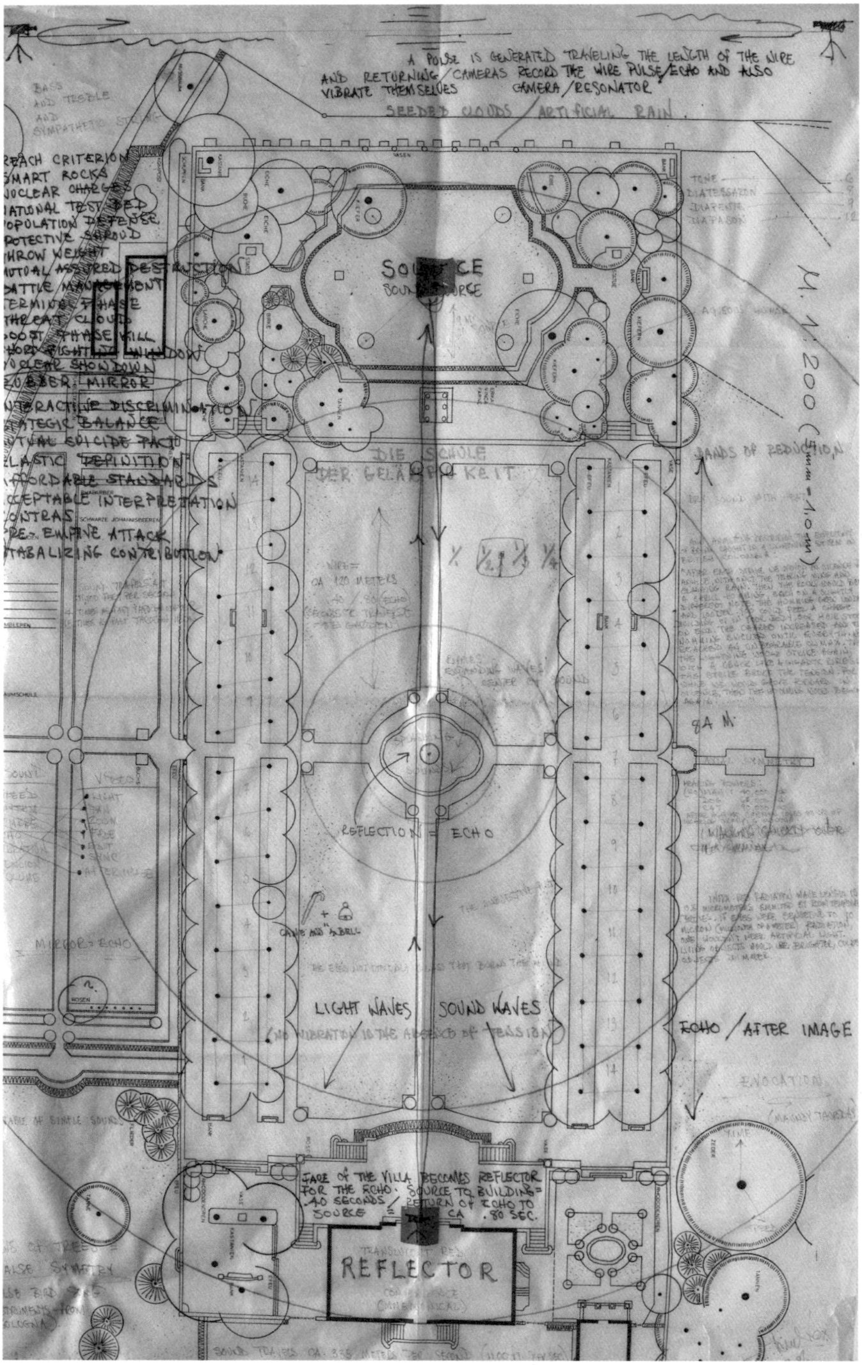

10 Terry Fox, *Die Schule der Geläufigkeit* (plan drawing for the workshop "The Intervention of Video and Sound in an Artificial Landscape"), 1986, 90 x 57.5 cm, layout of the French Garden in Wenkenpark, copied onto tracing paper, handwritten notes, drawings, and calculations, with black, red, and green pigment felt-tip pen.

Finally, I decided it doesn't relate at all to the garden and maybe there's a way to establish a relationship.

My main interest is sound—sound and language—and I thought the best thing is to transform the video by the use of sound, to humanize the video—not to use the video to take pictures in the garden but to find correlations of sound with video; what could some correlations be? For instance, if the garden's 132 meters long, it takes four-tenths of a second for sound to go from one end to the other—so here is the house, and there may be the possibility of a reflection with an echo coming back; it means eight-tenths of a second, almost a full second, it will take for the sound to travel back from one place to the other.

What is an echo in video? I thought what could be an echo? It's when you hold something on a bright object, you start to get a burn and move it, you have an after-image which corresponds to an echo. That's the first thing I thought was echo imagery.

Or to use the camera, which I did with the long string; I mounted the camera at one end of the wire so the camera becomes the resonator for the wire, and the image is no longer important at all: it doesn't matter what picture the camera's making, the camera has a whole other function because it's a box. This piano wire vibrates longitudinally so it needs a resonator at each end—it doesn't make a sound by itself. That's what I did: I strung the wire, put the camera on the wire and the camera became the resonator. Since it was aimed along the wire, it recorded its own experience which was the experience of the rhythm of the wire: so, you pluck the wire, the image you get depends on the rhythm of the wire.

Chris Dercon: You said you're unsure that the video still relates to the garden, or the image of the garden.

Terry Fox: Yes, I couldn't imagine making a video in this garden. For me, the garden had very powerful connotations after I started thinking about it; but the whole idea, the installation, was to work with ten people[5] for three days who don't know each other and try to make something, so, I only thought to give a pulse to this process hoping, ultimately, we would all be equal, that I would have no more power than them and that we would all do everything together—which is the way it worked.

Chris Dercon: Is it still possible, because you're working it? What would be an ideal reproduction of this garden, of this artificial situation.

Terry Fox: My idea was to make a tape which would be very aggressive and frightening using imagery from the garden. That was the first idea and that's the idea I presented at the workshop. The image of the vibration of this camera actually is a very frightening image; also, the sound of the wire is a sound like gunshot reverberation, or a *Star Wars* electronic sound; this sound doesn't sound acoustic. I thought I would make this in very fast cuts of shots with the after image—like echoes. That corresponds to a text I wrote, *Echo Porn Text*, but, during the process of working, it became completely turned around - well, not turned around, but that was just initiating the process—and then everything became turned around where

5 Terry Fox Workshop participants: André Aebi, Lukas Brunner, Greta Guntern, Gabriella Liner, Simon Lamunière, Eric Lanz, Tanja Merz, Omi Scheiderbauer, Urs Stöckli, Käthe Walser. Tech: Johannes Gfeller, Reinhard Manz.

the participants in the workshop all contributed their ideas and we did it like that. We all worked together.

Chris Dercon: In that sense, it's always been interesting in your work that you try to work on this almost impossible marriage between image and sound, and you're someone who puts to the fore that there's no possible way to marry, or combine, images of sounds.

Terry Fox: Yes, doing this was an experiment, and some worked; the wire worked. As I said, the idea became transformed and people came up with other ideas I wouldn't have, and they did it.

Another one was a lawn sprinkler at one end, and the lawn sprinkler's going choop-choop-choop ch-ch-ch-ch-ch- the way lawn sprinklers do—and we tied a camera to the sprinkler. The image of the camera became what the sprinkler looks at during it making this sound and, because it's making these jerks, it sets up a rhythm in direct correspondence to sound—besides the sprinkler making this wonderful sound—which was also used acoustically. The sound of the sprinkler was a clear, beautiful sound and the image was also a beautiful image: it was jerking, showing the whole garden—a panorama of the garden—and shooting back again, and showing it again.

11–16
Caption Sequence A
Project *Terry Fox and Workshop*, 1986, sound: Terry Fox
Video stills b/w from camera mounted on the vibrating piano wire

17–22
Caption Sequence B
Project *For Fanny* by Lukas Brunner and Omi Scheiderbauer, 1986, sound: Terry Fox, Video stills b/w from static camera, detail of vibrating piano wire, visualized for the control monitor on the gravestone

23–28
Caption Sequence C
Project *Sprinkler* by Käthe Walser, 1986, Video stills b/w from camera mounted on the water sprinkler, panning shot from left to right, 110-second sequence

29–34
Caption Sequence D
Project *Sprinkler* by Käthe Walser, 1986, Video stills b/w from camera mounted on the water sprinkler, panning shot from right to left, nine-second sequence

Video stills in b/w: original material from the installed b/w video cameras
Video stills in color: from video documentation of the Terry Fox Workshop
Videography/camera: Reinhard Manz, 1986
Selection of images and montage: René Pulfer, 2017

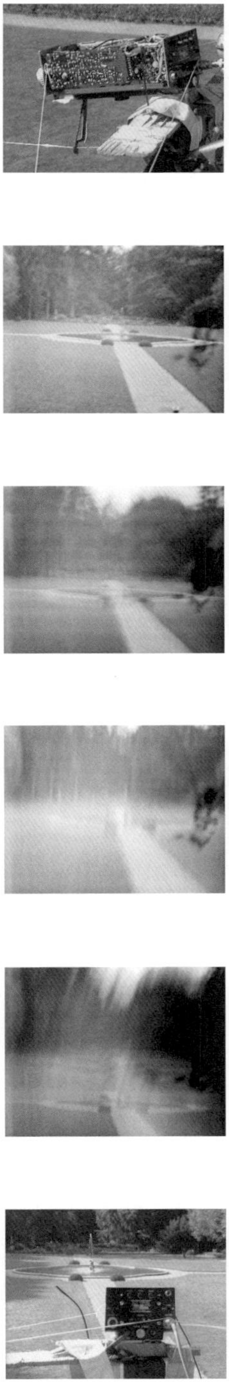

Sequence A
(Figs. 11–16)

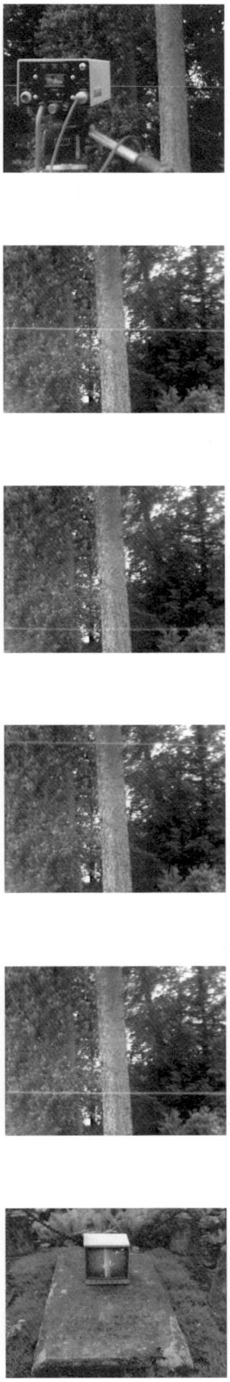

Sequence B
(Figs. 17–22)

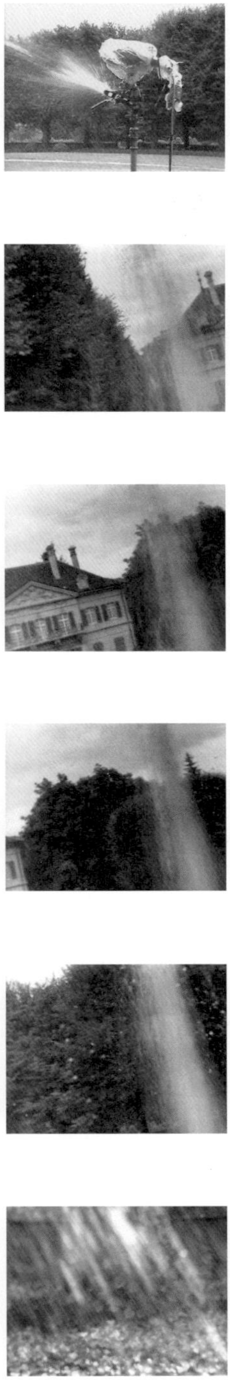

Sequence C
(Figs. 23–28)

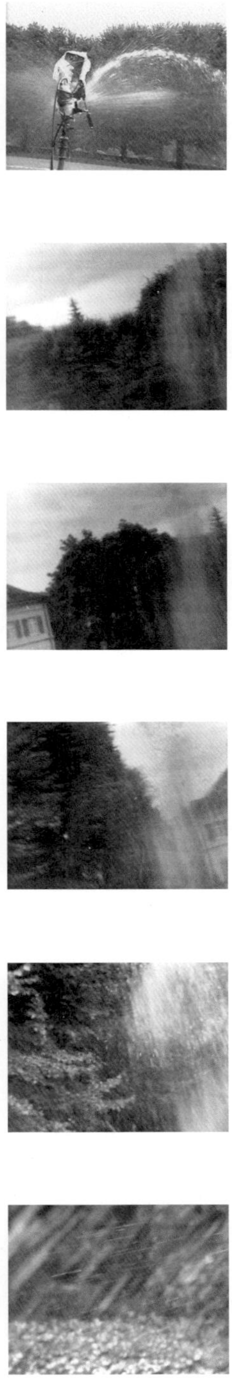

Sequence D
(Figs. 29–34)

Seraina Renz

They Are the Strangest Creatures: Terry Fox and Animals

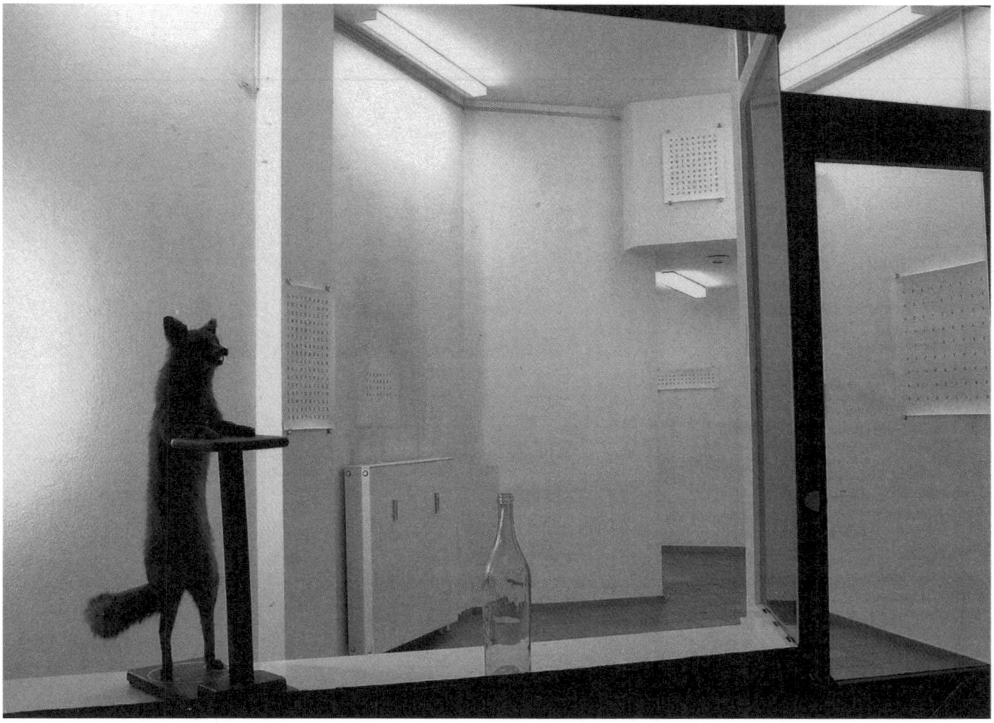

1 Terry Fox, *Lauschender Fuchs,* 2000, exhibition view *Raison d'être*, maly: service culturel & edition, 2001, Cologne, photo: Alexander Schmid

Metaphors and wordplay form one pillar of Terry Fox's oeuvre. The artist also treated his own surname as a symbol with which he activated a game of transference. In Cologne's artist's space called maly: Edition & Service Culturelle, Fox put a stuffed fox on display (fig. 1). It was certainly not evident to passersby who glanced into the gallery what the status of this fox was—whether it was an art object or something else—or, indeed, that it ought to be read as a rebus standing for the artist's name. Ultimately, of course, being obvious is not the aim of a riddle. Moreover, Fox's works seldom, if ever, aim at immediate visual recognition. Immediacy he reserved for performance and sound, whereas images, language, and symbols were for reading, deciphering, and thinking about. In the artist's space window display, there was a stuffed animal that embodies various stages of understanding. In the first instance, it's an individual living thing, although it's difficult to determine to what extent the stuffed fox skin still **is** the individual or instead stands for it. In the second instance, it represents the genus **fox**. It is necessary to **read** this connection between the thing and a particular genus in order for the third instance to emerge: the surname Fox, which in turn identifies the author of the exhibited works. The fact that the fox here is not simply **a fox** is characteristic of how works by Fox function. These and other configurations of transference in connection with animals in Fox's oeuvre are the subject of this text.

In the nineteen-seventies, when performance and later sound art were the initial focal points of his creative work, Fox included animals in some of his pieces. He was not alone in doing so at that time. The emergence of new art forms such as happenings, actions, and performance in the sixties thrust people's acts—not objects—onto center stage, and animals also made an entrance into art. Although the dead lambs in Hermann Nitsch's actions or the living horses of Jannis Kounellis (*Untitled, dodici cavalli*, 1969) in the Galleria l'Attico in Rome were still intended chiefly as a provocation to the arts audience, many artists in the seventies were beginning to investigate the question of human subjectivity. This included an examination of the relationship between human beings and nature, human nature included, as Joseph Beuys impressively demonstrated in his action *I Like America and America Likes Me* (1974). In the art of the seventies, dealings with animals were characterized on the whole by the fact that the animal was subject to injury and destruction. In many cases, the works impinged on the artists' own bodies, but most affected the animals' very existence. The vulnerable and mortal body, the experience of violence—these were summoned as elements linking human beings and animals. In a work such as *Death of a Chicken* (1972), a performance by Ana Mendieta, this is unambiguous. The artist had an assistant behead a chicken, which she then held by its legs in front of her so that its spurting blood splattered her naked skin and the white wall behind her. One might reproach her with essentialism for a work that is reminiscent of something akin to the origins of art (which, with John Berger, can be imagined as painting with animal blood), but that also links the female body with blood, with giving birth, with the constraints of physical being-in-the-world.[1] But intrinsic to the performance as well is a protest against the structure of victimization with which women's existence is traditionally bound up—there is a sisterhood with the animal, which is also excluded from the symbolic realm.

With Terry Fox, too, there is a destructive element, a connection with the animal via physical vulnerability and mortality, as will be shown. But the starting point for his interest in animals was the vital life force, perhaps the polar opposite of shared mortality. Once the artist abandoned painting in the late sixties in favor of activity-oriented forms, his own body became his artistic epicenter and fundamental

1 John Berger, "Warum sehen wir Tiere an?," *Das Leben der Bilder oder die Kunst des Sehens* (Berlin, 2009), pp. 12–35, esp. p. 17; originally published as: John Berger, "Why Look at Animals?," in *About Looking* (London, 1980), pp. 1–26.

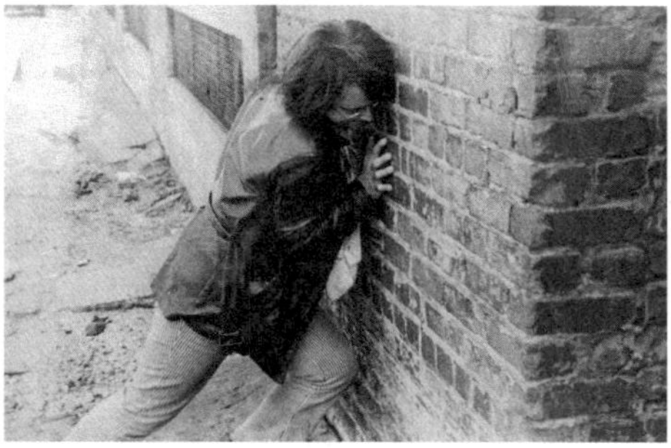

2 Terry Fox, *Wall Push (Push Piece)*, 1970, Minna Street, San Francisco, photo: Barry Klinger

material. In 1970, he carried out the action *Wall Push* (fig. 2). In an interview with Willoughby Sharp in 1971, he mentioned that one day, near where he always parked his car, he suddenly became aware of an inconspicuous brick wall. He touched it and sensed its body, its belly.[2] The action consisted of pushing against the wall as hard as he could for ten minutes. To Sharp's question whether, in such actions, he wanted to reduce his body to the level of other elements—in this case the wall—Fox answered: "No. I raise the other elements to the status of the body."[3] At this early stage in his activity as a performer, during which he—like Bruce Nauman a few years earlier—was primarily involved with minimal self-assigned physical tasks that were photographically documented but not performed in front of an audience, the equivalence of all materials and their treatment as a physical body were important. So it's not very surprising that other living things, along with his own body and diverse "material-bodies," became part of his art. At a solo exhibition in the Reese Palley Gallery in San Francisco in 1970, titled *Two Diffused Parallel Lines*, he set up a wire cage containing two pigeons (figs. 3, 4). The birds could perch on a wooden rod. The cage's floor was also wire mesh, for as the work's title suggests, Fox was concerned with the linear traces of digestion that the animals left on the gallery floor. The title, evocative of a formalistic drawing, stands in contrast to the base "product" that the two feathered artists produced on a daily basis. By introducing *the Other*, through animals, into the production of art, Fox undermined several parameters traditionally constitutive of art: genre, work, and authorship. The work changes in an ongoing process and is simultaneously painting and sculpture without, however, making use of even one single material that has connotations of art. But the work also borders on performance, even though the anticipated human performer is absent. There is no aesthetically and/or materially valuable object; rather, art appears here as the waste product of a life process. Authorship is transferred to two pigeons that unintentionally, in a formally aleatory procedure, produce *Two Diffused Parallel Lines*. Fox's involvement with the animal-as-Other nevertheless entails countless further implications, as the following will illustrate.

One factor that might have led Fox to integrate animals into his works is his physical, at times even vitalistic, understanding of material. It manifests, for instance, in the fact that he often worked with yeast dough in his performances during the seventies.

Like *Two Diffused Parallel Lines*, the work *Hefe* (*For Ute Klophaus*) (Yeast [For Ute Klophaus], 1971) is difficult to classify within any one genre (fig. 5). In close-up shots, the photographer Klophaus records how Fox takes flour, water, salt,

2 *Ocular Language*, p. 23; originally published as: Willoughby Sharp, "I Wanted to Have My Mood Affect their Looks," *Avalanche* (1971), pp. 70–81.

3 *Ocular Language*, p. 11.

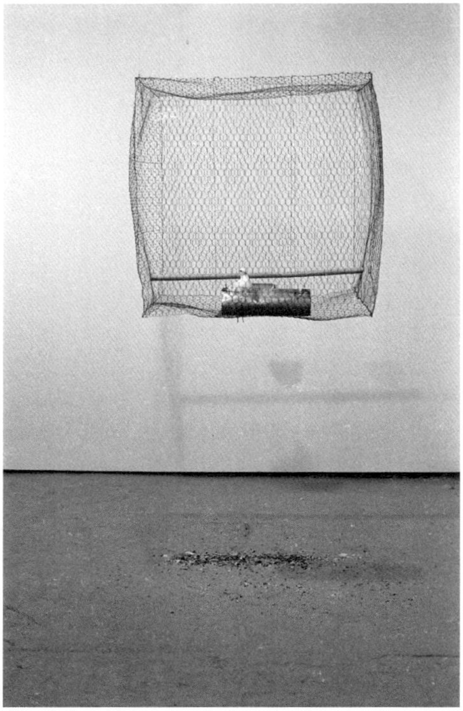

3 Terry Fox, *Two Diffused Parallel Lines*, 1970, 2 pigeons, wire cage, log, bird droppings, exhibition view, Reese Palley Gallery, San Francisco, photo: Terry Fox

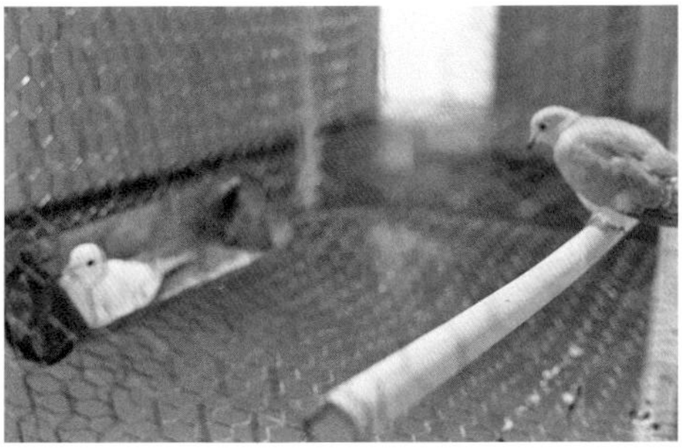

4 Terry Fox, *Two Diffused Parallel Lines*, 1970, 2 pigeons, wire cage, log, bird droppings, exhibition view (detail), Reese Palley Gallery, San Francisco, photo: Terry Fox

and yeast and mixes, kneads, forms, and allows a loaf of bread dough to rise. The prints' borders are torn, which both lends a performative character to the process of producing the photographs and makes each photo a unique specimen. Fox's actions and the yeast dough itself are performative, too. The work's essential core is the activity of the several active participants themselves, and/or perhaps the fact *that* they do something, move, live, are independently active.

Two years later, at the University Art Museum in Berkeley, Fox made the multipart performance *Yield* (1973), which lasted three days. Photographs taken by his twin brother Larry show the artist laying out paths of flour on the floor, which he drizzled with water from his mouth (fig. 6). This created a floury paste that then dried and hardened. Part of the path led over a mirror lying on the floor that reflected part of the room. The photos show that Fox worked during the day at times, but also at night with a spotlight. But the photography has no documentary ambitions in the sense that it might trace the process and formation of the flour trail. Rather, it is part of the process and chiefly depicts the artist in close-ups, *in actu*. Frequently, a perspective is chosen that makes no stable view of the space possible; indeed, it has a disorienting effect. In order to precisely grasp what Fox drew on the gallery floor, one can turn to his sketchbooks for help (fig. 7). They show that Fox drew an anthropomorphic form, a kind of skeleton, in which the chest and the hip bones were delineated in more detail. One sketch additionally contains a score that notates the spatial and temporal structures, together with puzzling materials and descriptions. Some of the elements (the bowls, the flour, and the bread) are seen in the photographs, while others (the eyetooth, the blood, and the labyrinth) cannot be explained.[4] The fact that they belonged to the work in its

4 The eyetooth, the blood, and the labyrinth belong to Fox's material iconography since his discovery of the labyrinth of Chartres (see below). The three elements were central components in the work *The Beginning of the "Dream of the Eyetooth in the Labyrinth"* (1975).

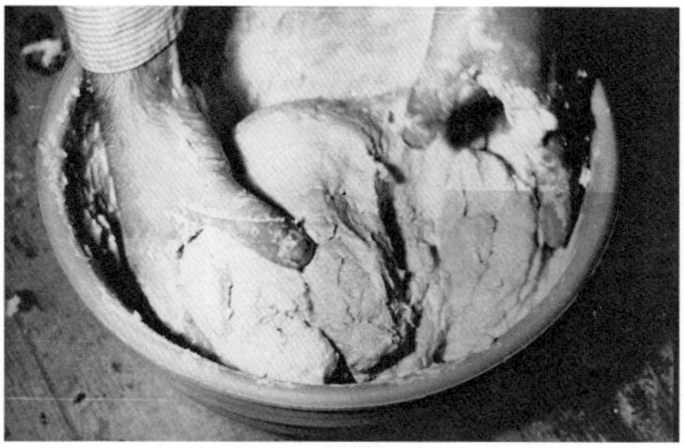

5 Terry Fox, *Hefe,* 1971, action for Ute Klophaus without an audience, photo: Ute Klophaus

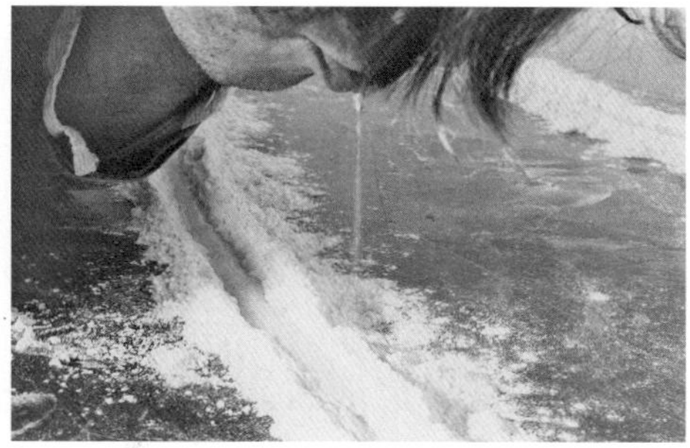

6 Terry Fox, *Yield*, 1973, action, University Art Museum, Berkeley, photo: Larry Fox

conceptual state clearly shows once again the central embrace of material and body in Fox's art. With Fox, changeability always also signifies vitality.

One of Fox's first complex performances also involved living things. The performance consisted of two parts. The first took place at the Museum of Conceptual Art in San Francisco, whose director Tom Marioni wrote a description of the course of events.[5] According to the account, Terry Fox bought two live fish in Chinatown in San Francisco on February 2, 1971. He placed the fish on the museum floor and tied a cord to each of their tails. He lay down and attached the other ends of the cords to his tongue and his penis. The fish wriggled in their death throes, tugging on the artist's body. Fox remained in position until the fish died. Then the artist used the dead fish, which he wrapped in white towels, for the second part of his performance in the de Saisset Museum at Santa Clara University. There, two lit flashlights lay on the floor in a semi-darkened room, their beams facing each other. The stream of light between them was dusted with flour. When the batteries were empty and the light extinguished, Fox lay down on the floor near the dead fish. Once again, he connected them to his body with string. One cord was fastened to a strand of his hair, the other to his teeth. Fox lay there for several hours during which, according to Marioni's description, he attempted to dream of the death of the fish (fig. 8).

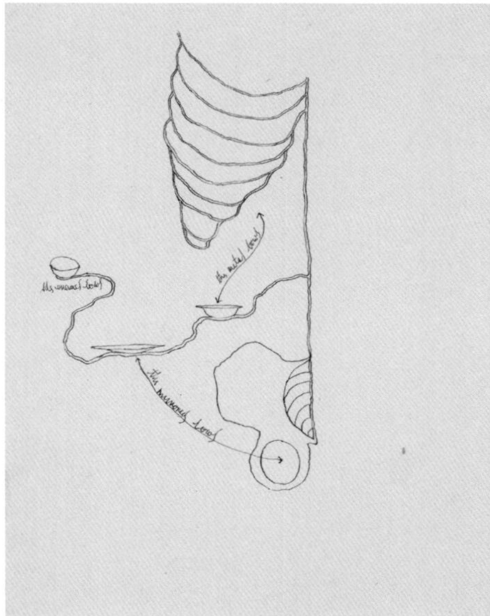

7 Terry Fox, (*Untitled*), sketch for *Yield*, 1973, 28 x 21.6 cm, Estate of Terry Fox, Cologne

5 *Ocular Language*, p. 34; originally published as: Tom Marioni, "Terry Fox: himself," *Art and Artists* (1973), p. 40. The first part of *Pisces* is not documented in photographs. The only document is the description by Marioni, upon which my interpretation is based. We can no longer know what in reality took place. I proceed from the assumption that Marioni described the performance based on his own viewpoint and that the artist shared support for the narrative. For my further dealing with the work, the question of whether or not it was a "reality" that the fish died on Fox's body, does not play a role. The narrative is today a constitutive part of the work, the truth that we have of it.

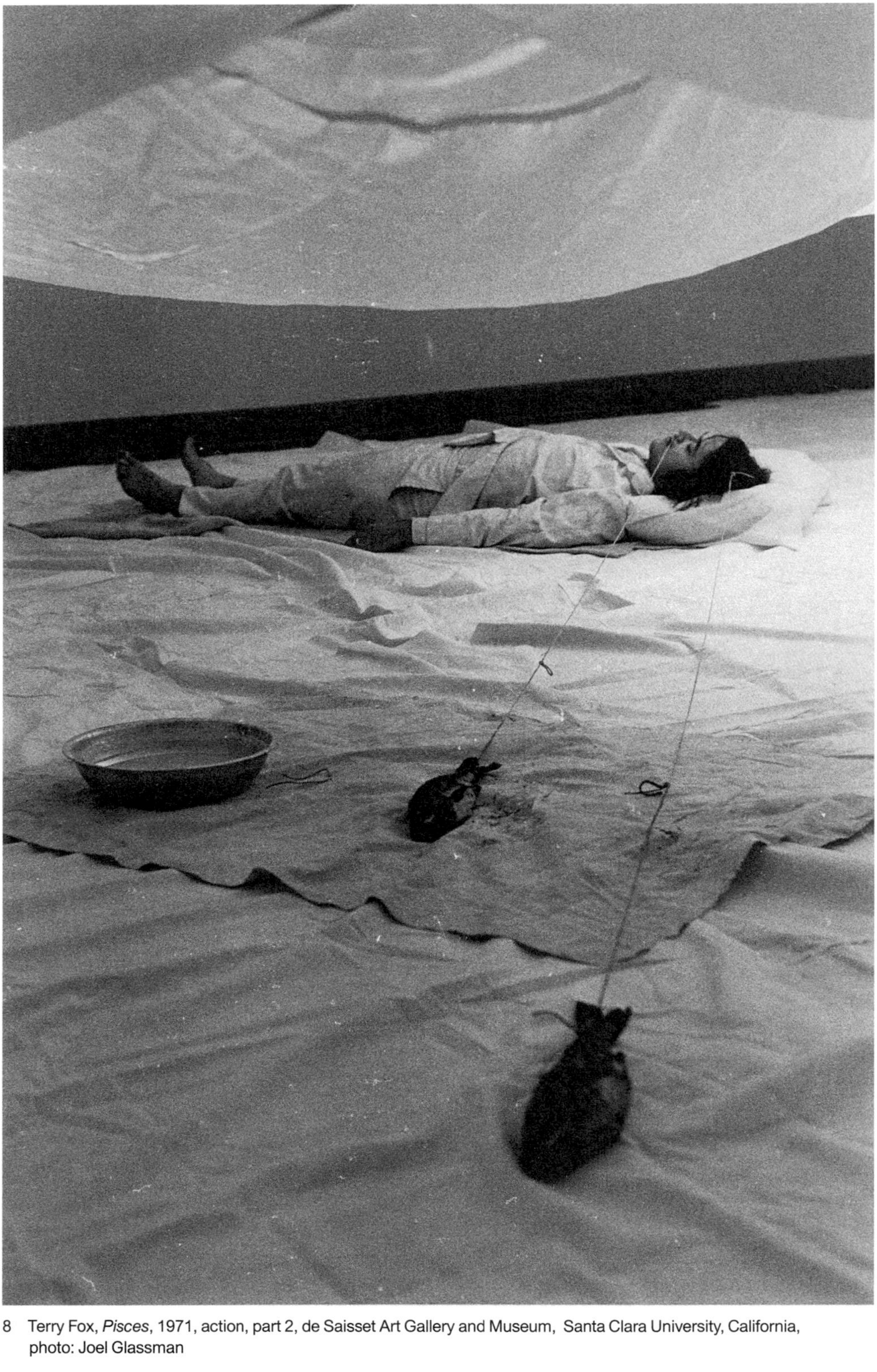

8 Terry Fox, *Pisces*, 1971, action, part 2, de Saisset Art Gallery and Museum, Santa Clara University, California, photo: Joel Glassman

As in many performances by the artist, time plays a significant role. It has to do with the remaining lifetime of the fish, with how long the flashlights will keep on shining, and finally with the hours the artist uses to rest, think, or dream. Fox, who had already had to struggle against a life-threatening illness as a young man, was all too aware of the fact that a limited lifetime was at his disposal. A work like *Pisces* is therefore based on an existential exigency. Fox entered into a physical bond with the fish. He could physically grasp their agony through the cords. He exposed himself—albeit in much lesser measure—to the torturous experience that he had in store for the fish. It may be assumed that Fox carried out this first part of the work alone. There was no audience present. The complete exclusion of an audience from the first part also means that there was no scope for the action of others. It is certainly possible that the brutal act of allowing two fish to suffocate might have led to interventions. When the second part of Fox's *Pisces* performance opened the exhibition *Fish, Fox, Kos* in the de Saisset Museum, an audience was admitted, although it could only follow the proceedings from the entrance; the gallery area was roped off. The gallery itself was horizontally subdivided by white cloth. A lightbulb in the upper part was illuminated, filtering through the cloth in a diffused glow. What could be seen was minimal: first of all, there was waiting. Fox had set up a space for himself in which, after the flashlights burned out, he could devote himself solitarily to sleeping and dreaming. The second part of *Pisces* adds a transcendental aspect to the first. Fox was not concerned with the raw act of killing, but with an examination of death and mortality, which he transposed to an intermediate existential zone, to sleep. To dream of killing can be interpreted as a spiritual surmounting of the act of killing, which neither neutralizes nor denies it. According to John Berger, who wrote his influential essay *Why Look at Animals?* in 1980, the parallel lines of the lives of human beings and animals cross in death.[6] For Berger, the lack of a (common) language conditions the difference between animal and human being; Berger thus situates himself within an intellectual tradition stretching back to antiquity. Human beings can always potentially bridge the abyss that yawns between two subjects via language. This possibility is not a given between human beings and animals. Fox thought similarly. The otherness of fish seemed to fascinate him, as he expressed in the interview with Sharp: "A fish's eye is always open, staring. They are the strangest creatures. They are an extreme case of an isolated kind of existence—a creature that fits only into its own environment."[7] Fox made this comment in relation to a visit to a market where the countless dead fish being sold had shocked him. "It's absurd to catch a fish and put him in the market. A creature like that, in the market! Beautiful colors and scales, cold, can't breathe in the air."[8] But didn't Fox himself also wrench the fish from its element? To Achille Bonito Oliva's question in a 1971 interview whether his performances were a kind of "magic land against death," Fox answered in the affirmative and added that they were also "against cruelty with the fish that is murdered and put in the market for money . . . I take him and make something else. . . . I bring the fish back to his real state,

6 Berger 2009 (see note 1), p. 15. Also see: Demian Berger and Seraina Renz, "Im Blick des Tieres: Adorno und Derrida zur Tierfrage," *Kritische Berichte* 2 (2017), pp. 55–64, esp. p. 56. See also the reflections on the role of the gaze in the video performance *Turgescent Sex* (1971), in which Fox had worked similarly with a fish.

7 *Ocular Language*, p. 17.

8 Ibid.

his pure state: his purity begins in the water, then he is murdered, and making an action is a way to return to a pure state."[9] Here Fox hints at what I have described as transcendental experience. Although dead fish do remain behind in his performance, binding the fish to his own body can be understood as a gesture of returning the fish to their "pure state." When the fish are connected to a strand of the artist's hair and his tongue, and he also establishes contact with them in his mind, together they all might possibly go beyond a state of being-in-the-world ensnared by immanence.

Concerning Fox's performances with fish—that same year he realized *Turgescent Sex*, a performative piece for video camera—the artist himself offers another approach to interpretation. In an interview, he makes a connection between the dead fish of the performance and the victims of the Vietnam War. ". . . It was a real, direct involvement for me, considering myself as a victim, and identifying with the Vietnamese people, and also considering myself as guilty. The fish represented the Vietnamese and also represented me. . . . You can't do anything about the war, you could go out in the street and get shot, or you could protest and sign petitions. But nothing was working. . . . I felt terrible. I wanted to release my guilt."[10] Here Fox, who said of himself that he understood nothing of politics and had created very few *explicitly* political works, in 1971 expressed alarm and indignation about the highly topical question of war, like so many US artists from that period. Martha Rosler, for example, made social mechanisms of repression and the effect of war propaganda visible in her collage series *Bringing the War Home: House Beautiful* (1967–72). She montaged pictures of the Vietnam War with portrayals of the American home produced and celebrated by lifestyle magazines such as *House Beautiful*. With her images, which were likewise published in a magazine, Rosler appealed directly to the public, as many artists had done in 1966 for the *Peace Tower* project. More than 400 artists had responded to a call from the Artists' Protest Committee and contributed paintings for an installation on temporary walls in a public space in Los Angeles, whose center was marked by an almost 20-meter-high abstract metal sculpture by Mark di Suvero.

Fox's approach to politics in art differs. His works foreground identification, individual guilt, and powerlessness. As part of *Turgescent Sex*, Fox released a dead fish, tangled in a knotted rope, from its fetters. It was a ritualistic action which began by moistening the wrapped-up bundle with the water he had previously used to wash his hands. Then Fox wrapped a white bandage around his head, covering his eyes. With his fingers, he felt for a small pool of blood on the floor in front of him and, with the blood, marked the position of his eyes on the bandage. When after much effort he had undone the knots in the rope and released the fish, he gave it a kind of burial. Loosely wrapped in the eye bandage and laid out on a bier of coiled rope, Fox blew cigarette smoke on the fish from all sides. After that, the performance was over (fig. 9).

Untying the rope signified, to him, release from guilt. The action is both a burial and a sacrificial ritual. Fox's act of laying

9 *Ocular Language*, p. 59; originally published as: Achille Bonito Oliva, "Terry Fox," *Domus* (1973), p. 45.

10 *Ocular Language*, p. 83; originally published as: Robin White, "An Interview with Terry Fox," *View* 2, no. 3, Oakland (1979).

the fish out and the treatment with smoke remind us of this. As the previous quote testifies, on the one hand Fox presents the fish as a sacrificial animal, while on the other, the fish represents the Vietnamese population as the victim of American aggression. And third, the fish represents the artist himself—qua identification with the Vietnamese. Here, too, an operation of transcendence seems to be underway. Through the ritual, deliverance of a sort becomes possible, even if the earthly act is not undone.

If we assume that Fox is concerned time after time with experiences of transcendence, then it is remarkable that he works with fish, of all things, in order to achieve them. Oxana Timofeeva, in her book *History of Animals*, devotes a brief chapter to the "Dialectics of Fish."[11] In it, she investigates what the animal might be, using selected philosophical positions from the history of evolving ideas of the fish. Historical access to an "idea of animal" liberates it from fixed and determined ontology. The fish is a special case, according to Timofeeva, because it almost invisibly and silently accompanies a major portion of philosophical reflection. "The fish is, so to say, negatively presented in the margins of metaphysics."[12] In metaphysical tradition, the role of providing a symbol for immanence falls to the fish. "The silent fish gliding through water appears as the very image of immanence, of the animal's conformity to its natural essence. Philosophers always speak of fish when they want to talk about the essence of animal being: a picture of water as the element par excellence with a fish swimming stupidly

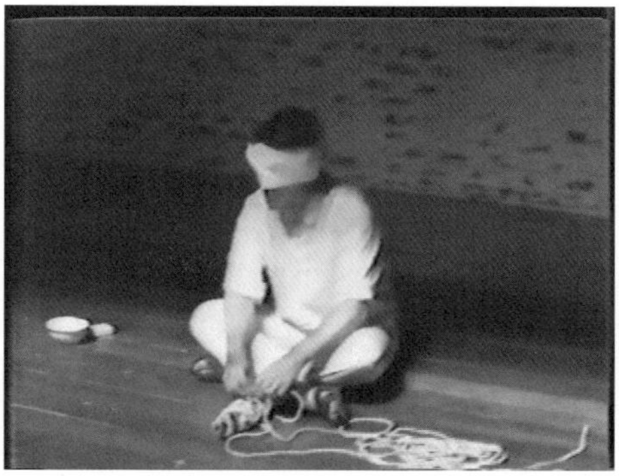

9 Terry Fox, *Turgescent Sex*, 1971, the artist's studio in San Francisco, video still, camera: George Bolling

is entirely convincing."[13] A culminating point in the immanence of fish is found in the works of Gilles Deleuze and Félix Guattari. However, for them the fish is a positive example of an "ontology of affirmation," the true model for becoming, as the two authors elaborated in the chapter "Devenir-intense, devenir-animal, devenir-imperceptible" (Becoming-Intense, Becoming-Animal, Becoming-Imperceptible) in *Mille plateaux* (1980). Thus, Timofeeva thinks, they raise the fish from the base nature of the subhuman to the peak of the philosophical universe.[14] With "pure state," Fox had an amazingly similar understanding of the fish's immanence, admittedly without using the term. But the affinity of thought goes even further. Deleuzian animals, as Timofeeva sees it, are immanent to such an extent that they are acquainted with death in a wholly different way than human beings. Counter to tradition, Deleuze maintains that it is not humans who know how to die, but animals.[15] Timofeeva sees a symbol of this in a story by Andrei Platonov about a fisherman who envies fish for their

11 Oxana Timofeeva, *History of Animals: An Essay on Negativity, Immanence and Freedom* (Maastricht, 2012).
12 Ibid., p. 111.

13 Ibid.
14 Ibid., p. 112.
15 Martin Heidegger would be an example of a philosopher who asked himself the question of whether animals die in the sense that humans die. His answer is that this is not the case. See Martin Heidegger, *On the Way to Language* (New York, 1982).

privileged knowledge about life and death. Out of curiosity and the urge to know, the fisherman ties a stone to his foot, follows them into the water, and drowns.

The question arises: Was Fox perhaps not concerned with an experience of transcendence, but rather with partaking of the absolute immanence of fish? And did he want to share in the fish-knowledge of death when he allowed the fish to die in physical contact with him and attempted to dream of their dying? In contrast to Platonov's fisherman, Fox doesn't give himself over. He only comes closer to the immanence of fish.

If we follow Timofeeva's thoughts further, we don't stop at immanence, either. She again calls Deleuze's thesis into question by way of Marx and Engels, who also made use of a fish metaphor. While human beings—like Platonov's fisherman—can at least try to experience the immanence of fish, a fish would never leave the water out of pure desire or curiosity. However, according to Timofeeva, "external factors" can call into question the unity of fish and water, as Marx and Engels describe. Water ceases to be the "essence" of the existence of fish when rivers are destroyed by industry. So suddenly one can think about what a fish and a worker share: the fact that essence and existence do not coincide. And in dialectical thinking, history arises from this non-coincidence. "The uneasiness of a single creature in the world is not only a problem of this very creature, but of the world itself, insofar as it is becoming unbearable."[16] As to whether it is possible for workers, for fish, to revolutionize the unbearable world—Timofeeva finesses this with a question mark, but she does insist that it is a historical necessity to overcome the impossibility.[17]

Upon more precise observation, what seemed at first glance like a simple, albeit radical gesture by Fox is actually a structure of overlapping, implicit, unspoken elements such as the artist's biography, projections, images adopted from the tradition of human-animal relationships, and counter-images of overcoming. In the end, we don't exactly know whether Fox achieves an experience of transcendence in which he makes use of fish, or whether he wants to come closer to the immanence—the "pure state"—of fish, or if he isn't even allowing the fish to slip out of their immanence and create another world with him, one characterized by an alternative image of the human–animal relationship. A great deal of movement is going on. Is it dialectical movement? One other work by Fox which involves animals may help us understand his movement more precisely.

It has to do with the sound installation *The Labyrinth Scored for the Purrs of 11 Different Cats* (1976). The work is a special variation on the labyrinth theme in Fox's oeuvre.[18] In 1972, he discovered the floor mosaic in Chartres Cathedral and it was so meaningful to him that the labyrinth as form and idea accompanied him for six years. He permuted it through all media and genres until, in 1976, it ultimately acquired acoustic form in a highly unusual instrument: the purring of cats. Composed originally as a two-channel installation, Fox worked with a dual structure: he assigned each cat one of the eleven concentric rings of the labyrinth (fig. 10).

16 Timofeeva 2012 (see note 11), p. 118.

17 Ibid.

18 See the essay by Ulli Seegers in this volume.

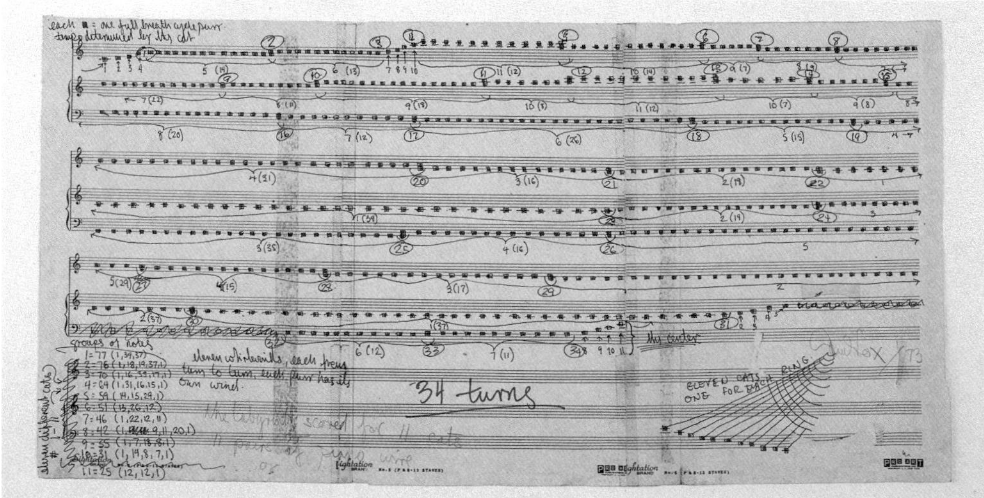

10 Terry Fox, *The Labyrinth Scored for the Purrs of 11 Different Cats*, 1973, pigment felt-tip pen, pencil on music paper, drawing / score, 31 x 60 cm, Estate of Terry Fox, Cologne

The installation makes it possible to acoustically walk the path: when a cat purrs alone for ten seconds, it corresponds to one of the 552 steps of the path. When the purring of two cats overlaps, it corresponds to one of the thirty-four turns in the path. The sounds wander from one loudspeaker to the other, just like the path in the labyrinth meanders back and forth. One arrives at the center of the labyrinth when all eleven cats are purring together.

Cats and the labyrinth of Chartres had already come together once before: in Villard de Honnecourt's church *Masons' guild book* from the early thirteenth century, with its architectural drawings and depictions of persons, plants, and animals.[19] In folio 7v, together with a drawing of the labyrinth of Chartres, there are depictions of a grasshopper, a fly, a dragonfly, a crayfish, and two cats, one of which is sitting while the other is licking its genitals (fig. 11).[20] Hans Hahnloser published a new edition of the manuscript in 1972, so it received considerable attention in the seventies.[21] Perhaps Fox, who was extremely interested in medieval art, was familiar with that puzzling drawing. Hahnloser's observation that the cats display anthropomorphic facial features might be of interest in our context.[22]

As Zdenek Felix remarks in the foreword to *Metaphorical Instruments*, the labyrinth is a "metaphor for human existence; Fox understood it as an instrument and as a measure, not as a maze, but as a metaphor for what happens in life . . ."[23] Fox himself wrote in a text for the publication that he associated the labyrinth with its

19 For showing me the drawing by Villard de Honnecourt, I thank Beate Fricke. On the guild book, see: Jean Wirth, *Villard de Honnecourt: Architecte du XIIIe siècle* (Geneva, 2015), p. 9.

20 On the description of the portrayals, see: Carl F. Barnes, *The Portfolio of Villard de Honnecourt* (Farnham, 2009), pp. 59–61.

21 Hans R. Hahnloser, *Villard de Honnecourt: Kritische Gesamtausgabe des Bauhüttenbuches ms. fr 19093 der Pariser Nationalbibliothek* (Graz, 1972).

22 Ibid., p. 37.

23 *Metaphorical Instruments*, p. 5.

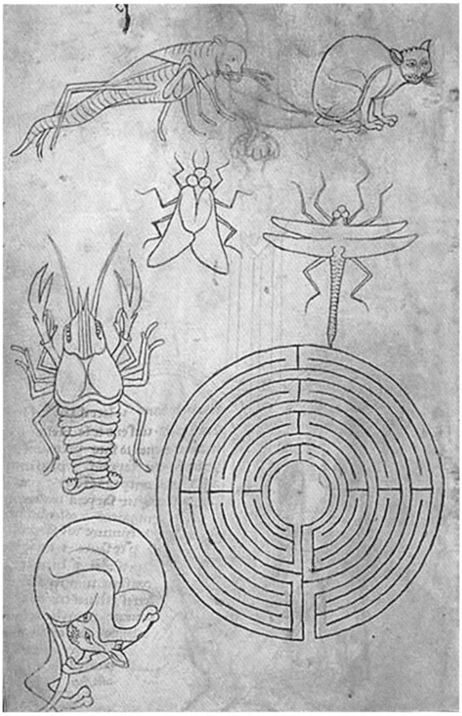

11 Villard de Honnecourt, *Masons' guild book,* fol. 7v

eleven rings with the eleven years of his battle against illness. When he discovered the labyrinth in 1972, he had overcome his illness—he had arrived at the center of the labyrinth and could traverse the path in reverse direction and work his way out.[24]

In contrast, listeners in the sound installation still have this path before them—and they embark on it with the guidance of the eleven cats. On one hand, the path is an abstraction, because the walk takes place only in the imagination. On the other, it is a sensory path, because the image is created via the sense of hearing, and above all because the purring evokes the physical feeling of hands petting the warm furry bodies of cats. Through polyphonic overlapping and movement of sound (in what was finally designed as a four-channel audio installation), Fox also manages to create a sculptural quality in the work. The labyrinth is given a body; listeners are addressed in their physicality. The connection with animals—an envisioned, imagined one—is here part of the audience's performative involvement, not that of the artist. Through the way in which Fox situationally or artistically shapes the relationship between human and animal in his works, he thwarts the idea that the human being is at one with him or herself. The cats are the ones leading the person to the center. The human desire to be at one with oneself has a long philosophical tradition, in which it always (also) has been a matter of erecting stable borders between human beings and animals. It was the "anthropological machine," as Giorgio Agamben calls it in *L'aperto*.[25] Human beings recognize themselves in the animal—or in the animal they recognize the human being—but philosophy has not been able to tolerate such closeness with the animal. Terry Fox seeks and examines it in his body of work, which has no interest in stable monads but allows things to interpenetrate. With Fox, the human being is not at one with him- or herself, nor at one with the animal. Fox upholds the tension between the two poles of possibility. The movement itself, the walking of the path, is the aim—and animals, as the Other *in us,* show us the way.

Translated from the German
by Andrea Lerner

24 Ibid., p. 61.

25 Giorgio Agamben, *Das Offene: Der Mensch und das Tier* (Frankfurt am Main, 2003), esp. pp. 42–48; originally published as: *L'aperto: L'uomo e l'animale* (Turin, 2002); English: *The Open: Man and Animal* (Stanford, 2002).

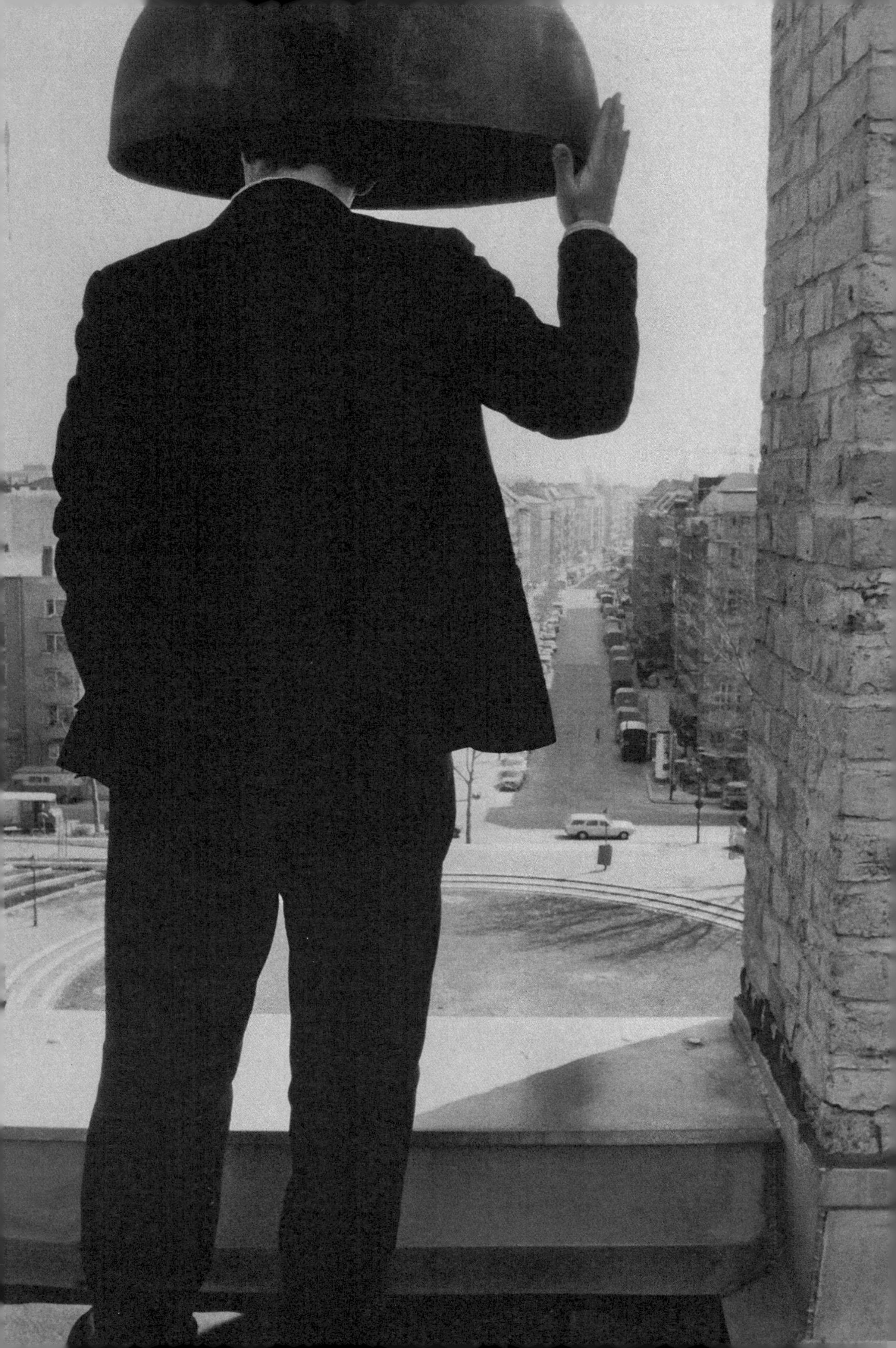

... and "Elsewhere"

Terry Fox, Künstlerhaus Bethanien, Berlin, 1982,
photo: Peter Hutton

Bernd Schulz

Ointment for the Knife

Terry Fox might call what I have to say here: “a stroll of thoughts.”

A Headless man had a letter to write:
’Twas read by one who lost his Sight:
The Dumb repeated it word for word,
And he was Deaf who listened and heard.

This riddle, cited more than once by Terry Fox, could be read on strips of paper against a blinded window in a niche at his exhibition in the Stadtgalerie Saarbrücken. A table with a bowl full of nuts and a nutcracker invited exhibition visitors to solve the riddle, that is, to crack one or more nuts. It of course goes without saying that the crunching sound of the shattering nuts would make it impossible to concentrate on any thoughts. It would also make it impossible to perceive the drops dripping from an infusion line onto a sponge. The construction of works of this kind, where very simple things are associated without much redundancy in order to arrive at a clear form, compels the beholder or listener to engage in a complex perceptual process that basically never ends—perhaps similar to a koan, which the Zen master uses in an attempt to bring his students to a state of awareness or enlightenment. *ATARAXIA*—calmness, peace of mind—was the main title of this exhibition in 1998. It was the first large show after his heart attack, the ramifications of which almost robbed him of the faculty of speech and forced him to live with a physical handicap from that point on. He accepted this with admirable, almost stoic composure, yes, one must even say that he embraced it as part, as new part of his life, which in his eyes, after battling cancer in early years, was nothing other than a winding path toward death.

There is a text by Terry Fox that reads like a description of physical collapse. He himself was even astonished, after writing this text and then rereading it later, that it was a description anticipating an actual state of collapse, which occurred when he went into cardiac arrest.[1] He had used excerpts from this text for a large steel sculpture showing a chest with ribs that appear to open or close in a way that resembles branches of the rose of Jericho. Whoever wishes to read the text must execute a movement that is both mental and real at once. In another exhibition, this text covered not only the inner surface of the steel strips forming the sculpture, but also the walls, where text with printed lettering ran without spacing or punctuation. It seems as if the text, in his reality, is continually dissolving and reforming. The real-world spatialization of

1 It was the text “BLOODLINE”; for more on this, see the contribution by Sabine Mainberger in this publication.

the text thus expands to become mountains of consciousness, in which one may veritably get lost. I'm mentioning these text works since they gained in importance for Terry Fox in recent years, and since, as compared to his performances and sound pieces, they have perhaps been granted too little attention to date. Maybe because they demand such tremendous effort on the part of the viewer, because they are often hard to decipher, and because the exposed meaning vanishes again and again, eluding the reader. Yet the text-works issue from the same passion for sound as his other artwork. Terry Fox loved not only the rapturous and physical theater of Artaud, but also the poetry of Verlaine and Rimbaud, for whom sound was the starting point for engendering meaning.

Terry Fox did not attend a proper, established art school, and he never really regretted it. He realized very early on that he enjoyed greater freedom, especially regarding concepts and materials, than others who had taken the classical path of art education. He had always distrusted the materials and concepts associated with art. He also distrusted the image, the likeness, as a possibility for mediation, as a possibility for communication. He especially picked up crude, cheap material—something that could be easily acquired at no cost or could be found along the way—so as to research its physical and metaphorical potential, and then to finally use these things in his work at the end of a long process of searching and exploring. Curators were always astonished at how little he needed, even when designing large spaces, giving rise to atmospheres, and creating labyrinths of consciousness.

Terry Fox loved sound. He once said that he was addicted to sound. He knew, as do we all, that humans are primarily auditive creatures, thanks to our time spent in the womb, having only secondarily mutated into visual people. Yet for him, this realization must have come to play a very significant role over the course of his artistic life, especially during his early years when, due to illness, he experienced and suffered through long phases of isolation, great pain, and, as he himself noted, strong boredom. The first performances, where he didn't really care much whether there was an audience or not, resembled spiritual exercitations, rapturous or meditative exercises that for him may have been a kind of game, a repeat of the liminal experiences he went through during his illness. So he didn't need a teacher for what one calls mindfulness in Buddhism, or for what is considered contemplation or meditation; these practices had become an integral part of his life. Maybe it is here that we find a secret to the impact of his performances, through which those of the audience who remained open were able to engage in a special experience of presence, an experience linked to the feeling of time standing still. This experience was the result of meditative clarity and rapturous concentration on the part of the artist, proving that empathy counts among the anthropological constants of our perception. The ability to connect our perception with that of other people, especially artists in this case, when we are open, simply allowing ourselves to go with the flow. Terry Fox's ability to concentrate was truly extraordinary. Any problem, any question, presented him with a challenge to enter a labyrinth, so as to revolve around a thought as if it were the heart of the labyrinth.

For him, of course, the labyrinth of Chartres was the ultimate metaphor for life, and for years it provided, at times quite obsessively, the fundamental structure for many of his works and performances. Perhaps we will at some point determine that he was thus also, as an aside, working on the rediscovery of the ornament as an expression of time, movement, and sentiment in the context of modern art.

For Terry Fox, suspense and silence were the goal of any situation he created—he loved the word situation more than performance. Suspense was, in his eyes, a sculptural concept. And the ideal material for this, both in real life and metaphorically, was the spanned steel wire which he used to yield sounds never before heard, or, better said, to imbue the spaces themselves with sound: through the resonance of the things creating or inhering within it.

It is typical for this utterly inquisitive artist that he spent a long time—several years, I would guess—thinking about what he could do with the concept of silence; with the concept of silence, without which the concept of sound would not even be conceivable. For these two of course belong together. This reflection resulted in the *Cones of Silence*, which he didn't actually produce until a few years ago: conical hollow forms made of ceramics (fig. 1). It seems to me that he must have used mathematical formulas from the field of acoustics to create this form: a pointed cone with a base curved inward. The form made it impossible for sound to spread within the cone. In order to prove this, we would have to destroy these objects, which nobody wants to do. I believe that we can trust Terry Fox, the careful researcher, on this as well.

His philanthropic nature was exceptional. It may be that he was only ever truly angry once during his artistic life, quite early on. This was when he held a performance in 1968 demonstrating against the Vietnam War, during which he burned a bed of jasmine in Berkeley with a flamethrower, in front of a classy restaurant. It was a defoliation action against the Vietnam War. Ever since, people interested in Terry Fox have occasionally called him a political artist. In my opinion, he would have probably, if he could still be here today, somewhat softened or dismissed this assessment. In the case of such a philanthropic man, if we really want to call him political, it is more fitting to consider a work that he had planned shortly before his passing as an edition for the Galerie Block: a healing ointment not for the wound, but for the knife making the wound. Terry came upon the idea thanks to Joseph Beuys, who, while the two were doing a joint performance in Düsseldorf in 1970, said to him while handling a knife: "If you cut yourself, then you'll have to bandage the knife."

Note:
Three months after the artist's death (October 14, 2008), *A Tribute to Terry Fox* was held in the Aktionsraum of the Hamburger Bahnhof in Berlin, with artistic contributions by Akio Suzuki, Arnold Dreyblatt / Thomas Ankersmit, David Moss, Hans Peter Kuhn / Junko Wada, Ivar Smedstad, Jörg Hiller, Lowell Darling, Peter Behrendsen, Peter Simon / Freya Hattenberger, Rolf Julius, Ron Meyers, Valerian Maly / Klara Schilliger, and Victor Meertens. The memorial event was organized by singuhr – hoergalerie berlin in collaboration with the Nationalgalerie Hamburger Bahnhof – Museum für Gegenwart – Berlin, supported by the DAAD Artists-in-Berlin Program and the Electronic Music Studio of the TU Berlin.

The text at hand derives from the speech given by Bernd Schulz on January 17, 2009, at the beginning of *A Tribute to Terry Fox*. It is an annotated and revised transcription by Marita Loosen-Fox, prepared based on a filmic recording of the event.

Translated from the German
by Dawn Michelle d'Atri

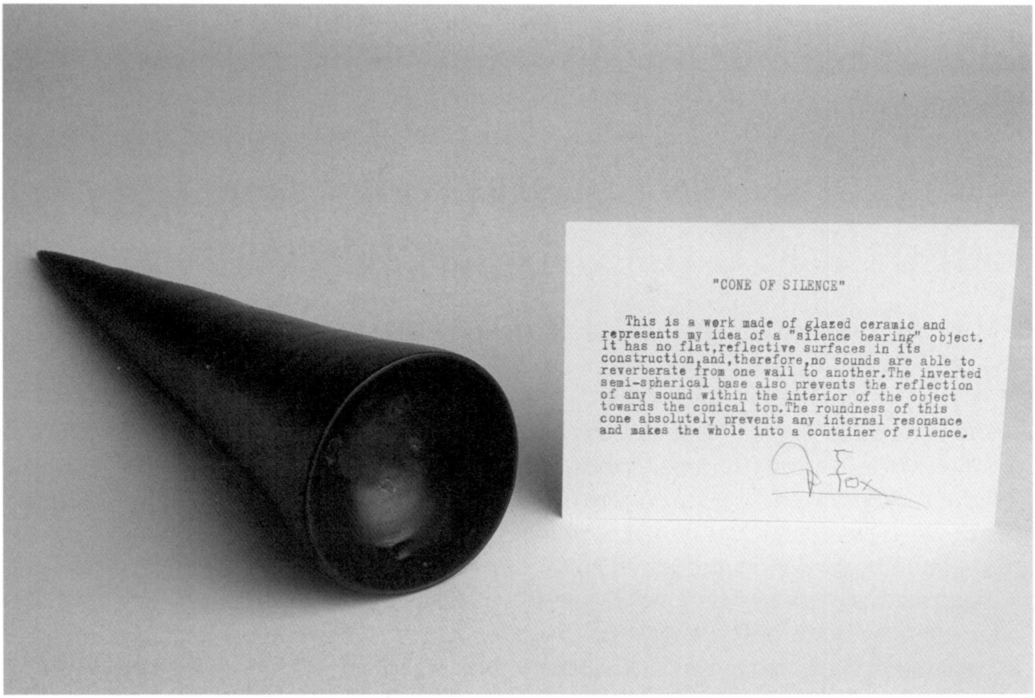

1 Terry Fox, *Cone of Silence*, 2000, edition, ceramic object, 31 x 8 cm, Estate of Terry Fox, Cologne

Ulli Seegers

The World as a Labyrinth: Bends and Circles, Metaphors and Amazement in the Work of Terry Fox

"When I went to Paris, for the show at Sonnabend's, I visited Chartres Cathedral. I saw the labyrinth and it just knocked me down to the floor. It has happened to me with other things too, but with this . . . it made such a correspondence with what I felt about my life up till then, and my life in general. And this labyrinth . . . I had no idea why it had such a powerful impact."[1] While working on preparations for his exhibition at Ileana Sonnabend in Paris, Terry Fox traveled in 1972 from San Francisco to Chartres for the first time, where he came across the extraordinary labyrinth on the floor of the famous Gothic cathedral. The labyrinth, made of light Beauce limestone and blackish-blue marble inlay, has a diameter of nearly thirteen meters and covers the entire width of the central nave. It is embedded in the stone floor near the West Portal and is considered to be the only fully preserved floor labyrinth in France (fig. 1). Might the reason behind Terry Fox's "revelation"[2] lie in this impressive instance of historical authenticity? What is the secret of the labyrinth that obviously made such a lasting impression on the artist that he explored this phenomenon almost exclusively during the following six years, and then touched upon it again and again, in very different ways, until his passing?

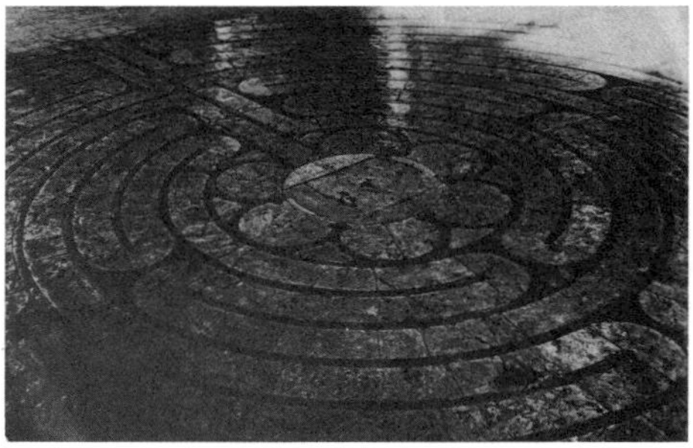

1 *Labyrinth in Chartres Cathedral*, 1972, floor mosaic

A labyrinth is generally defined as "a structure full of crossing passageways, but also a maze or a graphic figure with an intricate linear appearance, yet with only one path for accessing the center."[3] For over 5,000 years, the labyrinth has been leaving its traces in cultural history, though its precise origins are unknown. Also remaining in the dark are its use and meaning. The mysteriousness of the labyrinth has led to much speculation and, not least, has motivated a veritable flood of esoteric devotional literature.[4] In a

1 "'Die Grenzen erforschen / Exploring the Limits': Terry Fox im Gespräch mit René van Peer (1993)," in *Ocular Language*, pp. 156–83, esp. p. 167.

2 Terry Fox, "Arbeiten zum Labyrinth, 1972–1978," in *Metaphorical Instruments*, pp. 54–64, esp. pp. 54 and 61.

3 "Art: 'Labyrinth,'" in *Das ZEIT-Lexikon in 20 Bänden*, ed. Zeitverlag Gerd Bucerius, vol. 8 (Hamburg, 2005), p. 425.

4 Gernot Candolini, *Labyrinth: Wege der Erkenntnis und der Liebe*, 4th ed. (Munich, 2013).

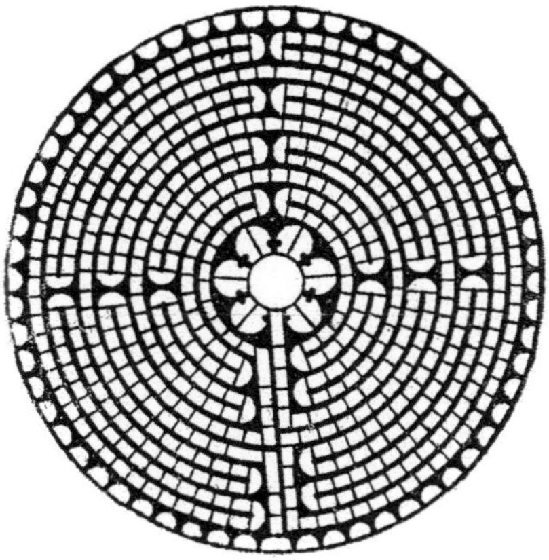

2 Terry Fox, *Labyrinth in Chartres Cathedral*, 1972, floor mosaic, stamp print, 7.4 cm in diameter

figurative sense, the term is used to describe an unclear or complex situation (fig. 2). The classical labyrinth apparently arose in the Mediterranean region, in the herding cultures of northern Africa or the Minoan seafaring culture of Crete. The more frequently the labyrinth appears in history, the more diverse are its places of application. It is found in highly diverse contexts like dances, initiation celebrations, weddings, funerals, foundations of cities, games, and more. Thus it almost always arises in transitional periods between phases of life, and in passageways: not without reason is it a part of ritualistic celebrations. The labyrinth plays a decisive role in the Greek myth of Theseus, where it is created by Daedalus, who is said to have built it in Knossos for King Minos of Crete, as a prison for the Minotaur. As a hybrid creature, half bull and half man, the Minotaur was a monster that demanded young sacrificial victims at regular intervals. Theseus, the Greek son of a king, entered the labyrinth and killed the Minotaur. Aided by the thread of his beloved Ariadne, he found his way back out again. Indeed, the labyrinth is associated with highly ambivalent connotations: from the very beginning, it has been a site of conflict and struggle, but also a place of liberation.

Against this backdrop, it is not surprising that the motif of the labyrinth was already present in the earliest churches, naturally under modified auspices: the triumph of the Greek hero over the monster quickly became Christ's victory over the Devil. From a Christological perspective, the Son of God was now viewed as the savior, entering the labyrinth of the soul in order to wrest power from evil, and to lead believers along the thread of love to a new life. Evident in the Middle Ages, however, were changes in form. Instead of eleven passageways, seven were now drawn around the center, all aligned in a cross. Around the year 1200, the labyrinth was in its prime, being integrated as a floor pattern in almost all cathedrals in the north of France. The labyrinth simultaneously symbolized the soul's path to salvation, and the pilgrimage to Jerusalem, which the penitent retraced here in prayer—sliding on his knees from bend to bend. The floor labyrinth in Chartres goes back to a drawing by Villard de Honnecourt, who worked for various Gothic Masons' guilds in the mid-third of the thirteenth century. This labyrinth measures 12.87 meters in diameter and elaborates a path running 261.5 meters, winding along 11 concentric circles and 34 bends before reaching the center. A circle of 113 regularly spaced notches form the outer edge. The round center, with a diameter of 3.1 meters, correlates with the inside section of the window from the main façade and is thus engaged in direct dialogue with the surrounding space in terms of proportion, structure, and dimensions. The number of stone slabs forming the paths is listed as 273, in the official rendering done by the local Masons' guild.

The Christian interpretation of the labyrinth thus harks back to a considerably older and more anthropologically universal constant. The labyrinth appears as an image of life in different cultures, regions, and time periods; as a symbol of existential conflicts and encounters, of the quest for the self and one's own center—as a metaphor for a labyrinthine life path that is not always easy and never direct, that is full of about-faces and detours, and that frequently displays evidence of a struggle between conflicting principles. The conflict between different principles was experienced firsthand by Terry Fox very early on. As an adolescent, a serious illness brought him face to face with his limits, directly confronting him with death. For eleven years, regular in-patient stays were necessary in hospital intensive-care and quarantine units. Isolated from the hustle and bustle of the world and sealed off from any kind of communication or information, Fox began to transcend the physical dimension. The boredom that set in after months of deprivation transformed into a new plane of perception, with "any tear in the wallpaper suddenly becoming interesting."[5] In an environment where external stimuli are reduced to a minimum, the experiencing and conception of time change. It appears as a meditative continuum of absolute present, rather than as a successive sequence of occurrences. Illness and suffering become a cathartic turning point, which in 1970 also manifested in the one-hour performance *Isolation Unit* (1970) in the cellar of the Kunstakademie Düsseldorf, together with Joseph Beuys: "My concern for the body has grown out of real experiences too. So many operations have been performed on me, I've been the object of action so many times that I became material. I was a piece of meat that people were acting upon."[6] The passive endurance of medical procedures and operations could now be transformed into active interventions in external processes. Associated with this was knowledge about the recognitivity of sensory perception: "I'm appealing to the mental space through the senses. It is tiring, it's painful, you get confused, you get lost, you have to retrace your steps over and over again, and this is also a physical experience. That is a lot different than reading a text in a book."[7] The body becomes a tool and medium of the act of making elementary processes visible. Art and reality coalesce in one's own existence.

It is no coincidence that encountering the Chartres labyrinth was a watershed moment in the life of Terry Fox, signifying the beginning of a new phase of work. In the intricate paths of the labyrinth he recognized a great parallel to his personal fate, a mirror image that heralded a process of reorientation: "I had undergone cycles of health, sickness, health, sickness, with attendant hospitalization, release, hospitalization, release, for 11 years. The labyrinth at Chartres has 11 concentric rings, which seemed to correspond to these 11 years. The 34 turns leading into the center of the labyrinth also corresponded to these cycles. I had just gone through a major operation that finished once and for all these cycles and seemed to have reached the center of the labyrinth. My energies

5 Terry Fox in conversation with the author on January 24, 2003, in Cologne.

6 "'Ich wollte, dass meine Stimmung ihr Aussehen beeinflusst / I Wanted to Have my Mood Affect their Looks': Terry Fox im Gespräch mit Willoughby Sharp (1971)," in *Ocular Language*, pp. 8–41, esp. p. 11.

7 "'Vom Boden zur Decke und von Wand zu Wand / From Floor to Ceiling and Wall to Wall': Terry Fox im Gespräch mit Lothar Schröder (1999)," in *Ocular Language*, pp. 192–209, esp. p. 203.

up to this point had been involved in reaching this center and I decided to reverse this process and work my way out by basing all my future work on the labyrinth at Chartres."[8] Here, the number eleven clearly played a special role, for Terry Fox continued: "And 11 had always been my number. My son was born at 11.44 on the 11th of September. Anyway, so I did an analysis of it for six years. Everything I did for six years was based on 11. Performance, sound work, drawings, sculptures, everything."[9]

Correspondence between one's own existence and aesthetic experience already embodied the leitmotif of his previous performance and video art; yet now—due to the exploration of the labyrinth in Chartres—objects, drawings, environments, and, most especially, sounds were added to the spectrum of mediums employed. In taking a partially scientific, partially pictorial-creative approach to probing its secrets, Terry Fox was on the trail of the potency of the mosaic. The 552 steps, 11 concentric circles, and 34 bends, which were analytically emphasized by the artist in the process, thus become a part of a pictorial whole that contains much more than the sum of its parts. "Because it's amazing. It's not a sculpture, it's not a decoration, it's really and truly a metaphor.... for something. But what?"[10] Fox cut the form of a labyrinth out of a piece of cardboard and pulled it apart in order to be able to study, through the suggestion of three-dimensionality, the individual twists and turns. He scraped the shape of the labyrinth out of a layer of soot on a pane of glass, allowing the contours to glow. He cast the labyrinth form in plaster and sought additional insight through the sense of touch (*Plaster Labyrinth*, 1972). He had the 552 steps chiseled into a cobblestone and placed it in the ground above a vein of water (*Podio del Mondo per l'Arte*, Middelburg, 1978) (fig. 3). In fact, during his extensive research, the artist discovered that an underground river flows under the cathedral at a depth of 37 meters, and that the spire of the architectural structure above the floor mosaic likewise measures exactly 37 meters. Terry Fox lent visual expression to this extraordinary labyrinth site with his stool object *A Metaphor* (1976): the rendering of the labyrinth on cardboard, suspended on a string, is situated precisely along the horizontal axis "in between these two incredible forces, moving water and the atmospheric forces,"[11] (fig. 4). The object was accompanied by an extended text[12] which gave the viewer detailed instructions for the imaginary overview of the cathedral, and which was meant to illustrate the localization of the labyrinth in space. Walking through the labyrinth led to rhythmic, spiraling movement in space, to movement "back and forth, where one believes to already be almost there and then to be led back along serpentines."[13] The path proceeds cyclically, rather than linearly, through continuous winding from beginning to end: it alters the experience of space and time. Not by chance was Terry Fox convinced that the floor mosaic in Chartres "must have been designed to be used as part of an initiation.... This kind of initiation doesn't seem Christian to me; pagan, rather."[14] The obvious relations-

8 Terry Fox, "Arbeiten zum Labyrinth," in *Metaphorical Instruments*, p. 61.

9 "'Die Grenzen erforschen / Exploring the Limits': Terry Fox im Gespräch mit René van Peer (1993)," in *Ocular Language*, pp. 167 and 171.

10 Ibid., p. 167.

11 Ibid., p. 171.

12 Reprinted in *Metaphorical Instruments*, pp. 56–57.

13 Terry Fox in conversation with the author on February 8, 2003, in Cologne.

14 "'Die Grenzen erforschen / Exploring the Limits': Terry Fox im Gespräch mit René van Peer (1993)," in *Ocular Language*, esp. pp. 171ff.

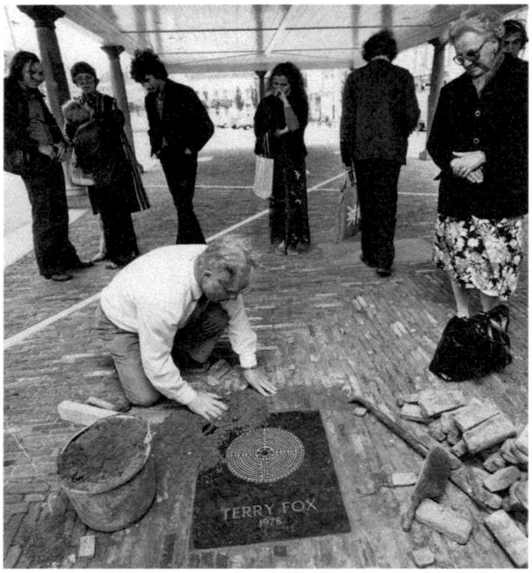

3 Terry Fox, *Untitled*, 1978, 1 x 1 m, floor plate, stone,permanent installation in exterior space, Podio del Mondo per l'Arte, Middelburg, Netherlands, photo: Wim Riemers

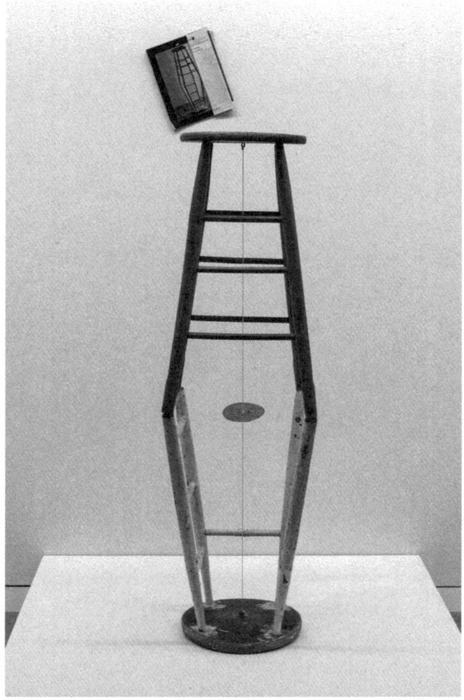

4 Terry Fox, *A Metaphor*, 1976, exhibition view *Elemental Gestures*, Von der Heydt-Museum, Wuppertal, sculpture, two wooden stools, newspaper text, string, paper, ink, sculpture, 142.2 x 42.5 x 40.6 cm, San Francisco Museum of Modern Art, photo: Antje Zeis-Loi

hip between movement and rhythm in the labyrinth inspired the artist to create various works of art using pendulums. A pendulum congenially traces the labyrinthine gyrations, steadily generating tones—especially while rotating around a water glass—and engaging in a state of constant vibration (*Metaphors for Falling,* 1977). Besides the dynamic element of the pendulum, Terry Fox was increasingly interested in its acoustic qualities. Against the backdrop of his obsessive dissection of the pictorial language of the labyrinth, the act of making the enigma of Chartres experienceable consequently took place, not only by means of visualization, but also of musical rendering. Indeed, many of his sound works, like *552 Steps through 11 Pairs of Strings* (1976) (see fig. p. 42) and *The Labyrinth Scored for the Purrs of 11 Cats* (1977) (see fig. p. 105), were inspired by the perception of the intricate floor pattern. Various means are employed in the translation of visual language into sound, such as taut piano strings or purring cats, yet all make use of the specific geometry of the labyrinth, to 552 steps, 11 circles, and 34 bends. Terry Fox described one of his performances, in terms of its clear reference to Chartres, as follows: "I also attempted, during this time, to make sound from the labyrinth. I made two sound works based on its path. '552 steps through 11 pairs of strings' was a performance in my loft in San Francisco in which I stretched 11 pairs of piano wire of 11 different thicknesses across the wooden floor of my studio. These were anchored by turn-buckles at either end, for tuning, and stretched over wooden bridges. The whole took the shape of a giant horizontal harp with the longest pair of wires being 34 feet and the shortest, 3 feet. These pairs of wires represented the 11 concentric rings of the labyrinth, the longest being the outside ring and the shortest representing the innermost ring. They are played with a soft mallet held in one hand and a score in the other. The score was a 34 foot string tied with 552 knots, each knot representing an actual step in the labyrinth with the 34 turns indicated by either a piece of wire in a knot (a move to the next longer pair or wires) or a rubberband around a knot (a move to the next shorter pair). This 4½ hour performance was done with the audience in the dark loft the next floor below. The sound moved in waves from their ceiling, which was also my floor."[15] The musical rendering of the labyrinth to which Fox committed himself here is found in the sound piece *The Labyrinth Scored for the Purrs of 11 Cats*, through exceedingly vibrant "instruments." He explained: "For this tape I recorded the continuous purring of 11 different cats. These 11 tapes were then mixed (joined) to follow the exact path of the labyrinth. Each cat represented one of the 11 concentric rings. The steps into the labyrinth were changed into 10 second segments of purring. The 34 turns were changed into 10 seconds of overlapping purrs as the path moved from one cat (ring) into the next. The tape follows exactly the path of the labyrinth and moves in stereo to the right or left speaker as the labyrinth path swings right or left. The center is the simultaneous purring of all 11 cats. This 90 minute tape took 2 years to produce and was finally finished in upstate New York by Z.B.S. with Bob Bielecki as engineer."[16]

Already the Documenta piece *Action for a Tower Room* (1972) in Kassel was positioned in the context of the synesthetic translation of visual experience. Over the course of three days, Terry Fox played the rather monotonous tamboura for six hours a day, thus filling the Turmzimmer with uninterrupted "circular sound." And, according to Fox, the series of thirty-four *Children's Tapes* gave rise to a "video labyrinth" that likewise represents the thirty-four twists of the real labyrinth. The labyrinth principle is—or so it seems—omnipresent and therefore to be found in the utterly mundane: "The actual labyrinth, I think, is also kind of an instrument. Because it's on the floor, and when you walk it, you make this very precise pattern in the air, and it works like a magnet, I think. Like, you could charge yourself by walking this thing."[17] An instrument allows something to resonate, makes it situationally experienceable, and evokes immediate sensations—"creating electricity,"[18] as Terry Fox phrased it. The energetic nature that had already sparked the interest of the artist in the floor labyrinth of Chartres now became a subject in his art. And the fact that the mesmerizing pull of the powerful labyrinth not only offered positive aspects, but must actually also be viewed with ambivalence, was felt by Terry Fox in 1978: "It got too obsessive, and I started drinking, heavily. I started to get into the labyrinth. I decided I really had to stop it. I made a piece in Middelburg, Holland. That was in '78. That was the last labyrinth I did."[19] This turned out to not be completely true, as demonstrated by the sound piece *Labyrinth of the Inner Ear*, from the year 2006, which transposed the labyrinth concept from the convoluted inner ear to the urban jungle, with the sounds of a blind person travers-

15 Terry Fox, "Arbeiten zum Labyrinth," in *Metaphorical Instruments*, p. 63.

16 Ibid., p. 63.

17 "'Es ist der Versuch einer neuen Kommunikation / It's an Attempt at a New Communication': Terry Fox im Gespräch mit Robin White (1979)," in *Ocular Language*, pp. 70–99, esp. p. 97.

18 Ibid., p. 99.

19 "'Die Grenzen erforschen / Exploring the Limits': Terry Fox im Gespräch mit René van Peer (1993)," in *Ocular Language*, esp. p. 171.

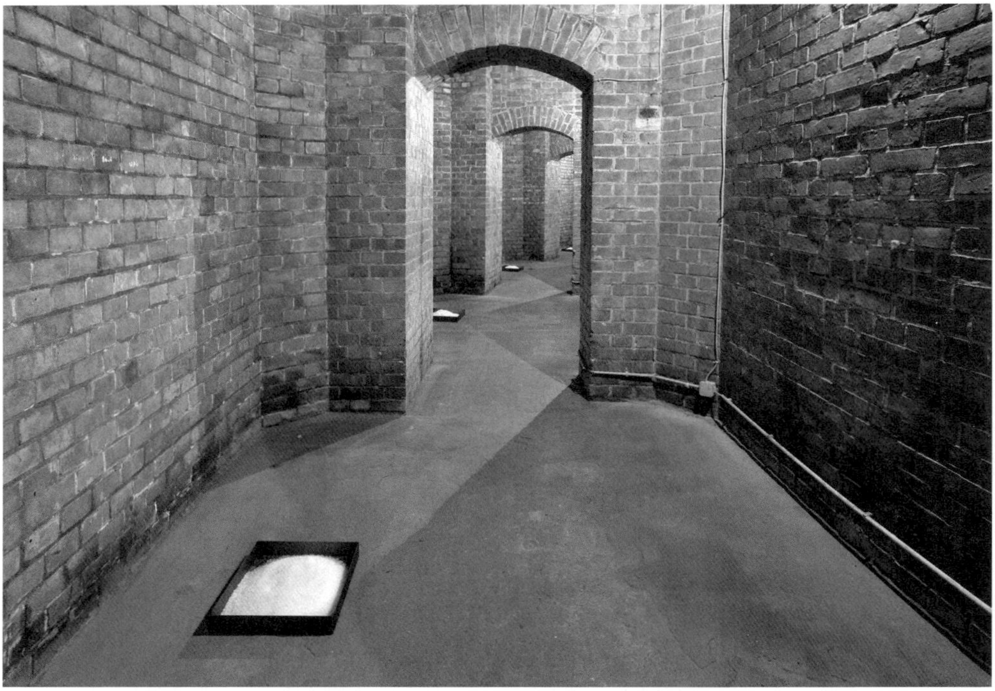

5 Terry Fox, *34 turns,* temporary installation with sound, singuhr – hoergalerie Berlin, realization: Marita Loosen-Fox and Carsten Seiffarth, 2009, 34 metal bowls (34 x 34 x 5.5 cm), steel plate, 34 x 3 kg salt crystals (sea salt), photo: Roman März

ing Berlin by tapping a white cane being recorded. Of course, the destination point is identical with the point of origin here. And in the last installation *34 Turns*, which Terry Fox had conceived in the spring of 2008 in Berlin while visiting an overground water reservoir, the labyrinth motif appears yet again (fig. 5). The thirty-four bends of the floor mosaic are mirrored in the thirty-four chambers of labyrinthine brick vaults that were to be transformed, through metal bowls filled with salt crystals, into a barely audible sound space—for the high humidity had transformed what were initially delicate crystals into a liquid aggregate. The installation was realized posthumously and illustrates how Terry Fox remained preoccupied with the labyrinth topic until the day he died. While the artist clearly subsumed different ways of being, phenomena, experiences, structures, and even situations under the term labyrinth, he was just as intent on a terminological demarcation. A labyrinth is not a maze, he emphasized repeatedly: "You're doing this revolving pattern and it's not maze-like. Most people associate labyrinth with mazes. . . . You're lost and you can't find your way out. But this is a unicursal path, you don't get lost at all. . . . That means an undeviating path."[20] Labyrinths thus preclude the possibility of getting lost; they have one single win-

20 "'Es ist der Versuch einer neuen Kommunikation / It's an Attempt at a New Communication': Terry Fox im Gespräch mit Robin White (1979)," in *Ocular Language*, p. 99; also see "Art: 'Labyrinth,'" in *Lexikon der christlichen Ikonographie*, ed. Engelbert Kirschbaum, vol. 3 (Freiburg im Breisgau, 1971), p. 2: "A certain goal is only reachable from a single starting point along a winding path. This sense of purpose sets the labyrinth apart from all linear ornaments, knots, and other convoluted lines resembling a circle, but in turn connects it with the spiral (yet differing due to repeated changes in path

ding path, which leads to the destination or center, along a route that runs as long as possible. In fact, a maze evokes a completely different experience than a labyrinth: while the latter entails more of an "inward movement," the maze aims for external orientation. Right and wrong become a predominant theme here.[21]

Labyrinthine patterns *with* bifurcations are found sporadically in Europe from the fifteenth century on, while real mazes were first created in the sixteenth century: for instance, the complexes in Verona around 1570, furnished with tall hedges in which one could get lost. These mazes are a phenomenon of Mannerism, which notoriously took pleasure in the grotesque, the surprising, the excessive, and sometimes even the warped. It is for good reason that Gustav René Hocke associated the labyrinthine mazes with Mannerist style. In the self-portrait by Parmigianino, for example, the true nature of things is first revealed through the warped perspective: the vantage point of the convex mirror shows the given reality visible at the time of painting—that is, with foreshortening. Yet in truth, according to Hocke, we must view reality from an inverted perspective in order to perceive it correctly. Through the many bends, circles, and turns in the labyrinth, precisely this twisting and turning is thematically and programmatically staged in the picture. It's no surprise that, in the culture, Hocke identifies the essential attribute of the labyrinth in the coincidence of opposites: he considered the labyrinth to be a "unifying metaphor for the calculable and the incalculable element in the world. The detour leads to the center. Only the detour leads to completeness."[22]

It was also Hocke who, in this context, elaborated on the dual meaning of the English word "maze." Not only does it mean "labyrinth," but, at the same time, it connotes "amazement."[23] Amazement and astonishment about utterly quotidian things and experiences, along with the act of becoming disoriented in the seemingly meaningless and unfathomable, are what constitute the labyrinth, and what at times challenge its beholder: understanding of the world and awareness of the self. And surely it is precisely this that Terry Fox considered his revelatory experience with the labyrinth: "I found a metaphor for my physical being, not my body, a labyrinth."[24] Preceding this realization was the existential threat of death or, in the language of the initiation rites, *symbolic death*. Thus, the new beginning equates to a kind of mystic rebirth, as per the "die and become" principle. The labyrinth fulfills these two contrary movements at once and, at first glance, seems paradoxical: entering, ascending, recognizing, and becoming on the one hand; and exiting, descending, and being on the other. The bipolar code of the universe is generally valid and recursive. Like Villard de Honnecourt, the inventor of the labyrinth in Chartres, Terry Fox also devoted himself to the quiet and transient, the commonplace and unspectacular; all the while understanding how to be connected to the grand and the universal at all times, for the very same

direction). Passage through a labyrinth can be combined with other figures (spirals, meanders). Crossings and bifurcations were mostly absent prior to the sixteenth century. So the old labyrinths offered no possibility of getting lost."

21 Candolini 2013 (see note 4), p. 27.

22 Gustav René Hocke, *Die Welt als Labyrinth: Manier und Manie in der europäischen Kunst* (Hamburg, 1957), p. 101.

23 Ibid., p. 102.

24 "'Es ist der Versuch einer neuen Kommunikation / It's an Attempt at a New Communication': Terry Fox im Gespräch mit Robin White (1979)," in *Ocular Language*, p. 95.

structures and correspondences recur. The labyrinth is simultaneously a cosmos, world, city, person, mental convolution, consciousness, heart, and path. Its paths run sometimes apart, sometimes together, causing disorientation through manifold shifts in perspective and direction. But they always move closer, step by step, to the target. In this respect, the labyrinth is also an invitation to experience decelerated time, a sign of hesitation, a place for oscillating back and forth, and an invitation to engage the external and internal sense of equilibrium.

It comes as no surprise that the import of labyrinths was no longer appreciated at the dawn of the Enlightenment, which resulted in more and more labyrinths being destroyed. Children and dalliers wandering along the winding patterns increasingly disturbed the regimented flow of church services, for which reason most of the labyrinths were removed without further ado. So it surprised the cathedral Canon of Chartres, Jean-Baptiste Souchet, who died in 1654, that the labyrinth there was to be retained, for in it he saw merely "a silly amusement for those who have nothing better to do than waste their time with insane turning, twisting, and running around."[25] So Terry Fox developed enthusiasm *for* the labyrinth for precisely the same reasons that some contemporaries of the seventeenth and eighteenth centuries apparently spoke *against* it: as the epitome of movement, rhythm, energy, and fluctuation in space, as a situative-corporeal experience of the vision of life, and as resistance against ideological paternalism.

25 Jean-Baptiste Souchet, *Histoire de Chartres*, vol. 1 (1866), p. 220.

In his oeuvre, Fox transformed the labyrinth as *metaphor* into various aggregate states, thus making it experienceable for (almost) all senses: for hearing, feeling, and seeing. The etymological origins of the word go back to the Greek *metaphérein* for *taking elsewhere*. Here, this *transfer* can imply either "the spiritualization of the sensory," or the "sensorialization of the spiritual."[26] This reciprocity of the metaphor as the "practice of figurative expression instead of that which signifies the matter itself"[27] is also evident in Terry Fox's work. His object *A Metaphor* had already proved to be a microcosmic model for Chartres Cathedral and its subsoil, with the bottom stool inverted, and the top and bottom stools' feet touching, intending to illustrate his conception of the visible and the invisible facets of the assumed building concept. "In order to grasp the object you need to make a few visual adjustments. Imagine the lower stool to be half imbedded in the earth and pretend an underground river flows along the floor and through the center of the stool. A well rises from the river along the string to ground level, half way up the stool."[28] The accompanying text, which the artist added to his work, makes the principle of the metaphor explicit: the metaphorical structure is an act of making visible "something as something."[29] Even if there is not a universal definition of *metaphor* within individual disciplines, and the term can hardly be operational in the charged

26 "Art: 'Metapher,'" in *Wörterbuch der philosophischen Begriffe*, ed. Arnim Regenbogen and Uwe Meyer (Hamburg, 2013), pp. 411–12, esp. p. 411.

27 Ibid.

28 Terry Fox, "Arbeiten zum Labyrinth," in *Metaphorical Instruments*, p. 61.

29 Stefan Majetschak, "Sichtbare Metaphern: Bemerkungen zur Bildlichkeit von Metaphern und zur Metaphorizität in Bildern," in *Logik der Bilder: Präsenz – Repräsentation – Erkenntnis*, ed. Richard Hoppe-Sailer et al. (Berlin, 2005), pp. 239–53, esp. p. 246.

context of visual and linguistic metaphors,[30] structurally, it does indeed thwart the strict dichotomy of separate areas of knowledge, and it opens up a new conceptual space that interconnects sensory and cognitive realms of experience. Since Terry Fox, with his eponymous object, quite obviously, and very consciously, initiated a multifaceted discourse about metaphorization in art, then—when it comes to *A Metaphor*—a connection can doubtlessly be made to Arthur Danto, with the dual structure of the metaphor reflecting the basic structure of artwork, evident essentially through viewing and conceptually eluding being paraphrased: "it is rather the power of the work which is implicated in the metaphor, and power is something that must be *felt*."[31] It is the situative sensation, such thinking in one's own body, that allows art to become a highly existential experience—both for the artist and the spectator. "But the greatest metaphors of art I believe to be those in which the spectator identifies himself with the attributes of the represented character" and those that culminate in "virtually the enactment of a metaphoric transformation with oneself as subject."[32] So in this interpretive approach, art is always created through an act of metaphor-formation that validates its ontological status as art in the first place.[33] It is precisely this metaphorical structure of art itself that Terry Fox poignantly visualizes for us, with his various *metaphorical instruments*, as a connection between up and down,

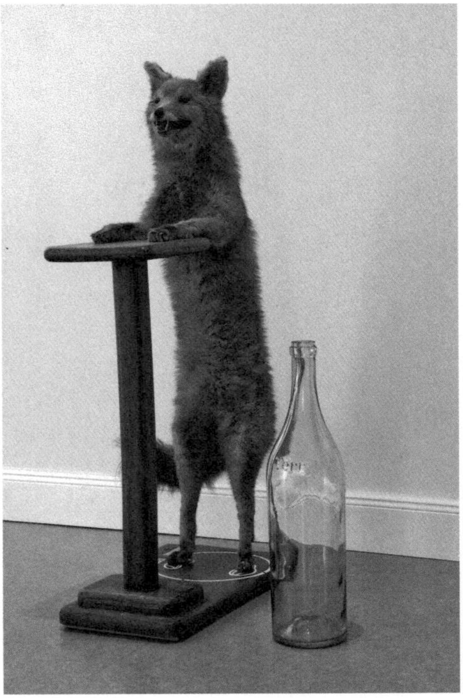

6 Terry Fox, *Lauschender Fuchs*, 1998, exhibition view *Terry Fox – Locus Solus*, at Barkenhoff / Heinrich-Vogeler Museum, 2011, taxidermied fox, 100 x 26 x 65 cm, glass bottle, 50 x 30 cm, Estate of Terry Fox, Cologne, photo: Kyra Witt

inside and outside, visible and invisible, conscious and subconscious. In the form of his self-portrait as *Lauschender Fuchs* (The Fox Listening, 1992) (fig. 6), he seems to have created the strongest metaphor: as coincidence of art and life.

Note: Revised version of a lecture given at the conference "Terry Fox: Situationen" on November 6, 2015, organized by the Terry Fox Association e. V., Cologne, at the Akademie der Künste, Berlin (at Hanseatenweg).

Translated from the German
by Dawn Michelle d'Atri

30 On this, see Marius Rimmele, "'Metapher' als Metapher: Zur Relevanz eines übertragenen Begriffs in der Analyse figurativer Bilder," *kunsttexte.de* 1 (2011).

31 Arthur C. Danto, *The Transfiguration of the Commonplace: A Philosophy of Art* (Cambridge, MA, and London: Harvard University Press, 1981), p. 174.

32 Ibid., pp. 172 and 173.

33 On the concept of the metaphor in the work of Arthur Danto, see Juliane Rebentisch, *Theorien der Gegenwartskunst* (Hamburg, 2013), pp. 122–35.

Michael Glasmeier

The Hardly and the Specific: *The School of Velocity* by Terry Fox

What relationship do you have to Nothingness?

Prick up your ears and maybe you'll hear the sound of a drop falling . . .

Giorgio Manganelli

In 1996, on the occasion of the international *sonambiente* sound festival in Berlin, American artist Terry Fox (1943–2008), who was living in Cologne at the time, presented *The School of Velocity* on the premises of the former East German Academy of the Arts at Pariser Platz. In this sound work, many references may be found not only to the artist's own oeuvre but also to a specific—at times loud, but for the most part essentially quiet—history of art in the second half of the twentieth century. Yet what is important to me here is to recall my first impression of this work; for I had seen it and remember being extremely fascinated. This led me to believe that it would be easy to put my impression into words. However, time erases memories and all I have left is a vague recollection of an enormous, high, disused space, bare and unpainted, with skylights. I also recall intravenous bottles suspended from the ceiling, a hot plate and a sponge in a bowl on the floor, as well as drops falling from the bottles onto these objects. Yet it was all almost inaudible, which was partly because the other visitors did not seem to care about listening and were instead themselves busy producing noise in the reverberating hall. Overall, I remember feeling a longing for silence that would allow me to follow the acoustic precision with which the drops were hitting the objects, and to appreciate the splendid contradiction between the subtlety of the events and the monumentality of the room. I also know that even back then I admired the courage with which a fragility had been made to enter and assert itself in the space, which resembled a former sculptor's studio.

Photographs and Fox's own text about the work made it clear to me that my memories, although correct, were less than half the story. And this was the case even though the piece was the starting point of my ever-renewed interest in the forms of this artist's actions: for even in the context of the many, very diverse artistic sound explorations in the *sonambiente* exhibition,[1] with works by artists ranging from Laurie Anderson to Nam June Paik and Sarkis, Fox was an

1 See *Klangkunst*, ed. Helga de la Motte-Haber and Golo Föllmer et al., exh. cat. *sonambiente: festival für hören und sehen*, Akademie der Künste Berlin (Munich and New York, 1996).

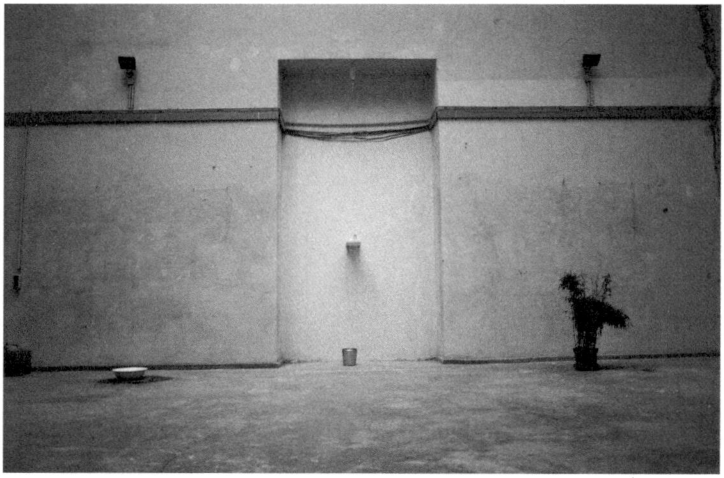

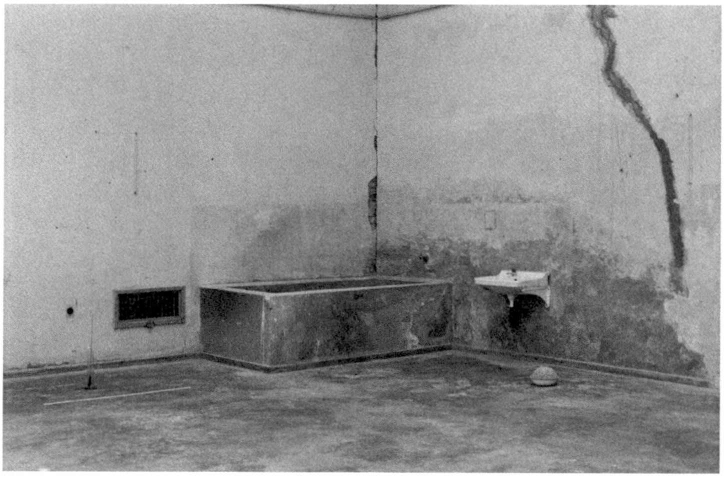

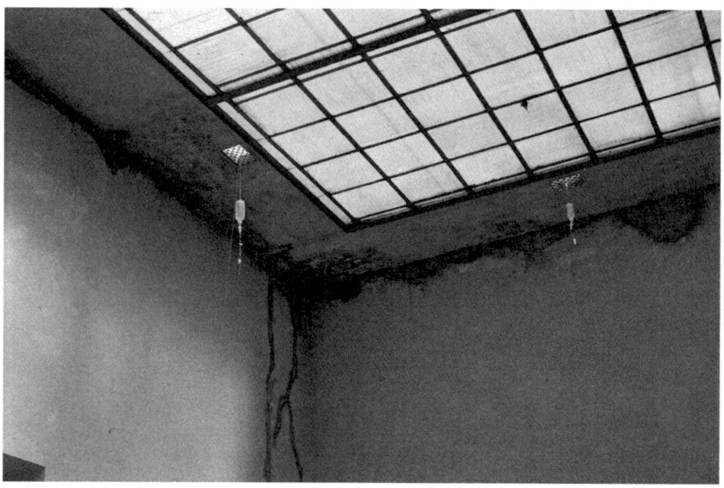

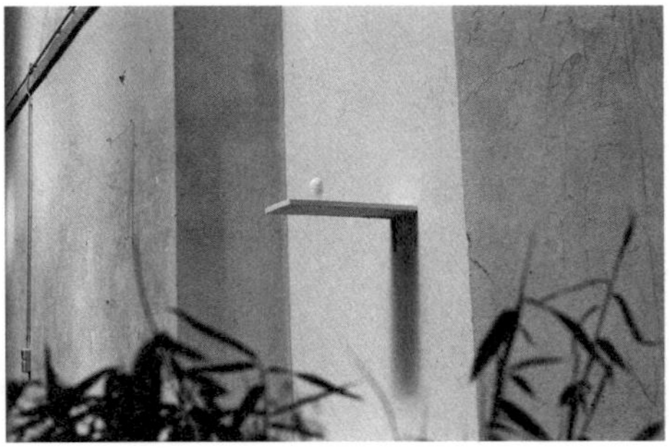

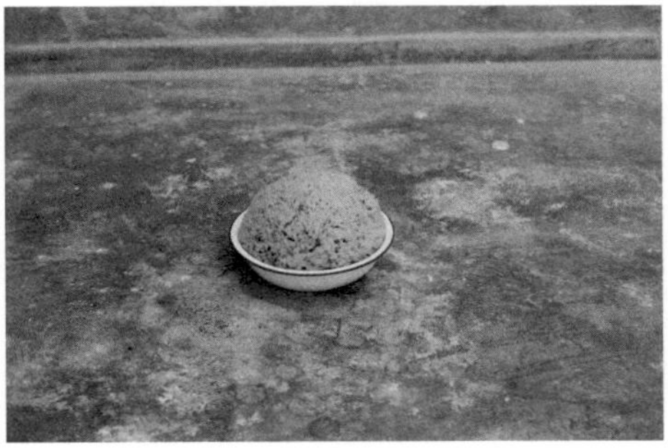

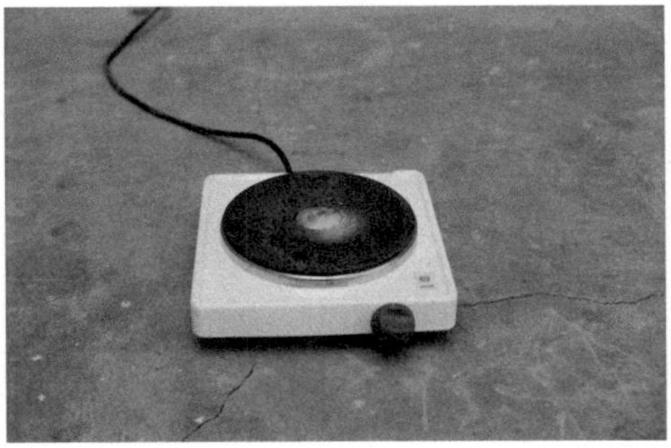

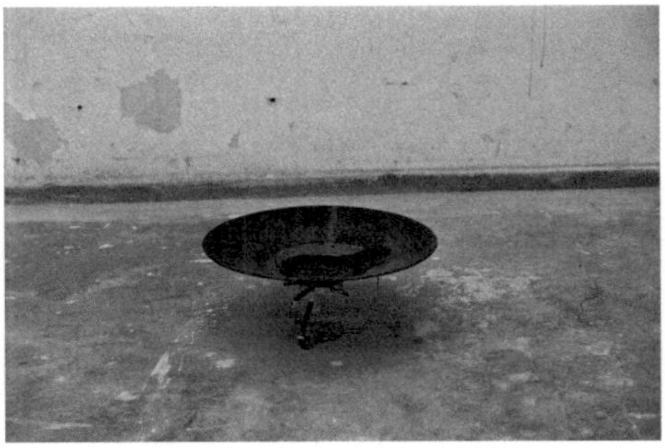

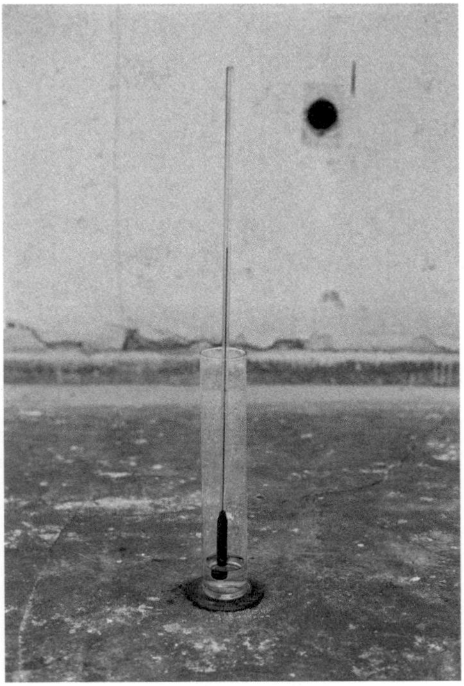

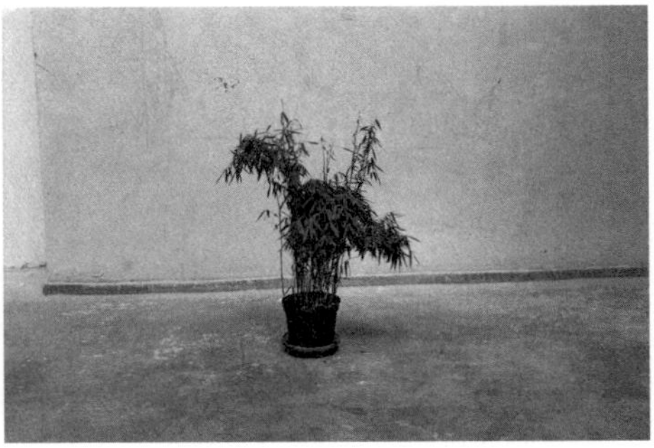

1–9 Terry Fox, *The School of Velocity*, exhibition views, Academy of the Arts (East), Berlin, 1996, photos: Marita Loosen-Fox

1 Exhibition view (wall with egg)
2 Exhibition view (sink)
3 Exhibition view (ceiling with dripper)
4 Egg in a cup
5 Natural sponge in enamel bowl
6 Hot plate
7 Gold-mining pan
8 Thermometer in a glass tube
9 Bamboo plant

extraordinary sound artist. This was largely because instruments, technical and acoustic devices, film and/or physical exertion did not as such form the basis of his work. Most akin to *The School of Velocity* was Akio Suzuki's quiet piece, which I will come back to later. But first, here is the short text Fox wrote about the work:

"For the sound show SONAMBIENTE in Berlin I worked in a large room in the Akademie der Künste Ost. It was a room without windows, in unrestored condition, but with skylights completely covering the ceiling. I decided to use intravenous bottles, hanging from the ceiling and dripping at different speeds onto various objects: an egg in a cup, a natural sponge in an enamel bowl, an active hot plate, a thermometer in a glass tube, a bamboo plant, an American gold-mining pan and a metal bucket.

Using combinations of very quiet sounds, some of which were almost inaudible, I wanted to emphasize the presence of the simple objects and their subtle sound qualities. The completely acoustic ambience helped to create a meditative, self-reflective environment. I wanted to invite the audience to walk through the space and search out the sounds, perhaps relating them to their own personal experiences."[2]

Admittedly, Fox has already formulated everything very precisely here. So what might there be left for me to say? One thing I find astonishing is how I could recall only two of the items listed: the hot plate and the sponge. They are the objects that react the most extremely when drops hit them. They cause the drops to disappear—that is, they are either absorbed or sizzle away.

But let me return to the beginning: I stood there in the large hall, which, after examining Marita Loosen's photographs, I now know was entirely gray, with gray cracked walls, a gray floor, a gray tub, a grayish-black ventilation shaft, and a grayish-white sink without a drain (figs. 1–9). Standing between an electrical socket and the ventilation shaft was a hardly visible glass tube with the thermometer mentioned by Fox; and next to the sink, the bowl with the sponge. I also remember things dripping, but neither from the faucet nor into the sink or tub, all of which are predestined dripping sites. Indeed, in images of motion and time, a dripping faucet is a symbol of what trickles *and* is motionless—a state of loneliness *and* isolation, such as seen in film noir.
And in a cult clip of Bert and Ernie from *Sesame Street*, dripping is a nerve-racking sound, one increasingly employed in real life as means of torture in places both known and unknown to us. Thus dripping, as symbolized by the faucet, is clearly not, in itself, an eagerly anticipated aesthetic event, especially when it is associated with a relentless regularity, for exactly then its sound hardly changes. Instead, it prolongs and marks time as well as a space of repetition which, when it is as gray and glum as this derelict room, can turn into hell.

Perhaps drops from these conspicuous room fixtures inspired Fox to want to show the other—so to speak—lively, arrhythmic side of dripping. His drops do not fall at regular intervals from the faucet but at different speeds from artistically positioned intravenous bottles directly onto specific objects that are, for the most part, set up on the floor. Drops hitting the

2 Terry Fox, "The School of Velocity (1996)," in *Works with Sound*, p. 96.

sponge sink in almost silently, while others land in the glass tube with the thermometer—after, perhaps, a high-pitched ping (depending on the water level)—to be carefully checked for fever. Another situation existing within this same space is created by a niche in one wall, and a wood and wire ledge, although they are actually irrelevant to the drip event. Installed here is the gold-mining pan which, if enough water were available, could be used to separate sand and ore. What makes this pan particularly special is its sculptural inner life. Hitting a variety of geometricized, three-dimensional elements, the drops sound different depending on the height and depth of the interior, whereas the drops falling on the bamboo plant splatter on its slender leaves, making them move gently. In Zen, a drop symbolizes rain and the lines nature draws in space. The egg in the cup, which is not on the floor but has its own little ledge, calls attention to itself by causing each drop to burst on its tip and break into tiny droplets, until they flow and converge with previously burst drops. Accumulating in a puddle on the ledge, they eventually, due to gravity, form new, larger drops that fall and collect with a clink in the metal bucket below. And when a drop finally hits the hot plate, it explodes and hisses upward as if into thermal nirvana.

Hence we have not just the different speeds of the drops, but above all, finely differentiated sound events when they land: almost inaudible, muffled, bright, hissing, clinking, splashing, or liquefying. But these words are mere euphemisms, resulting from a need to classify, a situation that has been pushed nearly to its limits, because the differences are not only too minimal but also verge on the inaudible. Optimally, the next drop at another spot in the room will bring out the difference, amplified by the gray resonating space which in its monumentality heightens the reverberations of even the tiniest event, though this includes not only the individual drops falling but also the noises made by the public. In other words, a highly sensitive space! If we were to close our eyes, as we do at a concert, we would—under ideal circumstances—have a symphony of minimal acoustic differences in both tone and beat. For as time passes, rhythms emerge and differences grow subtler, until they become, as it were, loud, autonomous, emancipated. I would like to speak here of a symphony of the "hardly," an adverb which at times I have, with all seriousness, nominalized,[3] in order to give the occurrence of the airy, the fleeting, and what is strenuous in art a commonality more complex than expressed, for example, by the terms "unremarkable" or "discreet" that I otherwise use. For the hardly also involves a temporal component which has been indispensable in my explorations of sound. Nevertheless, contrary to the "almost nothing" of philosopher Vladimir Jankélévitch, who passed away in 1985, the hardly does not operate at the boundary of death.[4] So it is not something perpetually inherent to humans, which then reveals itself in a specific instant. The hardly has to show itself or be shown. In exemplary fashion, Terry Fox achieves exactly that, and not just in this work. He repeatedly operates at the boundaries of what we call perception. He repeatedly teaches us through his actions that perception needs art, and not only to con-

3 See Michael Glasmeier, "'hmmm,'" in *Sandra Boeschenstein: Die ungelösten Kausalnähte tragen wir im Futter unserer Mäntel / The Unsolved Casual Seams We Wear in the Linings of Our Coats*, exh. cat. Künstlerhaus Bethanien (Berlin, 2015), n.p.

4 See Vladimir Jankélévitch, *The Forgiveness*, trans. Andrew Kelley (Chicago and London, 2005), pp. 34ff.

firm itself, but also to demonstrate at its boundaries its splendid subtlety and ability to differentiate; for perception is born from silence and emptiness, and leads back to them. And its mentor is the hardly.

Since the hardly is difficult to grasp, it requires the specific to show itself. The specific can be an object, a word, or an action that elevates what is hardly there to a perceptible state, which is here the sound of dripping—since that is primarily what this is all about. Fox speaks of his "sound show," a peculiar choice of words for what has come to be known as "sound art." But, unlike in art, in this light and entertaining show the form of showing something through the specific manifests itself brilliantly as an activity that is able to transcend the variety show. To begin with, Fox, like the variety artist, needs the absolute specificity of, let's say, a cloth to make a coin appear or disappear. In other words, he requires specific objects to bring about the appearance of the hardly. In most cases, these are simple and inexpensive items that are themselves already en route to the hardly, such as a sponge or an egg. Although even a hot plate is on the brink of disappearing when the space is as impressively large and gray as here.

Now the specific is per se the chosen, and since it appears in this kind of show it is always more than just a prop. For as soon as a prop becomes visible and assumes its role, it emerges from its shadowy existence and confirms the specific as a condition for the hardly, a condition that can itself become quite symbolic, elementary, narrative. It tends toward imagery, toward a tableau vivant, especially if, as here, it holds, as fitting in a sculptor's studio, sculpturally still. To appreciate the hardly—as I have already said—we need time. Fox also addressed this matter, and so it is worth remembering that he "… wanted to invite the audience to walk through the space and search out the sounds, perhaps relating them to their own personal experiences."

In this sound show, the experience of the hardly leads without fail to our appreciating specific objects, not only as instruments, which they are to a certain extent—that is, resonators—but also as objects transferred from the context in which they normally function to that of art; in other words, almost readymades. And in this tension between readymade and resonator, there is room for the symbolic, which we inevitably will or must ascribe to the objects presented here. Charged, so to speak, by the hardly, and present umpteen times in the dripping, they radiate in the splendor of their own personal significance. I have already described the plant as being Zen-like, although here it stands more generally for nature and its history; as does the egg for growth, the sponge for absorption, the thermometer for measurement and research, the gold-mining pan for quest, as well as alchemy and the hot plate for transformation and heat. If we see these things as symbols, then Fox's work expands into a cosmos for the forms of action of human existence; or to put it less heroically, of artistic practice, in particular the historical practice of the Renaissance and the Baroque, such as reflected in art and curiosity cabinets and chambers from the period, and later passed on to Modernism by Marcel Duchamp, Man Ray, and Francis Picabia. Hence, what is being dripped upon is ultimately the essence of art and natural history, reflected in exemplary objects. They enhance one another, or as drip analyst Leonardo da Vinci remarked on the topic in 1500: "If a drop of water falls into the sea when it is calm, it must of necessity follow that the whole surface of the sea is raised imperceptibly . . ."[5]

Now it is finally clear what is dispensing and controlling the drops: those intravenous bottles hanging high overhead. Suspended above the objects—yet at such a height that when a drop succeeds in hitting the object below, the attentive listener feels quite pleased. In other words, the great distance of a dispenser from an object makes the situation extra fragile and uncertain, though not arbitrary. As a rule, intravenous bottles are extremely practical, for they must reliably and regularly release drops at set intervals. And eventually, when a bottle is empty, it only has to be exchanged for a full one; this especially makes sense in hospitals, since then there is no need to reconnect the tube to the vein again. And as someone who was often ill and in danger of dying, Terry Fox was well acquainted with what trickled drop by drop from intravenous bottles into his bloodstream. On the poster for *Hospital* (1971), one of his earliest performances, the artist featured an infusion tube as well as a quote (fig. 10) by Antonin Artaud—the founder of the Theater of Cruelty, of pain and noise, of the fragmentary and the deficient—from his text collection *Electroshock* (1943–48): "This sin consisted of a temptation visited upon me to pass the breath of my heart through a tube to both sides of the surface."[6]

I admit that I have always found Artaud too overblown, existential, and, ultimately, too emotional. In the same way, I find Surrealism, in comparison to Dadaism in its purer forms, too affected and narcissistic, especially when it comes to André Breton and others in his circle. Yet in the end what speaks in Artaud's favor is the relentless artistic and anarchic consequence of his own physical and spiritual experiences. And exactly this is reflected in the quote that Fox selected. Indeed, through his earlier performances, Terry Fox could make Artaud's work more accessible to us, to me, independent of any sort of trendy intellectual understanding of it. Alas, this is another topic I would have enjoyed discussing with Fox. No matter: in a text for *Hospital*, written to accompany the poster, it becomes apparent that he projected his own sick body into the space at the Reese Palley Gallery in San Francisco (fig. 11)—indeed brought his body and the space into alignment there.

"The bases are isolated from the energy of the floor and walls by electrical tape.
How many units in the backbone?
A relationship with hospital or isolation experience rather than with art (history) experience while (viewing) the piece.
Anxiety, depression, pain, fear, the corporate states of the experience which is this piece.
An instrument in the service of infinite grace.
That is the interpretation of the infinite as a sweet continuous flow of heart and mind tracking.
Blood.
The tube maybe is the cord.
The door provides the location of the (skin's) membrane that separates the outer from the inner.
In relationship to the needle which is the arbitrator and also the sound.
The umbilical cord functions in relation to a support system as the electric cord here."[7]

By the way, the cord ensures that the tape

5 Leonardo da Vinci, *Notebooks*, Oxford World's Classics (Oxford and New York, 2008), p. 25.

6 Quoted from *Works with Sound*, p. 61.

7 Terry Fox, "Statement," in *Ocular Language*, pp. 5 and 7.

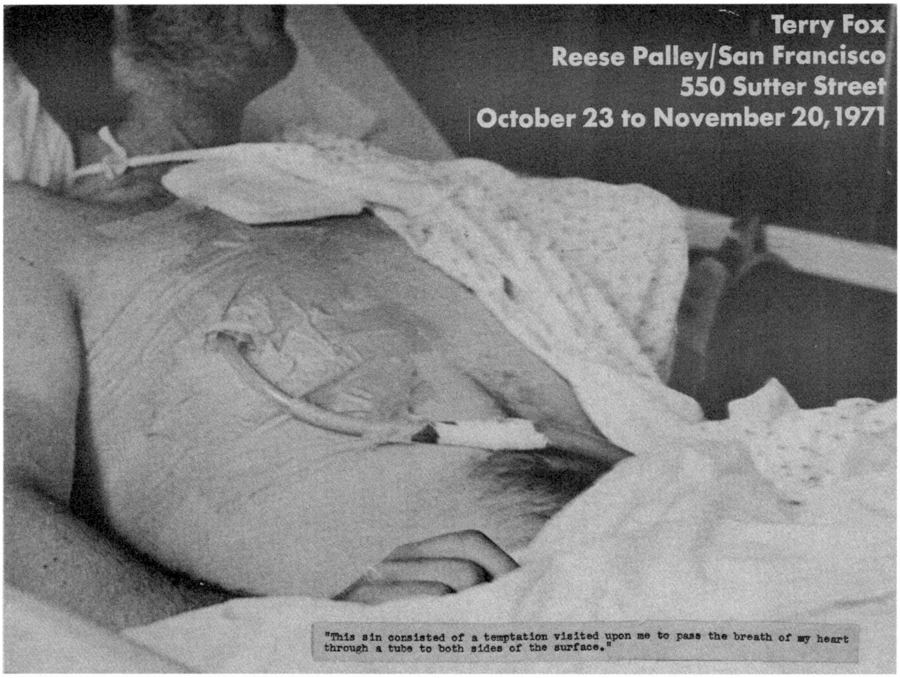

10 Terry Fox, *Hospital*, 1971, exhibition poster, Reese Palley Gallery, San Francisco, Estate of Terry Fox, Cologne, photo: Larry Fox

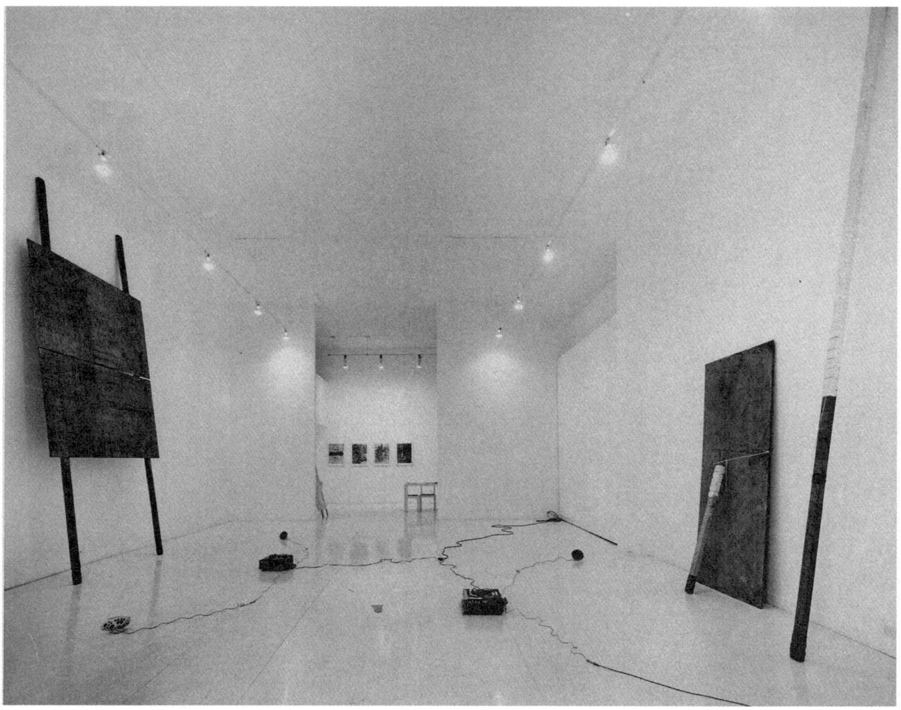

11 Terry Fox, *Hospital*, 1971, exhibition view, Reese Palley Gallery, San Francisco, photo: Schopplein Studio

recorder plays not only a text spoken by Fox, but also the pulsating sounds of breathing, which fill the space and bring the objects and images to life. By localizing the anthropomorphism of sickness pervading this performative installation, the tubes in the text and poster become life-sustaining dispensers of drops in the fight for the vital forces determining the human pulse and, as with Artaud, art as evidence of energy. Now viewed from the perspective of this early work, are my notions of the hardly and the specific too light, too airy, in themselves too hardly? Just as art helps you to persevere in the face of illness, to transform it as energy, it also helps you to focus on what is most essential. Existential experiences in hospital crystalize perception, or as Fox put it after a three-month stay in isolation: ". . . I may get bored by something, but I know I can get through it and that whatever is boring me, is actually going to turn out to be interesting."[8] There, when a drop falls from the ceiling, it is an acoustic and optical sensation, independent of illness, death, and, of course, also boredom.

An automatism of genius and illness à la Van Gogh does not exist. How many ailing artists have gotten bogged down in symbolism! However, there is a special form of perceptual intensity that need not always express itself in pathologies, but instead, by emphasizing the hardly, fires the imagination. In this sense, illness can constitute the concentrated experience of the poetry of a "lifetime," of which Vladimir Jankélévitch says: "More insipid, inodorous and colorless than pure water, more intangible and imponderable than atmospheric air, time becomes, when sparingly doled out to us, priceless. For the person dying of thirst in the desert would undoubtedly give all the gold in the world for a few drops of water at the bottom of a flask . . . Just as rarity and, at the edge of nothingness, a uniqueness, which is an almost-nothing, makes things more precious and endows them with value, so do the brevity of the term and, in extreme circumstances, a semelfactive instant that is an almost-never enhance the value of becoming . . ."[9]

In the hardly there is always the *memento mori*, especially when it bespeaks sickness, death, and suffering; and yet in dripping it joyfully divests itself. And this is why there is no need here for the "confession drops" mentioned by the American poet Walt Whitman in 1860.[10]

Or have I strayed and overdone it? For the tube, so prominently featured twenty-five years ago, is now missing in *The School of Velocity*. Instead, there is just a stub with the dripper on the intravenous bottle. A tube that might connect directly to the recipient has been replaced by a long stretch of nothingness. The insertion, the infusion, and, in fact, the intravenous moment have literally been omitted. Without a tube, the intravenous bottle is almost any old bottle, hanging there with a flow-regulator. Thus, in reality, only the visuals are about infusion, which becomes evident in the text on the work in the *sonambiente* catalogue. In it, the title *The School of Velocity* is typed in four languages, in four parallel vertical lines of capitals, a style often used by Fox. And while three of the final four letters of each

8 Terry Fox, "Exploring the Limits: Interview by René van Peer," in *Ocular Language*, pp. 157–83, esp. p. 163.

9 Vladimir Jankélévitch, *La mort* (Paris, 2015), p. 95, first published in 1977; trans. Catherine Kerkhoff-Saxon (C. K.-S.).

10 See the poem "Trickle Drops" in Walt Whitman, *Leaves of Grass: The 1892 Edition*, (New York, 1983), p. 101.

word appear to be approaching free fall, their final letters demarcate the ground. The words "CITY," "CITE," "KEIT," and "CITA" are made to trickle through what looks like a dripper (see fig. IV in plate section). In other words, not too poor a result when it comes to the ambiguity of multilinguality—or when it comes to a pointer in the direction of urban bicycling, which cannot be plugged often enough. But if I were to propose just one interpretation here, I would have to bring the concepts and the objects into alignment—a process that might lead to my drawing fatal conclusions, and to my having to seek advice from the two Jacques, Lacan and Derrida, which is really not my thing. And as far as the "velo-city" goes, I would prefer calling attention to the wonderful strips of tape, the "skylights," above the individual sequences of letters, to the "pattern poetry" as Dick Higgins calls it,[11] the visual poetry, text imagery, and typographical adventure. I will stick with Roland Barthes here.

Dripping as it does, *The School of Velocity* cites a work (originally titled *Die Schule der Geläufigkeit*) by Carl Czerny, a Viennese composer and student of Beethoven. Published as a collection of exercises for piano students in the eighteen-thirties, it is still in wide use today. Nevertheless, the word velocity as it relates to Fox initially meant the opposite of trickling: these exercises were to be played until they "flowed smoothly." Applied to Fox and the Academy in Berlin, it might be described as a kind of school, an art school in the original Platonic sense, one with a universal claim to the union of science and art. Something academies obviously still need to practice. Knowledge exists, if at all, drop by drop. The goal is to get it to flow.

"Velocity," the traditional English translation of this Viennese *Geläufigkeit*, places greater emphasis on the speed to be practiced or, as I learn from Wiktionary, on "the relationship between the distance traveled and the time it takes." In this sense, Fox's work in Berlin might be more of an exercise for the spectator, who learns to see the route from the intravenous bottle to the object as a perceptual unit, one that includes the tone produced, whereby a special meaning of the following term should be mentioned: "expression" (for example, on electronic keyboard instruments as the kind of pressure that is applied to the keys). When it comes to drops, their strength, of course, also depends on the height of the fall.

Fox made a wise choice with this title, as it considerably expands the frames of interpretation: ascribable to the location yet still so open, we no longer know for sure who or what has begun practicing. Is it we, the spectators, with our sometimes less and sometimes more receptive perceptual skills; or the objects in their differentiated functions; the subtle sounds; or, ultimately, the space, the location, the grayness, the sickness, the imagination, the poetical, or the joy, for instance, that arises when something drips on an egg? Since "practicing" has been central to my concept of artistic formation for some time now, it affects everything equally, nothing less or more, and culminates in the experience of the "hardly."[12]
Here Fox has selected a title whose musical associations wash over the piece

11 See Dick Higgins, *Pattern Poetry: Guide to an Unknown Literature* (New York, 1987).

12 See Michael Glasmeier, *Üben: Essays zur Kunst* (Cologne, 2000).

as it goes about its work. Moreover, it gives both study and practice—which ideally may be called learning by exploring—a place in art. Also, Fox is obviously not after the pianistic extremism of a Lang Lang, a spiritual brother of Czerny, but sound itself, which is why he favors the piano wire over the piano in other spatial works. As Fox says:
". . . I like the idea of a lot of tension in the place and everything very silent. To try [to practice] and exaggerate the kind of silence it has. To make it even more silent than it is. Make it more silent than silent. It has the potential of sounding. I think sculpturally it could be an interesting concept."[13]

Like Marcel Duchamp, Terry Fox has an essentially sculptural and spatial understanding of sound. Thus the efficacy of the hardly involves working on and with the silence he considers so indispensable, enacted by the specific. In this sense, *Capillary Action* (fig. 12) is a direct forerunner of *The School of Velocity*. Here is the artist's description of the former: "[It] was an installation in the Galleria Schema in Florence in 1975. I had two large clay bowls, one placed above the other on top of a box. A red cloth drew the water out of the top bowl by capillary action, and slowly emptied it, drop by drop, into the lower bowl. This created a constant water music in the gallery. As the water filled the lower bowl, the tone of the dripping sound changed slowly from high to low. In this process, it took eight hours for the upper bowl to be drawn dry. The bowls were reversed each day for the four weeks of the show."[14]

In this early exploration, the space was smaller, and the situation closer and more with one another. The red cloth "takes and gives at once," as Conrad Ferdinand Meyer so memorably formulated it in his poem "The Roman Fountain" in 1882. The tightly interwoven movements are silent to begin with, but then develop into an ever more dramatic "water music," though only if you lean your ear toward it, since then perception may tune in more finely. A similar situation of the hardly, with a spoon and a fork as intermediate pieces, and a melting ice cube joining the ensemble, is found in a study on balance from one year earlier, Fox's splendid *Children's Tapes* (1974). Later, for Ferrara, this work was transformed and radically enlarged in *Suono con Tensione* (1979):

". . . by replacing the bent fork with a two meter high ladder, the spoon by a three meter wooden board with a metal bucket fixed to one end, and the ice cube by a ten kilo block of ice. . . . This 'spoon' was balanced on the top of the ladder with a red towel over its edge to draw the melting water out."[15]

In other words, a fairly wobbly affair more reminiscent of a dripstone cave, and yet it demonstrates that Fox also had a command of pursuing the hardly on a large scale. For again, nothing but drops of water were produced here. Providing the blueprint for a piano string performance, this work can be seen as the link between *Capillary Action* and the work at the Academy of Arts in the GDR, where height and free fall play a major role.

And so now we have arrived at Fox's contemporaries. In the same year as

13 Terry Fox in *Ocular Language*, p. 173.
14 Terry Fox, *Capillary Action* (1975), in *Works with Sound*, p. 64.
15 Terry Fox, *Suono con Tensione*, in *Ocular Language*, p. 149.

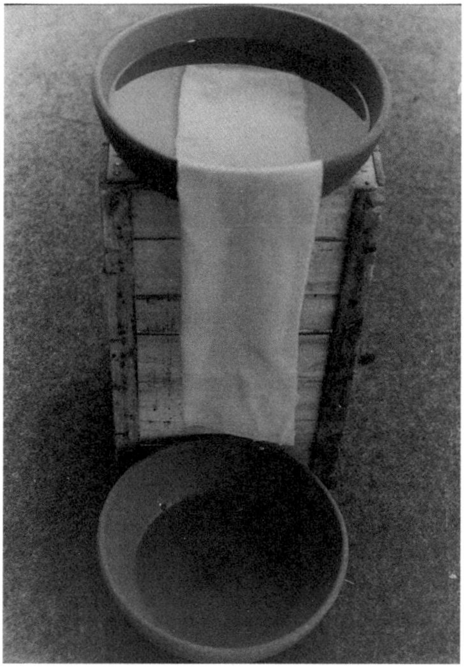

12 Terry Fox, *Capillary Action*, 1975, exhibition view, Galerie Schema, Florence, photo: Terry Fox

Capillary Action went into operation, a certain Bill Viola filmed Fox's sound show *Lunedi* in Florence. A year later, in 1976, Viola delivered one of his first video sculptures. A drop of water falls from a faucet onto a drumhead. The fall itself, in the form of a close-up in which the viewer is reflected, is projected onto a screen; and the sound of its landing amplified. Everything here still takes place in real time, whereas later Viola turns to transforming simple actions or artworks (by, for example, Bellini, Botticelli, or Pontormo), into incredible kitsch using cheap effects, such as slow motion and rewind video, multichannel sound and gigantic projections. What later became so bombastic in its symbolism was already apparent in the title of this relatively innocent drip work: *He Weeps for You*. Jankélévitch, whom I mentioned earlier, would have spoken in this context of an "affective incontinence."[16] Here the specific obscures the hardly, destroying it and every form of intellectual and sensory openness, including interpretation. The artist's intention in specifying the specific converges in a hackneyed symbol of so-called concern about some matter or other. To weep and to bleed: in the wake of the precision of their iconography in the Renaissance and Baroque, these highly contrived Western-religious drops should always be handled with utmost caution.

Yet, sadly, the end of Postmodernism is still not in sight, as Doug Aitken's latest drip installation made clear. *Sonic Fountain II* was presented recently in the atrium of the Schirn Kunsthalle in Frankfurt. What was once done by analogue intravenous bottles is now controlled by an electronic system; both the dripping and spurting have been scored and are channeled toward a large pool. What results is a sound between pianissimo and crescendo, a pattering and trickling, a decidedly unironic water music, more reminiscent of the—acoustically also interesting—Baroque water displays in Versailles, or choreographed fountains in Las Vegas, even though there they all spout in the opposite direction. In this respect, the basin with the milky water goes very nicely with the Postmodernist architecture of Axel Schulte's Schirn Kunsthalle. So it could all be worse.

While Bill Viola (who evidently finds the simplicity and intensity of Terry Fox's drip works unbearable) goes at it with pathos and grandeur, the clever Japanese artist Akio Suzuki, whom I mentioned earlier, responds directly and oppositely to *The School of Velocity.* Suzuki—an artist who continues to receive far too little recognition—has largely devoted himself

16 Vladimir Jankélévitch, "Satie et le matin," in *La musiques et les heures*, Paris 1988, p. 26.

to listening perception. By making it visible, he shifts attention to it, as one can see in the various "listening points" he set up across the city of Berlin for the *sonambiente* sound festival. Naturally, on this occasion, he also saw the work of his colleague Terry Fox. A year later, Suzuki reinterpreted it in *Ku (Verse)*, a piece for his solo exhibition in Saarbrücken. Here I would like to quote Matthias Osterwold's detailed description more extensively:
"Ten water faucets that do *not* drip are mounted on the room's longer wall. Under the water faucets are objects that evoke the idea of very specific dripping noises, for example a conical pile of sand, an avocado seed half-immerged to sprout in a glass of water, a bucket balanced as if by a magical hand on the edge of a pillar; from another faucet a chain of pearl-shaped bells 'drips.' A clothes hanger with a hand towel is suspended from another water faucet, which is turned upward, with a bowl placed beneath it. Asked by a young woman why precisely this faucet is turned upward, Akio Suzuki answered: 'Ah, only a hook.' Akio Suzuki knew that his artist friend Terry Fox would come to Saarbrücken for the opening of the showing."

Osterwold goes on to speak of the *School of Velocity* and then remarks:
"Akio Suzuki greeted Terry Fox in front of his work, said, 'I am sorry' and giggled with embarrassment... Of course he knew Terry Fox's installation. And of course both knew *Drip Music* and *Drip Event* by George Brecht, whose first, 1959 version was described as: 'A source of dripping water and an empty vessel are arranged so that the water falls into the vessel'; the second, 1962 version was called merely 'Dripping.'"[17]

Suzuki's approach to dripping does not, as one might expect, shift to non-dripping, but to the prolongation of the possibility of dripping, which must be compensated for by the imagination and may be equated with the need for evocation referred to by Osterwold. At the same time, Suzuki's work is substantially more narrative, playful, cheerful. As in Asian philosophies, its efficacy evolves by means of an absence and is ". . . all the greater, the more *discreet* it is."[18] Yet the energies in the works of these two artists have fundamentally different emphases. In Fox's piece they are essentially focused on the occurrence of dripping and its acoustic realization within the scope of a constellation of objects set up in a dilapidated former sculptor's studio. Suzuki's response, on the other hand, lies closer to John Cage's *4'33"*, that is, in the space of cultural representation; to unfold, it needs the museum, much like Cage needed the concert hall. The dripping we do not hear allows us to see better and to hear something different inside the white cube, including the noise of the visitors, which, unlike in the Academy (East), is perceived not as a disruption, but as an aesthetic event in itself.

What is important for both of these approaches, as Osterwold sees it, is how they refer back to George Brecht's *Drip Music* (1959) and *Drip Event* (1962). In these performances, Brecht stands on a ladder, for example, and lets water drip directly into a bucket. In this context Gabriele Knapstein and Douglas Kahn cite *Water Music* (1952) by John Cage and, of course, painter Jackson Pollock's dripping technique—which is basically considered the birth of performance to-

17 Matthias Osterwold, "Akio the Cat," in *Akio Suzuki: Sound Works Throwing and Following*, exh. cat. Stadtgalerie Saarbrücken (XX, 1998), pp. 42–52, esp. pp. 47 and 48.

18 François Jullien, *A Treatise on Efficacy: Between Western and Chinese Thinking* (Honolulu, 2004), p. 58.

day.[19] With Cage, water in very diverse objects begins to free itself as sound. Imitation, required by composers such as Schubert or Smetana, is no longer necessary. Thank god! And if we watch Cage's performance of *Water Music* on YouTube—incidentally, as a segment of a network TV show—we grasp how precise, cool, and comical anarchy in art can be. George Brecht, as a student of Cage, went on to simplify matters even more and brought them to an endpoint. To a certain extent he perfected Cage's Zen-like approach with his "events," which I would like to call "sensations of the hardly." They were scored on many different-sized little cards collected in a cardboard box, titled *Water Yam*. Water—and, of course, dripping in particular here—epitomizes the time in which an action, sound, and object become intermedially one. Fluxus, flowing, giving, taking: *Yam*. The fluidifying of a sculpture as a subtle enactment of sound. In the piece *zyklus for water pails (or bottles)* (1962) by Tomas Schmit, this aspect is emphatically celebrated. Ten to thirty pails or bottles were set up in a circle, one of which was filled with water. Schmit poured the contents from one container to the next until everything had either spilled or evaporated—a procedure that could take some time, and which, by the way, Fox reinterpreted in 1971.[20]

In 1967, in hot Southern California, Allan Kaprow presented *Fluids*, a happening in which a rectangular walled structure built of ice blocks was left to melt. From 1963–70, George Brecht steadily worked on his sculpture *Drip Music—Fountain*, using a water faucet and a container. In 1966, another artist had already portrayed himself dripping—Bruce Nauman in *Self-Portrait as a Fountain*. In my view, what is important about this work is that the fountain does not actually flow; instead, an arc of water shoots from the mouth of the naked, manneristically posed body, and dissolves into oddly dispersed individual drops. And then in the nineteen-sixties, Alighiero Boetti conceived a life-size self-portrait in bronze. One hand holds up a hose that spews a small stream of water. It trickles onto the head, which contains a heating element, causing the water to evaporate into a cloud of steam and surround the thinker with what looks like an aureole—and this is precisely what makes art so perplexing: here thought, energy, and stillness are transformed into movement as perception.

With the artistic treatment of water and dripping, we might also open up a plethora of interpretations that focus on religion and alchemy. With Boetti, we might think of some kind of self-baptism; with transformations from ice to water and water to steam, of alchemical processes; and with Nauman's self-enactment, of the power of giving and exhausting oneself artistically. Yet let us return to George Brecht, who wisely gets to the bottom of things and brings them into immediate reality:
WATER. coming from, staying, going to
THREE AQUEOUS EVENTS. ice, water, steam[21]
And naturally: raining, pissing.[22] Naturally this last line takes us to Marcel Duchamp's *Fountain* (1917), itself the silent precursor of his own final work, *Given: 1. The Waterfall, 2. The Illuminating Gas* (1947–66); and to Cage's *Water Music*. To me, *The School of Velocity* seems the

19 See Gabriele Knapstein, *George Brecht: Events* (Berlin, 1999) and Douglas Kahn, *Noise. Water. Meat.: A History of Sound in the Arts* (Cambridge, MA, and London, 1999).

20 See Lisa Steib, "Terry Fox: A World Traveler in Europe," in *Elemental Gestures*, p. 45–51, esp. p. 45.

21 Event cards from George Brecht's *Water Yam*, Editions Lebeer-Hossmann, Brussels and Hamburg, 1996.

22 Ibid.

summation of all these art-historical events, albeit conceived as a compelling situation in which, through dripping, the experience of space becomes an experience of time. Here in the Academy (East), the hardly of George Brecht turns into something enduring, just as does the *Water Music* of John Cage, the spilling and evaporating of Tomas Schmit, the creative exhaustion in Bruce Nauman's work, the transformation of Allan Kaprow (though in reverse), the giving figure of an artist in Boetti's work, and last but not least, Nauman again, whom we may (as previously noted), detect in the presence of the intravenous bottles. *The School of Velocity* has once again captured the essence of different concepts in the course of the art-historical treatment of water and thus—in the middle of the Postmodern era—brought them to an intense and contemplative preliminary conclusion. Terry Fox presents us with a performance on permanence without the presence of the artist. The dripping into this emptiness and silence may show the "mutual fusion taking place between the different sense-functions," which Cage's Zen teacher, D. T. Suzuki, wrote about in 1949. He then went on to quote the following lines by the Zen poet Daito:

If you see with the ears
And hear with the eyes,
No doubts you will ever cherish:
How naturally falls
The rain dripping from the eaves![23]

It would be inappropriate and far too easy to let ideas about *The School of Velocity* end in Zen mysticism, but we cannot exclude the possibility that the naturalness required to prepare for the satori experience was more than merely present in the Academy (East). In fact, it was celebrated continuously from August 9 to September 8, 1996, as a reality that could at all times be visited and probed, contemplated and meditated. The possibility of experiencing a situation of contemplation existed, both musically and sculpturally, in a utopia of unperturbed constancy. Nevertheless, I think for Fox it was less about the "mutual fusions taking place between those different sense-functions" that D.T. Suzuki saw coalescing in dripping, and more about synesthesia, about seeing through hearing and hearing through seeing. In this respect, media do not dissolve in water, as Douglas Kahn surmised,[24] but reaffirm themselves as the respectively specific en route to the hardly. Indeed, there is too much too-much, and too little too-little, and I would have liked for this splendid, simple and sensitive work, this optimal situation for the fundamental experience of reality to have been preserved, including the room, right at the heart of Berlin. It would then still be dripping today, nonstop, as beat poet Allen Ginsberg said in 1956, in his poem "Transcription of Organ Music": ". . . because it has to, to stay alive, to continue to the last drop of joy."[25]

Note: Revised version of a lecture given at the conference "Terry Fox: Situationen" on November 6, 2015, organized by the Terry Fox Association e. V., Cologne, at the Akademie der Künste, Berlin (at Hanseatenweg). Originally published in Michael Glasmeier, *Geräusche, Ritornelle für eine Kunstgeschichte des Klangs: Von Fra Angelico und Claudio Monteverdi zu Marcel Duchamp und Terry Fox*, ed. Tania Prill and Andrea Sick (Hamburg, 2016), pp. 169–188.

Translated from German
by Catherine Kerkhoff-Saxon

23 Quoted from Kahn 1999 (see note 19), p. 281.

24 See Douglas Kahn, "Wasser und die Auflösung des Mediums," in *Klangkunst* (see note 1), pp. 222–25, esp. p. 224.

25 Allen Ginsberg, "Transcription of Organ Music," in *HOWL and other Poems* (San Francisco, 1956), pp. 25–27, esp. p. 26.

Sabine Mainberger

Word—Body—Art: On Terry Fox

". . . I feel the urge to participate in the world via lines."[1] This is how the slender book *Émergences Résurgences* by the Belgian writer and artist Henri Michaux begins. Written in 1972, it offers a kind of history of his painting activity. For Michaux, "to participate in the world through lines" is a synonym for drawing (*dessiner*), which in turn refers to numerous different graphic activities in his oeuvre, particularly his way of working *between* drawing or painting and writing. Michaux's art is chiefly nonfigurative. His best-known works are manifestations of bodily-gestural action: their figurative attributes, like the grotesque heads and faces, only emerge *post festum,* or they recall writing in which the individual characters, however, remain illegible. The mescaline drawings testify to a perception accelerated to a point of torment and, in the most extreme case, an experience of madness. Yet Michaux always remains an artist that *draws* lines.

Terry Fox knew the Belgian's work.[2] And like him, the American performance and (non-) video artist participated in the world through lines. These are, however, only in part graphic. Fox also, and especially, connected to the world through *three-dimensional* lines, or to be more precise, through line-like things such as string and wire. And he created line-objects as well: things in which lines have volume, traverse rooms, provide instructions for actions to be carried out in linear manner, and more. Fox's oeuvre consists of performances, videotapes, sound events, works with writing and with signs unrelated to writing, sculptures in the wider meaning of the word. While at first glance these various articulations seem heterogeneous, their common denominator lies in the "participatory" functions of the not-only-graphic line. Even Fox's key private mythologem, the labyrinth of Chartres, fits in here: a structure of lines par excellence, both as a two-dimensional drawing and print and as a three-dimensional plaster model. In the sense of a *contrainte*, a formal constraint, it also generates other line objects such as the musical score of purring cats (*The Labyrinth Scored for the Purrs of 11 Different Cats*, 1973) or the fragile, filigree construction made of two stools (*A Metaphor*, 1976) that refers to the real site of the labyrinth: in the middle, where their legs touch, a round slip of paper with the labyrinth depicted on it is suspended

1 ". . . il me vient une envie . . . de participer au monde par des lignes." Henri Michaux, "Émergences Résurgences" (1972), in *Œuvres complètes*, ed. Raymond Bellour, with Ysé Tran, 3 vols. (Paris, 1998–2004), vol. 3, p. 545. Paraphrased from the English translation by Richard Sieburth, The Drawing Center, New York, published by Skira (Milan, 2000), p. 10.

2 Among other things, catalogues of Michaux's art were lying on his "last desk." (As reported by Marita Loosen-Fox.)

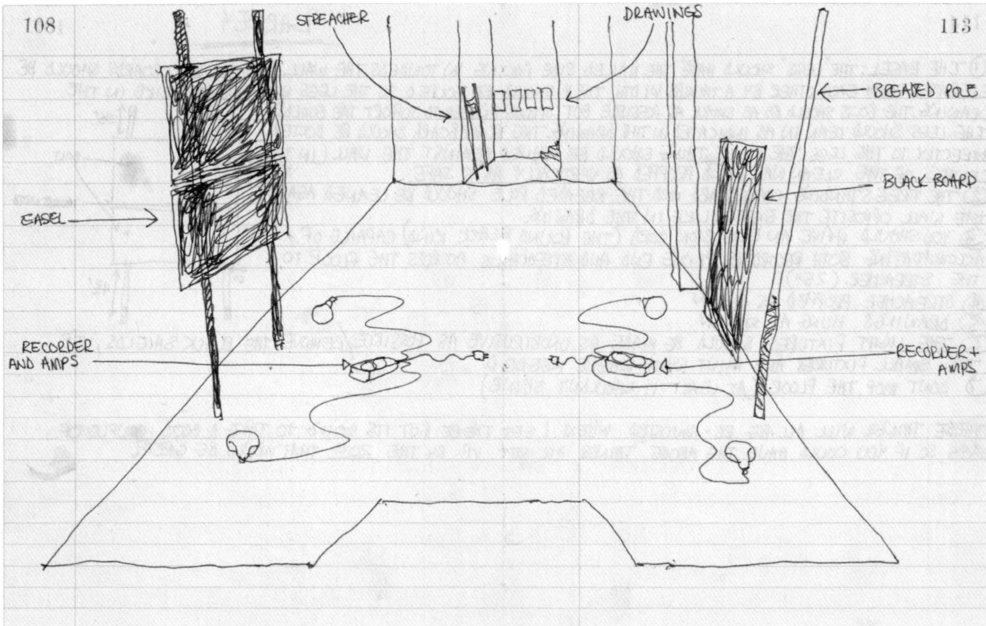

1 Terry Fox, sketch for the exhibition *Hospital*, 1971, Reese Palley Gallery, San Francisco, drawing, pigment felt-tip pen on paper, 23.4 x 37.4 cm, Estate of Terry Fox, Cologne

on a taut string, while on the wall is a photograph of the same stool object printed in a magazine.

Fox connects with the world via line-shaped things, for instance the strings and wires in his installations and performances. The drawing (fig. 1) and photograph titled *Hospital* (1971, see fig. p. 132)[3] depict objects leaning against the walls or lying on the floor: single and dual blackboards, recorders, amplifiers, drawings, a kind of long rod or pole. In the drawing, the electric cables create an almost symmetrical wave structure, with the disconnected plugs facing one another, as though they were supposed to engage in dialogue. In the photograph, the lines of cables seem to flow through the white expanse of the large room, which is illuminated by two rows of light bulbs, but are connected in the middle. In these two-dimensional images, and these are what generally remain from the actions, the cables draw lines that border on the ornamental and interact with the vertical and horizontal lines of the architecture. In the carefully drawn sketch of the objects' arrangement and in the sharp black-and-white photograph, they stand out as an assertive, yet delicate form.

Cassette recorders and tape recording devices record sound, while video footage records images on tape. The acoustic and optical are transformed into traces. The long thin tapes can be wound onto and off of spools or stuffed into drinking glasses. Video stills are presented in strips: images in series, in succession. The tapes give Fox's mechanical experiments using the simplest, most everyday things—fork, candle, flame, a piece of cloth, matches, glass, bowl—their name: *Children's Tapes*

3 *Elemental Gestures*, pp. 58–59.

(1974). Tape makes its appearance in Fox's work in less technical functions as well: as adhesive strips, for instance, that attach drawings and photos to their background in the simplest possible way. It's the most primitive means of collage, the unifying of heterogeneous components. *L'unità* is the title of a work from 1972 that connects two images of the labyrinth with a slip of paper bearing this title.[4] Over time, the strips of tape have become discolored, and the adhesive has etched into the paper like acid: nothing comes across as older, more obsolete, poorer, and more miserable than a sheet of paper taped together. It openly shows the limited shelf life of its tenuous adhesion.

Broad wrinkled strips of white bandages taped over one another also hold something else together: a naked male torso and a thick tube. On the right side of the chest is a hole in the bandages, through which the tube enters the body. The device it leads to is taped in place and its first turn affixed beneath the rib cage to allow fluids to flow through it and prevent it from falling out, slipping away, or getting a kink that might cause a backup in the system of inner and outer fluids. The body taped in this way cannot move; only the right hand can pull aside the patterned hospital gown to reveal the point of connection—the wound in the chest. The invitation card to the exhibition *Hospital* (1970, see fig. p. 132) presents this body-tube ensemble; the head is cropped off, while the image that catches the viewer's attention is the torso and tube. In medical terms, the photo depicts an intercostal catheter,[5] but the combination of photo and writing calls something else to mind: the picture is accompanied by a quote from Antonin Artaud that speaks, among other things, of an apparatus-induced exteriorization of vital functions: ". . . to pass the breath of my heart through a tube . . ." The patient and artist Fox is mirrored by the patient and artist Artaud, the cult figure and icon of suffering for the nineteen-seventies. The arrangement is aptly reversed: the tube is placed not on the left side, where the heart is, but rather on the right, and passing through it is not breath, but blood or secretions. The photograph of the performance *Levitation* from 1970, by means of which Fox sought to leave his illness behind, portrays him inscribed in a circle like Leonardo's male figure in his drawing of human proportions, but, instead of standing up, lying on scattered soil. The circle is not an ideal geometrical circle, but irregular; the person stretched out is surrounded by numerous tubes filled with water, milk, blood, and urine. If this scene is intended to express the *conditio humana,* then it's living within a system through which elementary fluids flow: man is connected to his surroundings, the world, through line-shaped transmitters.

Another prominent "conduit," this time to another living being, as well as an attempt

4 Ibid., p. 18.

5 To be more precise: "From the anterior one sees an intercostal catheter in the right thorax. It is approximately in the midclavicular line. The exact height is undetermined, as the mamilla and costal arch are covered. In all probability it is a thoracentesis, which is applied postoperatively to re-expand the lung after iatrogenic pneumothorax, or it may be applied in order to drain a hemothorax. The operation may have been performed in connection with a lymphoma and would have been to gain lymph node tissue and/or a lung biopsy. A further indication for such a thoracentesis would be a pleural effusion, which could be aspirated in this way to contribute to the diagnostic process after cytological examination. As a bandage can be seen in the upper area of the sternum, it can be assumed that a mediastinoscopy was first performed to remove lymph node tissue and that the aspiration was a subsequent surgical procedure." My thanks to Dr. Reinhard Stroele for this information.

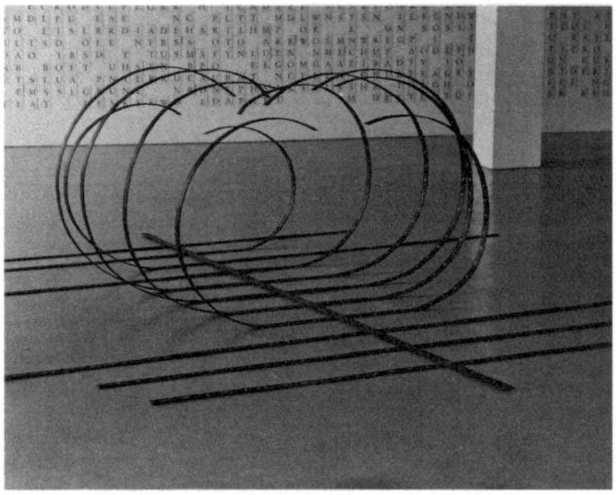

2 Terry Fox, *Vortex*, 1992, floor sculpture with text, exhibition view *Terry Fox: Elementary Parallelism*, Gesellschaft für Aktuelle Kunst, Bremen, 1997, metal, paint, 450 x 240 x 130 cm, San Francisco Museum of Modern Art, photo: Joachim Fliegner

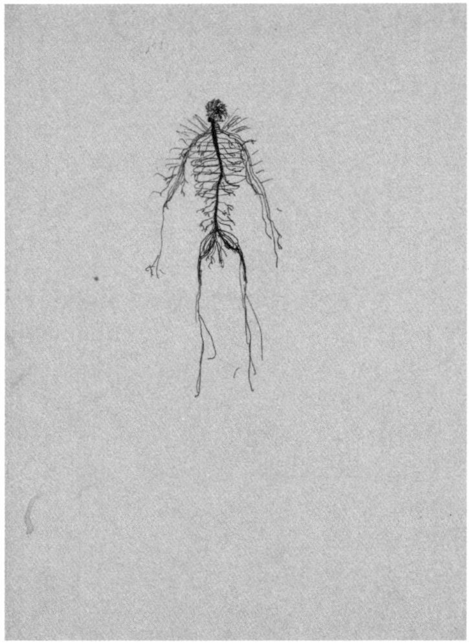

3 Terry Fox, (*Untitled,* mentioned in archives as: *Human figure*), n.d., drawing on paper, 27.9 x 21.7 cm, Estate of Terry Fox, Cologne

to participate in their experience as directly as possible, can be seen in the performance *Pisces* (1971, see fig. p. 100).[6] Two fish are attached to Fox's body with string, or to be more precise: to his head and mouth (to an incisor?); transmitted through the strings, he can directly feel the fish twitch in their hours-long death struggle.

The invitation photo for *Hospital* depicts the upper body from the outside. It is open only at the point where the tube is attached and an alarming hole can be seen. In contrast, other images and three-dimensional enactments depict the body from the inside, as an X-ray image of the chest[7] or as a *Rib Cage* (figs. 2, 3) made from bent strips of metal:[8] lying on the floor, attached to a long brace at a right angle—like a kind of backbone that carries the ribs—they bend toward one another. Their arced curves, however, remain open: the part that would correspond to the breastbone is missing, like Fox's sternum, damaged by too much radiation. In this way, they form a filigree "cage" that contains nothing. What is inside this body, permeated and surrounded by emptiness, is already on the outside. And a being with a skeleton of this kind would be entirely at the mercy of its surroundings: receptive to a maximum degree, vulnerable to a maximum degree. The air would pass through it, just as it would itself pass through the air. The small undated drawing *Human figure* (fig. 4) reduces the human form to ribs, vertebrae, and dark pathways that reach to the tips of the hands and feet. At first glance, one is reminded of one of those didactic medical pictures that depict the branching system of human arteries and veins. For a diagram of circulation, however, the most important thing is missing: the heart. Perhaps, then, the small sketch of the body's interior is of something less known: the lymph channels. For medical purposes, they can be made visible in an X-ray

6 See, for example, *Elemental Gestures,* pp. 104–5.
7 See ibid., p. 245.
8 See ibid., pp. 115 and 171 (undated) and *Ataraxia: The Fox Room*, in Ulli Seegers, "Terry Fox," *Künstler: Kritisches Lexikon der Gegenwart* 62, no. 10 (Spring 2003), Munich (henceforth abbreviated: KLG), fig. 12.

by injecting a liquid contrast agent. Fox, who had been diagnosed with Hodgkin's disease, had to undergo precisely this: "There's one test that I've had frequently where I lie motionless on a table for about six hours, with tubes inserted into my feet. Two giant injectors pump a blue fluid into my lymph system for about an hour."[9] Technologies of visualization, and in any case those of modern medicine, are extraordinarily inventive: the spectrum of images and graphs is broad, and the procedure Fox describes is only one of many. It might well have inspired the small figure made up of ribs, vertebrae, and branching lines; *Human figure* would then be something akin to an imaginary lymphangiogram.

Other linear objects can be found in the *Catch Phrases* (1984): bent and welded metal rods. On a regular grid of paper, letters of catch phrases heard on radio broadcasts by the American Armed Forces Network Europe are applied. The expressions are euphemisms for terrible political and military events. Drawn over these are large illegible characters or graffiti-like signs that Fox collected from walls in Italy; according to his own account, they have political meaning as variations on the hammer and sickle or the dollar sign.[10] A sculptural plane is superimposed over this graphic plane: linear forms made from metal rods, similar to graffiti but not legible, are attached to the paper with a few nails. They maintain a distance of several millimeters above the surface of the graphic marks. These three-dimensional "signs" cast shadows on their two-dimensional counterparts and the paper surface beneath them—with the effect of doubling the lines. The metal forms become less sharp and the sfumato even gives rise to a kind of motion effect.

In this way, the overall piece consists of multiple visual layers: the paper containing the grid; the letters written in pencil, some of which are inside the boxes, and some on the grid lines; the large, illegible forms drawn over these; the forms made from metal rods; their shadows. The layer of letters is also open to deciphering. As there is nothing to mark individual word units, it takes some effort to read the regularly spaced letters. On one of the large formats,[11] for instance (see fig. p. 48), are the phrases "spasm war," "punitive war," "cold war," "holy war," and many other variations of "war." Proceeding from this, one might consider the phrases of the mass media, which range from formulaic to outright false, and wonder whether Fox is denouncing this language when he impedes their normal everyday consumption. The fact that these words, like the non-writing signs, are *readymades* seems to be important in this context: any other type of text or form would provide a gateway for interpretation, for conjecturing messages or an expression of some kind. This, however, can be ruled out here. If anything at all is legible, then it's the anonymous snatches of speech caught from a public language circulating in the ether, formulaic words with neither author nor addressee. Captured here, these catch phrases become disempowered, as it were: because they are subdivided into a cumbersome visual form, it's difficult to differentiate them from a meaningless bit pattern. As a result, they lose all impact. As surface-spanning graphemes, the phrases, which would

9 *Ocular Language*, p. 11.

10 See the artist's text in Terry Fox, *Catch Phrases*, exh. cat. Kunstraum München (Munich, 1985), unpaginated.

11 On the first, which is also printed on the cover. A plastic magnifying glass is enclosed for deciphering in the magazine-like catalogue.

otherwise be acoustic, work in a visual way, as a wallpaper of the everyday. Fox's arrangements disturb normal semiotic activities. We only gradually become aware of the continuous underlying current of signs—the phraseological background noise. The individual signals immediately sink back into a structureless uniformity. In any case, the various components of this arrangement make the viewer alternate between deciphering and viewing, between perceiving the whole as a surface and as a relief. The graphic becomes sculptural, writing becomes plastic and even, to a degree, kinetic. Over the paper, however, it's not space per se that opens up, but rather a flat zone: the rods lift up a little from the background, and so the *Catch Phrases* offer a new variation on the bas relief. With the shadows, however, they create drawing effects: the sculpture becomes graphic.

Metal bands and rods (with letters), strips of wood, springs, laths, chair legs, pendulums, walking sticks, ladders and their rungs, tracks in flour, traces from spraying and spitting, traces of light, smoke rings, stilts, et cetera, are further line-shaped objects that Fox employs. I'd like to call attention to one of these: piano wires. A photo of the performance *Erossore* from 1978[12] shows one such wire strung taut through the space, which Fox's hand is about to make vibrate. In *Radiation* (1979),[13] one can see him testing the strung wire. In the photo *Chorda Tympani* from the same year,[14] he seems to be holding two glow sticks or rays of light. For the performance *Suono Interno* (1979),[15] over several hours, Fox created sounds with two parallel hundred-meter-long piano wires strung through the entire church interior. Visitors could only watch the performance from the outside, through a hole in the door. If they were able to see the wires from their fixed standpoint, these must have seemed like the lines of a construction drawing in perspective, converging at the vanishing point: the wires were resonating vanishing lines.[16]

Fox not only used line-formed things but also created line objects: lines were installed in space, for instance in *Delineation* (1990, fig. 5), or made into objects that stand, hang, lean, or lie as in *Cynosure* (1990), *Ovum Anguinum* (1990), *Mock up* (1991), *Le décapité parlant* (1993), and others. To the extent that these objects have to do with writing, their linear character is to a certain degree unavoidable; if writing is to be legible, then it takes on a direction that cannot be reversed. Letters have to be applied in a certain sequence for them to function as writing. On the other hand, it's a known fact that reading itself is *not* a linear process. The eye does not register each character successively. Readers do not spell a word letter by letter but recognize the visual form of clusters, a *gestalt*. Reading a line of text, the eye jumps rapidly back and forth, and it takes breaks; saccades alternate with fixations. The empirical research on reading examines the lengths of the jumps and the duration of the fixations; this knowledge allows reading aptitude to be measured and reading conditions to be optimized. The fact that the latter are not ideal in Fox's writing pieces is clear. Yet on the other hand, reading them is not impossible; on the con-

12 See KLG (see note 8), fig. 7.
13 See *Ocular Language*, p. 140f.
14 Ibid., p. 2.
15 See the description in, *TERRY FOX: Articulations*, exh. cat. Goldie Paley Gallery (Philadelphia, 1992), p. 28.
16 The function of the strings does not, of course, lie in their visual appearance, but this cannot be ignored, either. Fox's musical notes are also evocative line drawings. On his works with piano strings, see the essay by Michael Glasmeier in this publication.

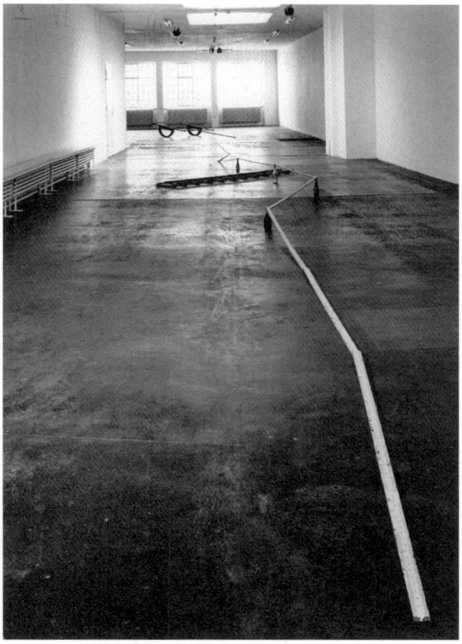

4 Terry Fox, *Delineation*, installation with text, 1990, exhibition view Syndikat Halle, Bonn, 1990, oil paint, acrylic paint, ink on wood, 10 parts, 240 x 4.5 x 1.3 cm each, private collection. Photo: Galerie Löhrl

trary, the letters ask to be deciphered, and the words to be understood. For this reason, it would probably be interesting to study the eye movements of a viewer. The measurements would certainly differ from the ordinary, but what would the differences be in a concrete sense: Does the eye linger longer when the reading is more difficult, or does it return to the same point more frequently? Are the saccades to the left and right larger, more frequent, faster? Fox has explained why he presents his viewer/reader with an array of obstacles—and every exhibition catalogue reports it anew—but the actual effects of these reading barriers have never been properly analyzed.

Bloodline (fig. 6) incorporates the polyvalent word *line* in its title and makes reading difficult in several ways. The German translation *Blutzeile*[17] arises from the fact that letters form legible words and syntagmas and are arranged on the wall in such a way that the normal sequence of characters remains intact, even while capitalization and an occasional vertical configuration[18] make the reading process more difficult. The letters extend from one corner of the room to the other, entirely filling up the wall space in between. The edges function like a column of type or the borders of a page: once a line reaches the right margin, the writing jumps to the next line and back to the left-hand margin. Apart from these contingent restrictions on the letter sequences, the "text"—if one can call this sequence of words a text—has no interruptions; there are no spaces between words, no diacritics, and of course no pilcrows: nowhere does a new line or paragraph begin. The writing covers the entire available surface, with a new line the result of a lack of space and not an organizing parameter of the text layout. The "text," in this sense, is a surface text—with all the semantic consequences that implies. Even when one doesn't know the source of the text, one quickly surmises that this, too, is found material,[19] although the rules according to which it's been selected and applied to the wall remain unclear. Despite the leveling, non-hierarchical disposition of the words, certain key words do stand out and seem to emit a cry: they speak of illness and death. At the same time, they are

17 As it appears in *Ocular Language*, p. 184. On the other hand, Britta E. Buhlmann and Jochen Gerz speculate on the meaning of the title as "origin / source / kinship, but blood trail, as well" in *Terry Fox*, exh. cat. Galerie Löhrl, Mönchengladbach / Pfalzgalerie, Kaiserslautern (Mönchengladbach, 1996), unpaginated.

18 See the photo of the installation in Bremen, 1997, in *Ocular Language*, p. 185.

19 The source is an English textbook titled *The Little Londoner: A Concise Account of the Life and Ways of the English with Special Reference to London* (Freiburg im Breisgau, 1921). (Information from Marita Loosen-Fox.)

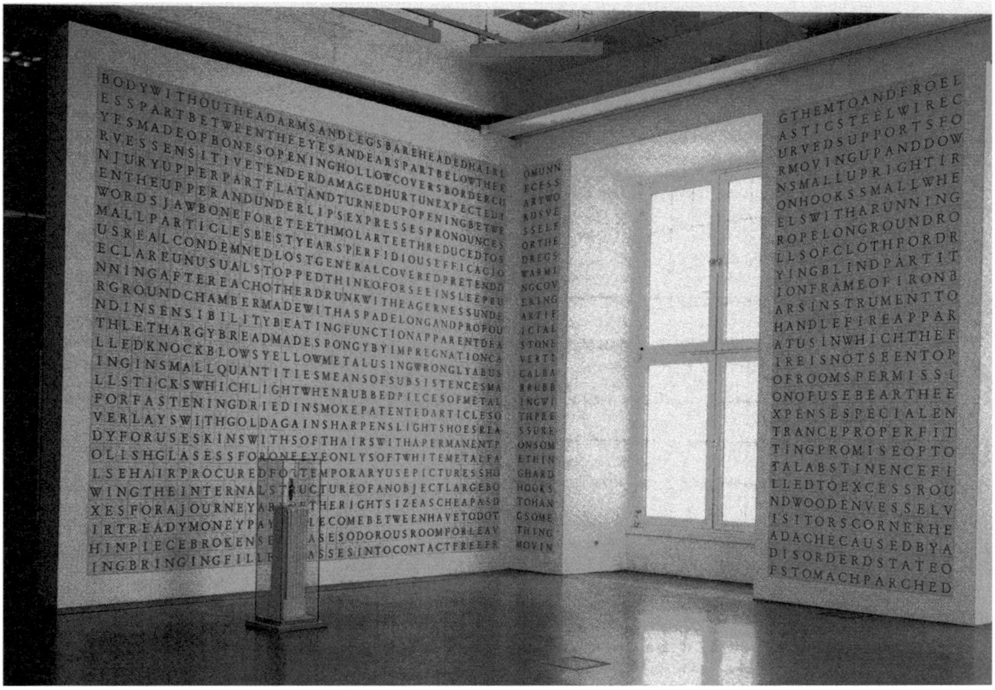

5 Terry Fox, *Bloodline,* 1996, installation with text, Kunsthalle Fridericianum, Kassel 2003, 7.126 letters on cardboard, 14 x 11.5 cm each; 2 display cases, glass, wood, paper, printing ink, 110 x 35 x 35 cm each, University of California, Berkeley Art Museum and Pacific Film Archive. Photo: Ludger Paffrath

situated next to words of banal content and rhetorical syntagmas; they are not marked for the eye and only stand out when the text is read. Yet the act of reading—at least as it pertains to the overall "text"—is the least probable act of reception that can be expected here. Viewers will make attempts and soon give up. They will succeed in picking out one or more words here or there from the letter cards on the wall. The eye seeks an anchor, but finds it more in the architectonic elements: a window, a threshold, in any case not in the writing. The beginning and end, though, might enjoy a certain privilege here: potential readers optimistically search for a point of entry, rules, objectives. In this sense, the first words, "body without head arms and legs," seem to offer orientation: just as a body of this kind is no more than a torso, the text also lacks limbs: it's a trunk text. It is without articulation: a torso text, a rib cage of words. There are regular formal elements—distinct characters, homogenous font and color, placement next to and below one another, legibility, the uniform use of English—but the arrangement as a whole is far too open to contain something like meaning. The textual is reduced to very few factors: a couple of ribs or lines. Beyond semantics, the monumental character—the type is reminiscent of an inscription—and simultaneous ephemerality are what stand out: the letter cards are individually pinned to the walls with nails. And they evoke decrepitude all the more when they are dumped on the floor as a knee-high pile: meaning has broken down here, or it has as yet to be constructed.

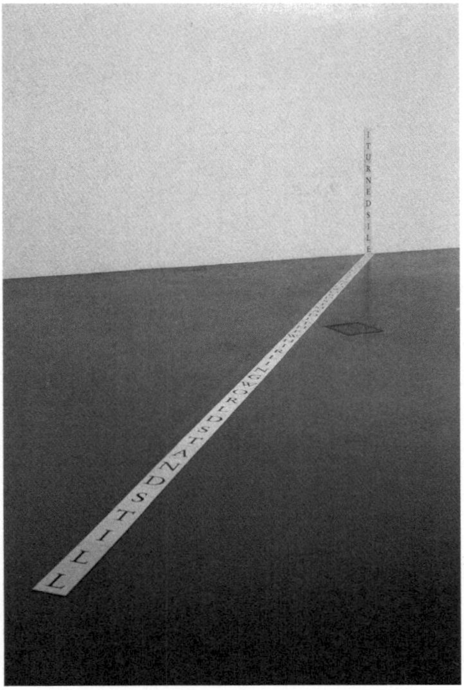

6 Terry Fox, *Lever*, installation with text, 2002, exhibition view, Kunsthalle Fridericianum, Kassel, 2003, printing ink on cardboard, 64 cards, 14 x 11.5 cm each, Estate of Terry Fox, Cologne. Photo: Ludger Paffrath

A minimalistic version of this *Bloodline* is the Arthur Rimbaud line in *Alchemy of the Verb* (2002, fig. 7).[20] Fox quotes the text in English and arranges the letters one beneath the next, without space in between. A long band of this vertical writing begins on the wall of a large space in Turin and continues several meters onto the floor. The letters form sentences: "I turned silences and nights into words. I made the whirling world stand still."[21] The writing remains on the surface, but the surface itself changes direction by 90 degrees; in this way, the band of letters, the long thin line, proceeds through three dimensions.

There is yet another way in which Fox has used writing extracted from its attachment to the surface or to a surface: in *Transparent Abelard* (2005, fig. 8), he once again—and, he surmises, for the last time—borrows a text by Artaud. In the English translation it reads: "Strange defeat. How to get away? Quick, the eye of a needle! The smallest needle's eye, so Abelard won't be able to come looking for us. He renounces the chaste coitus permitted by God."[22] Fox himself describes what he created from this: "The quote is laid out on a grid of 143 squares drawn on a sheet of heavy paper. The paper is twisted into a cone-shaped form with a needle inserted in the small end of the object. The needle itself refers to the 'needle's eye' in the text. I found the way to fold the paper into this shape in an old book that I have on geometrical experiments. It was a way of folding the paper into a cone shape where the squares followed one another in a spiral around the cone, so that the text could be read from the point all the way to the bottom in a linear order. This idea enabled me to give the text a physical body by combining its two-dimensional structure with the three-dimensional form of the cone through the spiraling order of the words: an instance of the body recoiling in upon itself, like the

20 "Alchimie du verbe" is a title from Rimbaud's *Une Saison en Enfer: Délires II*. Fox's specification "from 'The Drunken Boat'" evidently refers to a collection of texts.

21 In the original: "J'écrivais des silences, des nuits, je notais l'inexprimable. Je fixais des vertiges." Fox transcribed the text himself on a typewriter, with one word per line and a period between "words" and "I." The period does not appear on the white cards with the red letters. Regarding the illustrations, see *(Re/De) Constructions & c.*, exh. cat. Kunsthalle Fridericianum (Kassel, 2003), fig. 13: *(Reconstructed) Vocale Vocale*, 2002.

22 According to his own account, he is quoting from the *Artaud Anthology* (San Francisco, 1963), p. 53. In the original, it is the early text with the title "Le clair Abélard": "Étrange déroute. Par où disparaître? Dieu! vite, un trou d'aiguille. Le plus mince trou d'aiguille par lequel Abélard ne pourra plus venir nous chercher. / . . . / Il renonce au coït chaste et *permis* de Dieu." Antonin Artaud, Œuvres, ed. Évelyne Grossmann (Paris, 2004), p. 197.

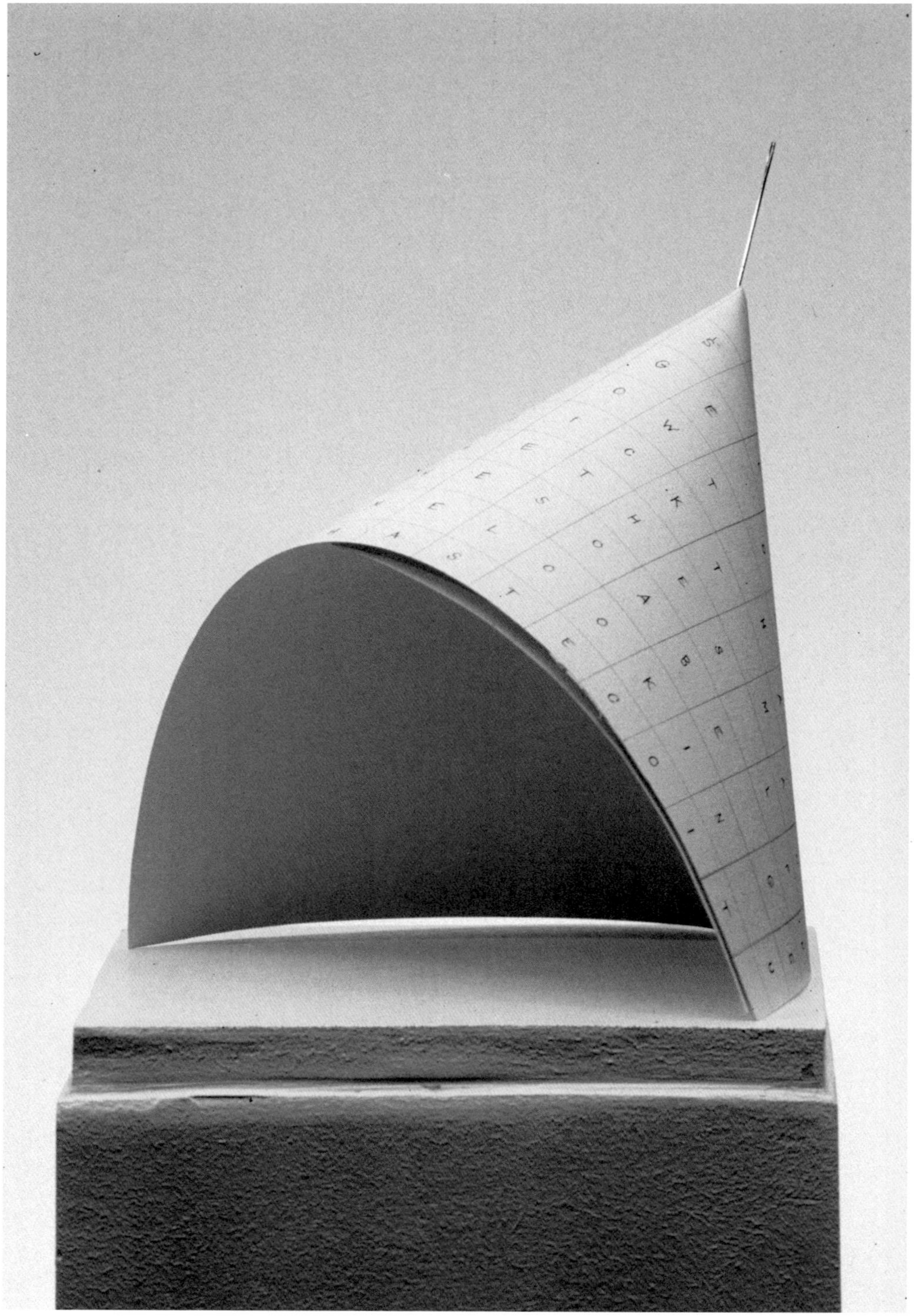

7 Terry Fox, *Transparent Abelard*, 2005, drawing with text, graphite; paper, needle, on pedestal under a Plexiglas display case, 132.08 x 20.3 x 20.3 cm, University of California, Berkeley Art Museum and Pacific Film Archive. Photo: Anglim Gilbert Gallery

cone torqued, or twisted on itself to make the strange shape of this textual sculpture."[23]

The written-upon paper, twisted into a cone, and with a new, but nevertheless legible direction of letters gives rise to a hybrid species that is both old and new: the text sculpture. One could also call it poetry in space, poem sculpture, word-body art.

The above-mentioned line of text with the Rimbaud quote, which has been inserted in the strict exclusivity of planes that meet in rectilinear fashion, speaks of making the whirling world stand still. In the conical object, the line of text begins from the point and, in a spiral-formed movement, winds down the surface of the cone. While the world is made still in a grid of squares, it once again is made to whirl.

Acknowledgments
My thanks to Marita Loosen-Fox for allowing me to view the artist's estate, for her explanations, and for the materials she gave to me.

Translated from the German
by Andrea Scrima

23 Terry Fox, information sheet, Paule Anglim Gallery, San Francisco, exhibition *Solid Concept*, 2005.

From the Archives

Color Plates

I Terry Fox, *Untitled*, n.d., pencil, typewriting on paper, 27.9 x 21.6 cm, Estate of Terry Fox, Cologne

II Terry Fox, *School of Velocity*, n.d., pencil, typewriting, watercolor on paper, 29.6 x 20.8 cm, Estate of Terry Fox, Cologne

III Terry Fox, *School of Velocity*, n.d., pencil, typewriting, watercolor on paper, 29.6 x 20.6 cm, Estate of Terry Fox, Cologne

IV Terry Fox, *School of Velocity*, 1996, typewriting on paper, colored paper, adhesive strip, 29.0 x 20.3 cm, Estate of Terry Fox, Cologne

V Terry Fox, *Untitled*, n.d., pencil, pigment felt-tip pen, typewriting on paper, 29.8 x 21.1 cm, Estate of Terry Fox, Cologne

VI Terry Fox, *Untitled*, n.d., pencil on paper, paper strips with text, 27.9 x 21 cm, Estate of Terry Fox, Cologne

VII–IX Terry Fox, *TEXTUM (WEB) Original*, 1989, pages from artist's book with handwritten corrections, 29.7 x 20.8 cm, Estate of Terry Fox, Cologne

X–XV Terry Fox, *Untitled*, n.d., sketches for the solo exhibition at Kunstmuseum Luzern, 1982, pencil, pigment felt-tip pen on paper, mixed media, 29 x 21 cm each, Estate of Terry Fox, Cologne

XVI Robert Walser, *Masquerade and Other Stories*, book cover, John Hopkins University Press, 1990, Estate of Terry Fox, Cologne

XVII Terry Fox, *Colored Silences, Articulated Silences*, 2000, ink, graphite, rubber stamp ink on paper, drawing, stamp print with text, 50 x 36 cm, Estate of Terry Fox, Cologne

XVIII Terry Fox, *Silence Helps Secrets*, 2000, ink, graphite, rubber stamp ink on paper, drawing, stamp print with text, 50 x 36 cm, Estate of Terry Fox, Cologne

XIX Terry Fox, *Pendulum Swings to Time*, 1999, ink, graphite, rubber stamp ink on paper, drawing, stamp print with text, 50 x 36 cm, Estate of Terry Fox, Cologne

XX Terry Fox, *Small Mysteries Unfold*, 1999, ink, graphite, rubber stamp ink on paper, drawing, stamp print with text, 50 x 36 cm, Estate of Terry Fox, Cologne

XXI–XXIV Terry Fox, letter to Petr Stembera, n.d., 25.3 x 20 cm, Estate of Terry Fox, Cologne

XXV Terry Fox, *A Metaphor* (drawing with instructions for the installation), 1976, pigment felt-tip pen on paper, 33.5 x 25.8 cm, San Francisco Museum of Modern Art

Terry Fox

When vessel A is sounding its simplest and deepest note the air alternately rushes in and out of the opening. When it rushes in it compresses the air in the vessel, the pressure increases, and presently has increased so much that the tide is turned and the air is forced out again. Its momentum carries it too far, and after a time the tide begins to flow once more; the constant repetition of these events constitutes the vibrating motion. Suppose that the same effects were occurring in the vessel B of the same size as A but having a wider opening, and that the same amount of air was flowing in and out, then the maximum pressure would be the same as in A; but since the opening in B is wider the in-and-out motions of the air are less restricted and the vessel will empty and refill itself more quickly. The pitch of the note is therefore higher.

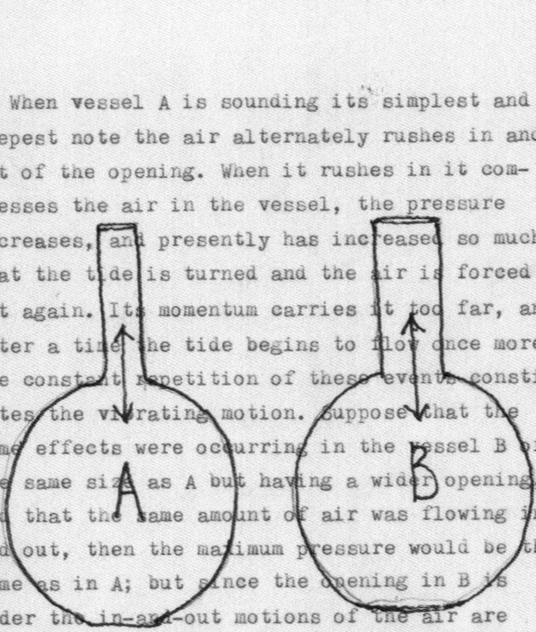

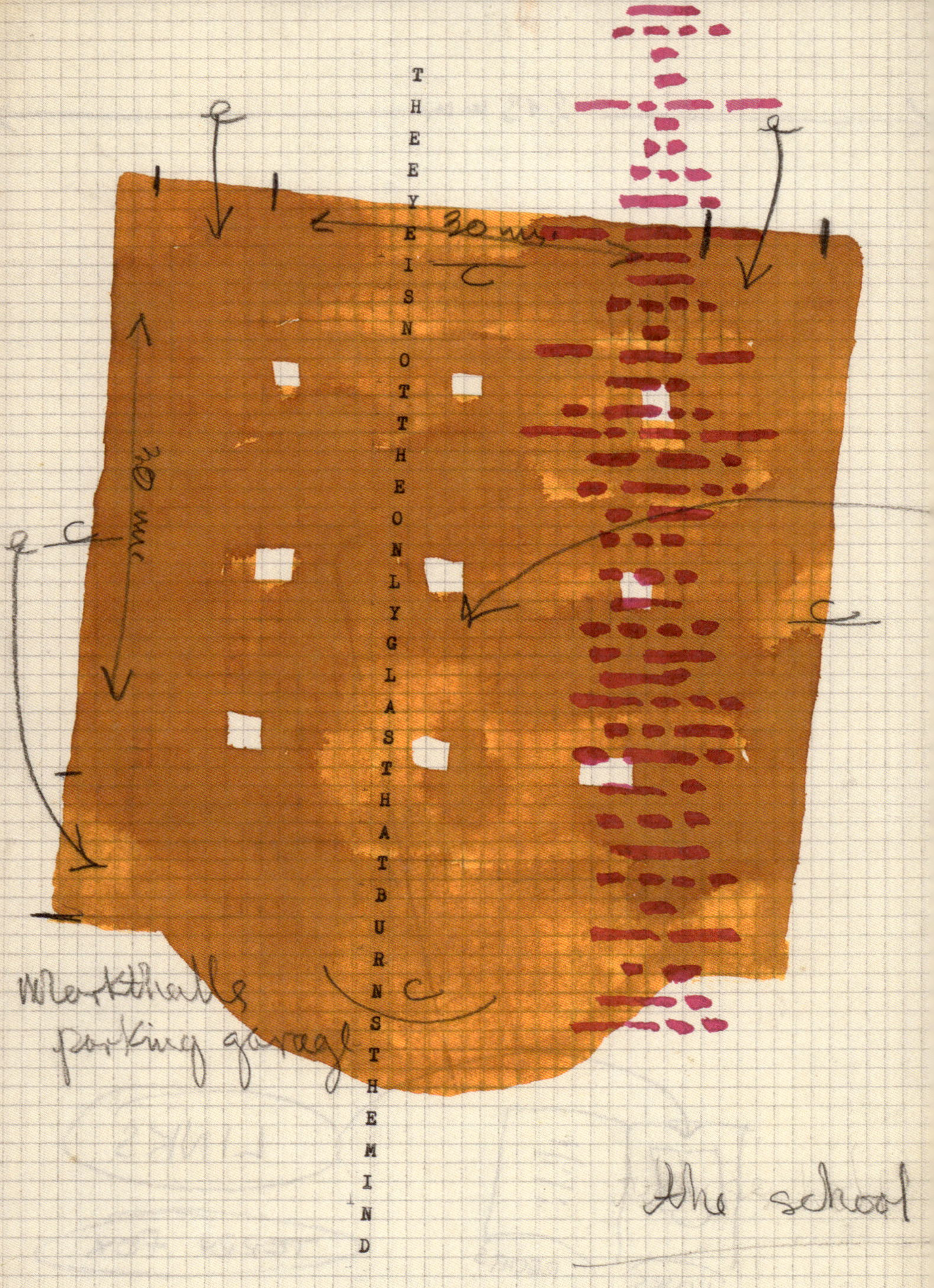
THEEYEISNOTTHEONLYGLASSTHATBURNSTHEMIND
30 m
30 m
c
c
c
c
Markthalle
parking garage
the school

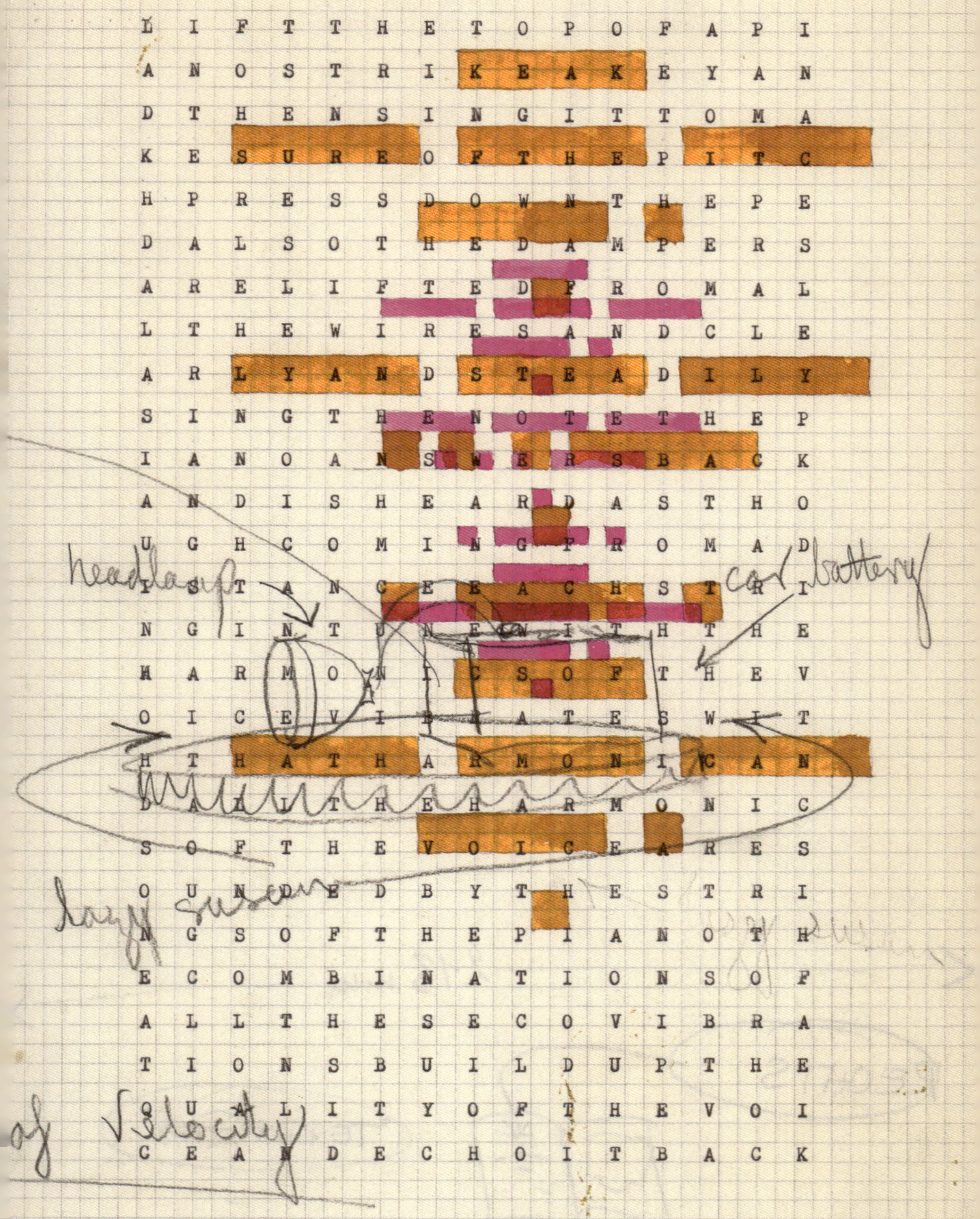
L I F T T H E T O P O F A P I
A N O S T R I K E A K E Y A N
D T H E N S I N G I T T O M A
K E S U R E O F T H E P I T C
H P R E S S D O W N T H E P E
D A L S O T H E D A M P E R S
A R E L I F T E D F R O M A L
L T H E W I R E S A N D C L E
A R L Y A N D S T E A D I L Y
S I N G T H E N O T E T H E P
I A N O A N S W E R S B A C K
A N D I S H E A R D A S T H O
U G H C O M I N G F R O M A D
I S T A N C E E A C H S T R I
N G I N T U N E W I T H T H E
H A R M O N I C S O F T H E V
O I C E V I B R A T E S W I T
H T H A T H A R M O N I C A N
D A L L T H E H A R M O N I C
S O F T H E V O I C E A R E S
O U N D E D B Y T H E S T R I
N G S O F T H E P I A N O T H
E C O M B I N A T I O N S O F
A L L T H E S E C O V I B R A
T I O N S B U I L D U P T H E
Q U A L I T Y O F T H E V O I
C E A N D E C H O I T B A C K
headlamp
car battery

THESCHOOLOFVELO C I T Y

LECOLEDELAVELO C I T E

DIESCHULEDERGELÄUFIG K E I T

LASCUOLADELLAVELO C I T A

F.'96

A T A B L E O F S I M P L E S O U
N D S E C H O E S S H A D O W S R
E F L E C T I O N S C O N C R E T E
C I E L I N G S S T E E L W A L L S
L E A D W I N D O W S S T O N E D
O O R P A P E R F L O O R T H R E
E O B J E C T S T H E M A N D U S
T W O I D E O L O G I E S A N D O
N E T H O U G H T B A S S A N D T
R E B L E A N D S Y M P A T H E T
I C S T R I N G S T H E M O N L O
T H S I D E S U S I N T H E M I D
D L E T W O F A C I N G S C R E E
N S W H O S E P R O J E C T E D M
I C R O W A V E S B L E N D A T T
H E C E N T E R B L A C K A N D W
H I T E A N D C O L O R E D A S I
L E N T A R B I T E R A N I N T R
U D E R S O U N D A N D N O I S E
O N B O T H S I D E S S I L E N C
E A T T H E C O N F L U E N C E V
I B R A T I O N S B E L O W O D O
R L E S S C O L O R L E S S T A S
T E L E S S F O R M L E S S T H O
U G H T L E S S A N D S I L E N T

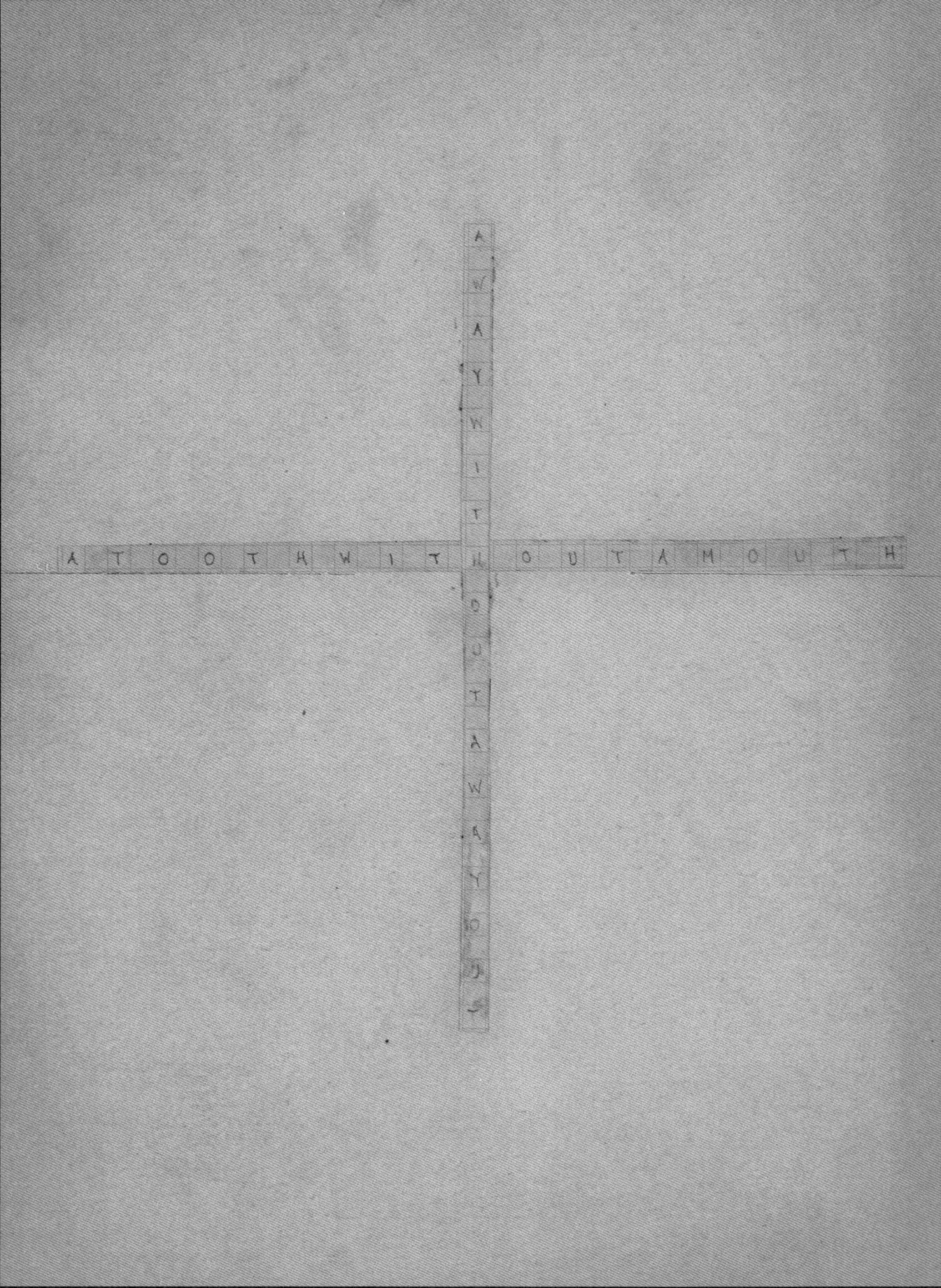

VI

HOURGLASS

T

M A N C U T S H I S H

S O U N D S E

E A D O F F W I T H A

R

C H A I N S A W A N D

L I V E S W I F E B U

Y

R I E D A L I V E W I

T H D E A D H U S B U

N D O W N E R B U I L

E

D S P O O C H A W H E

Y

E L C H A I R A F T E

R H E I S C R I P P L

E

E D B Y A G U N M A N

S

E

Y

E

S

O

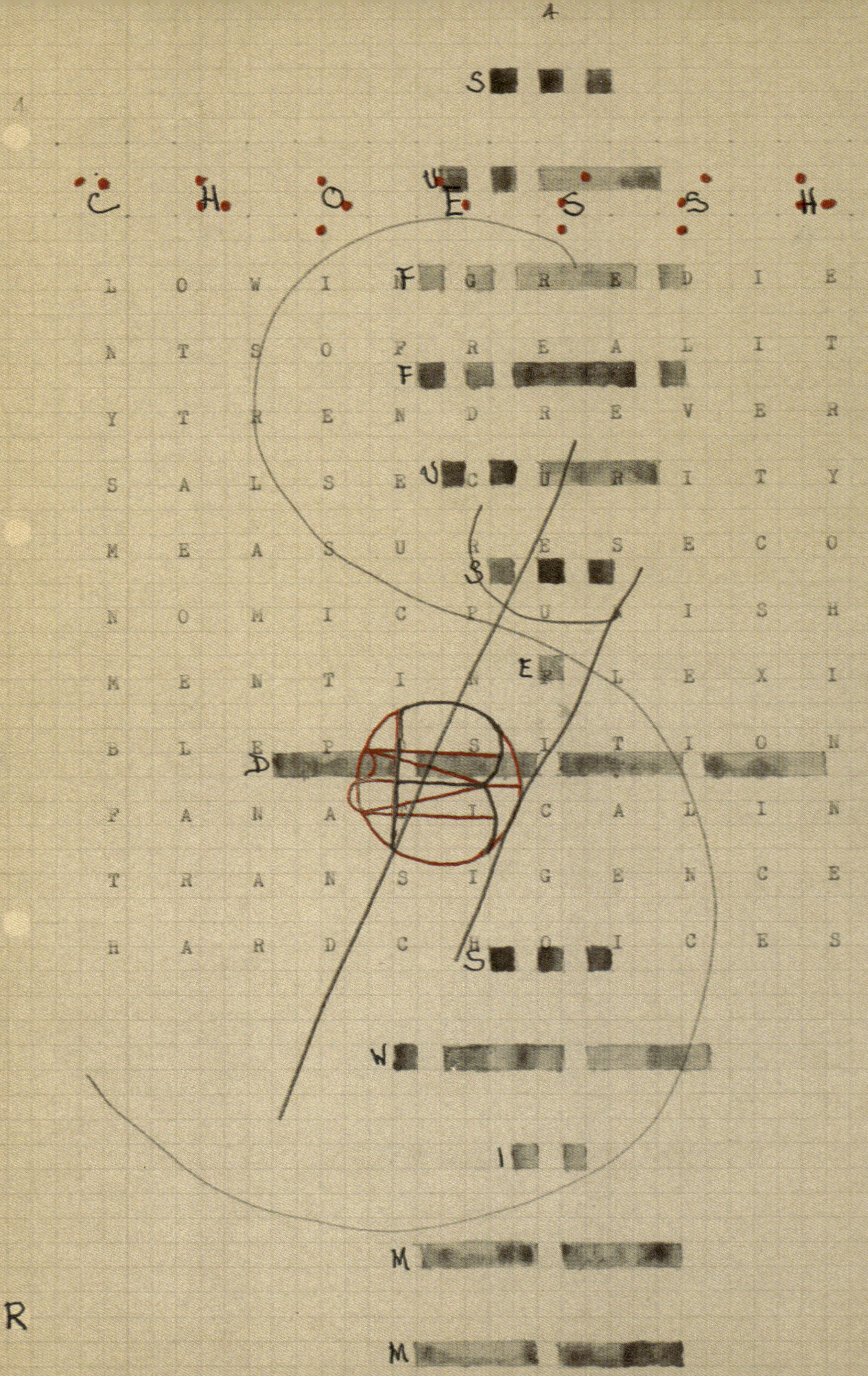

A
S
C H O E S S H
U
L O W I N G R E D I E
F
N T S O F R E A L I T
F
Y T R E N D R E V E R
U
S A L S E C U R I T Y
M E A S U R E S E C O
S
N O M I C P U N I S H
E
M E N T I N F L E X I
B L E P O S I T I O N
D
F A N A T I C A L I N
T R A N S I G E N C E
H A R D C H O I C E S
S
W
I
M
R
M

I

N

A D O W S R E

G

B A L A N C E O F T E

R R O R S H I F T I N

B

G T H E T H R E A T U

R

N L I M I T E D R E T

A L I A T I O N N A T

I

I O N A L T E S T B E

D B L A C K P R O G R

M

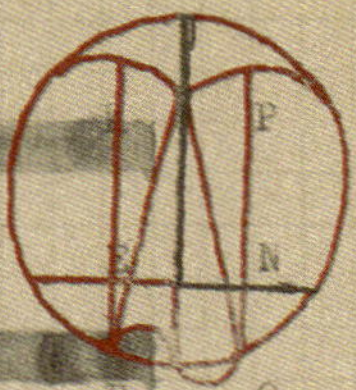

A M P O T E N T I A L

M

F L A S H P O I N T S

I

E L E C T I V E D I S

C R I M I N A T I O N

N

G

L

W

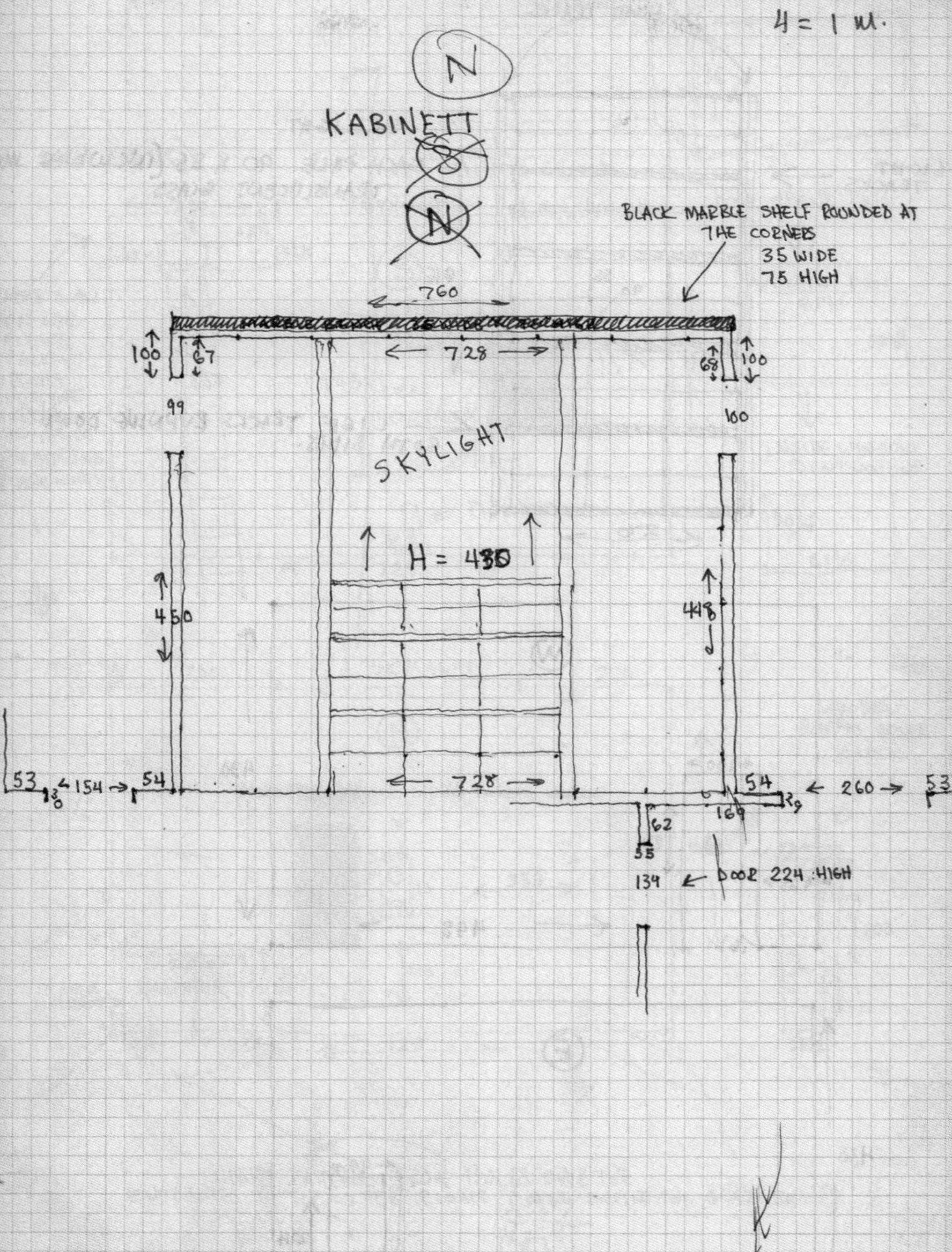
4 = 1 m.
N
KABINETT
BLACK MARBLE SHELF ROUNDED AT THE CORNERS
35 WIDE
75 HIGH
760
100
67
728
68
100
99
100
SKYLIGHT
H = 430
450
418
53
154
54
728
54
260
53
62
169
55
134
DOOR 224 HIGH

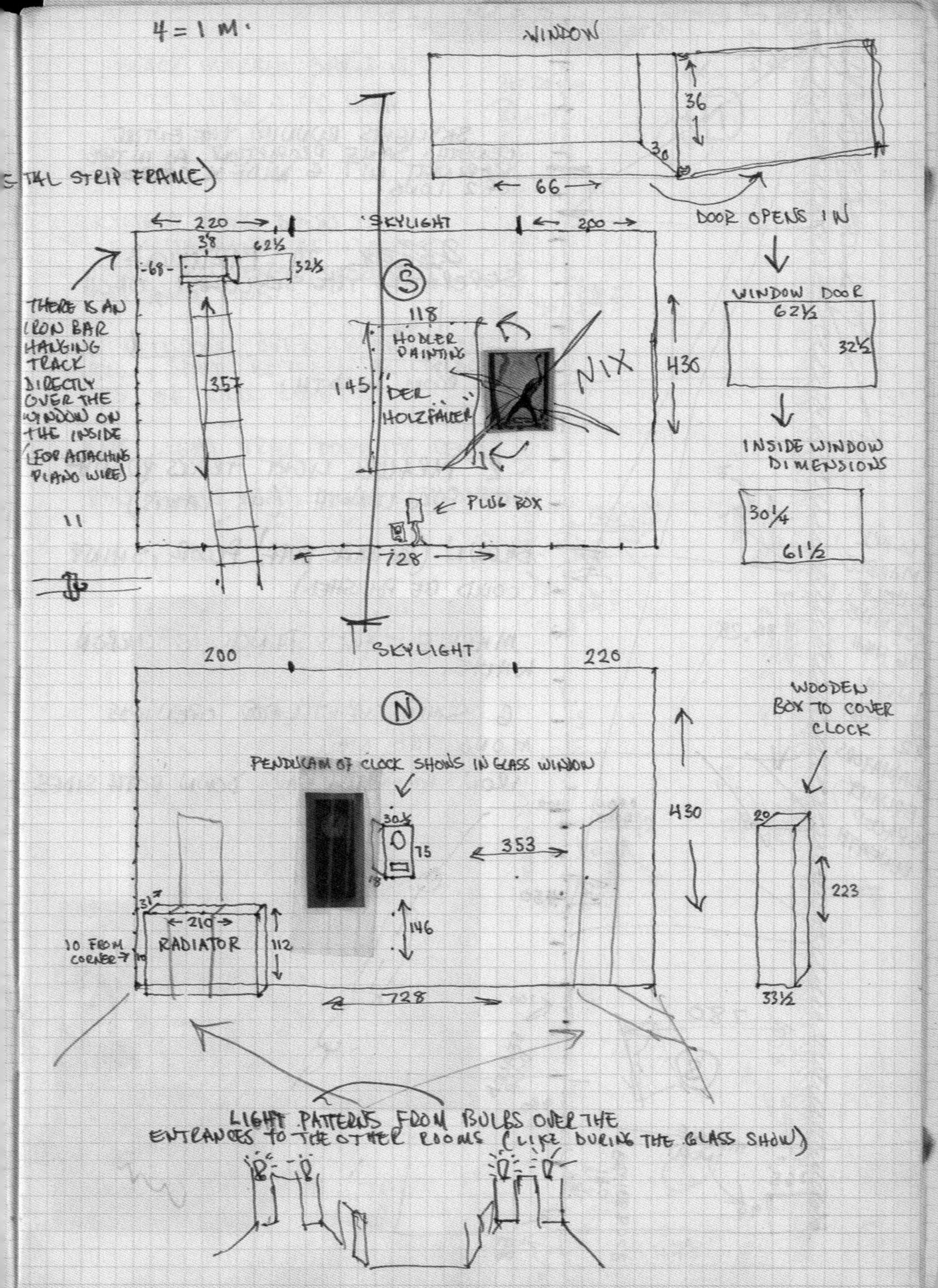

4 = 1 M.
WINDOW
36
30
66
DOOR OPENS IN
TAL STRIP FRAME)
220
SKYLIGHT
200
38
62½
-68-
32½
THERE IS AN IRON BAR HANGING TRACK DIRECTLY OVER THE WINDOW ON THE INSIDE (FOR ATTACHING PIANO WIRE)
357
S
118
HODLER PAINTING
145
DER HOLZFÄLLER
NIX
430
WINDOW DOOR
62½
32½
INSIDE WINDOW DIMENSIONS
30¼
61½
PLUG BOX
728
200
SKYLIGHT
220
N
WOODEN BOX TO COVER CLOCK
PENDULUM OF CLOCK SHOWS IN GLASS WINDOW
30½
75
353
430
20
223
31
210
RADIATOR
112
10 FROM CORNER
146
728
33½
LIGHT PATTERNS FROM BULBS OVER THE ENTRANCES TO THE OTHER ROOMS (LIKE DURING THE GLASS SHOW)

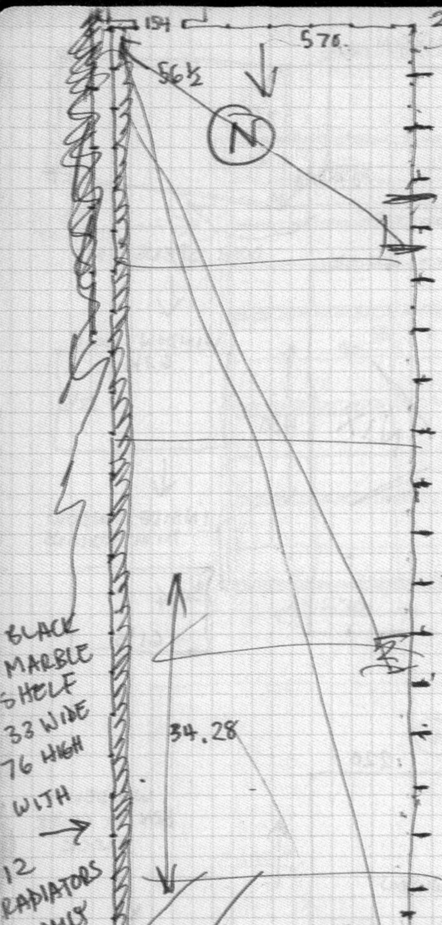

SKYLIGHTS RUNNING THE ENTIRE LENGTH. SAME PROPORTIONS AS IN THE KABINETT BUT 6 WIDE X 23 SETS OF 2 LONG.

~~23 22~~ 24 PARTITIONS SEPERATING THE SKYLIGHST, EACH

94
17

FULL ROOM WIDTH.

2 PARALLEL LIGHT TRACKS RUNNING THE FULL LENGTH (48 LAMPS)

BROWN (~~DA~~ DARK BUFF) FLOOR, SHINY (COULD BE POLISHED)

MARBLE TAKES PENCIL AS CARBON WHITE.

6 SMALL VENTILATOR OPENINGS ALONG THE WALL

IRON HANGING BARS DOWN BOTH SIDES

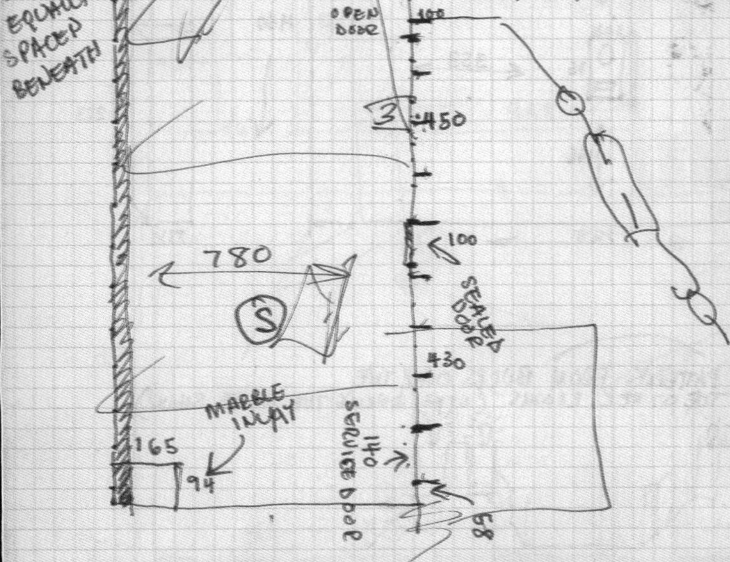

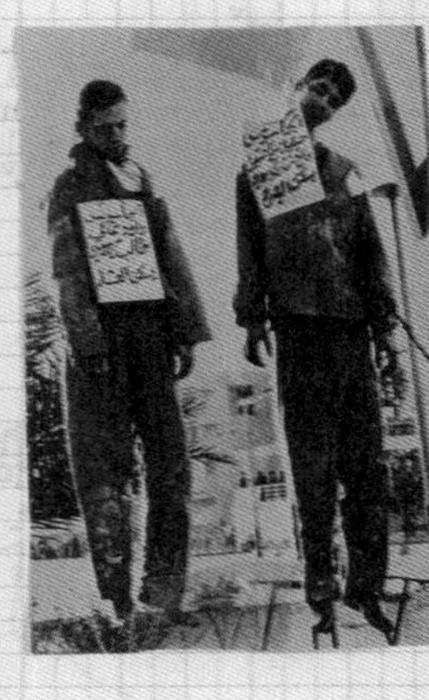

BLACK MARBLE SHELF IS
33 WIDE & 76 HIGH

SKYLIGHT RUNS DOWN THE MIDDLE WITH PANES AS IN THE KABINETT FULL LENGTH, SHORT BY 1.30 AT EACH END.

3 WINDOWS OPENING ONTO FIRE WELL, SPACE BETWEEN BUILDINGS LOTS OF WELL LIGHT.

ONE LIGHT TRACK DOWN THE CENTER.

IRON HANGING BARS DOWN BOTH SIDES.

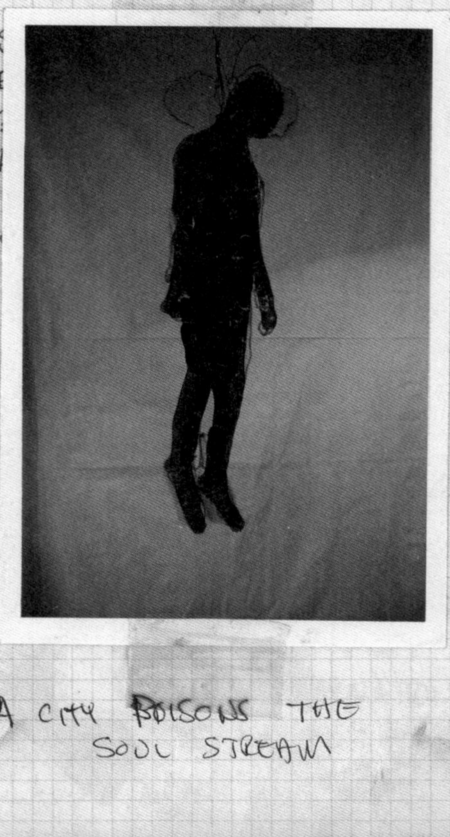

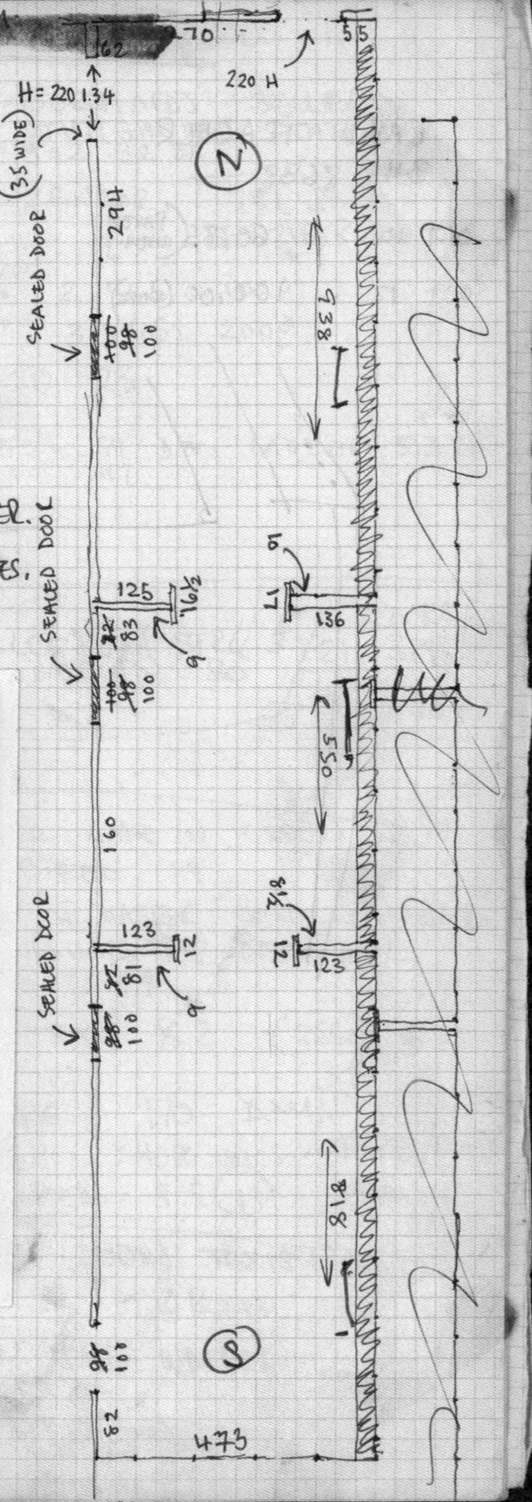

A CITY POISONS THE
SOUL STREAM

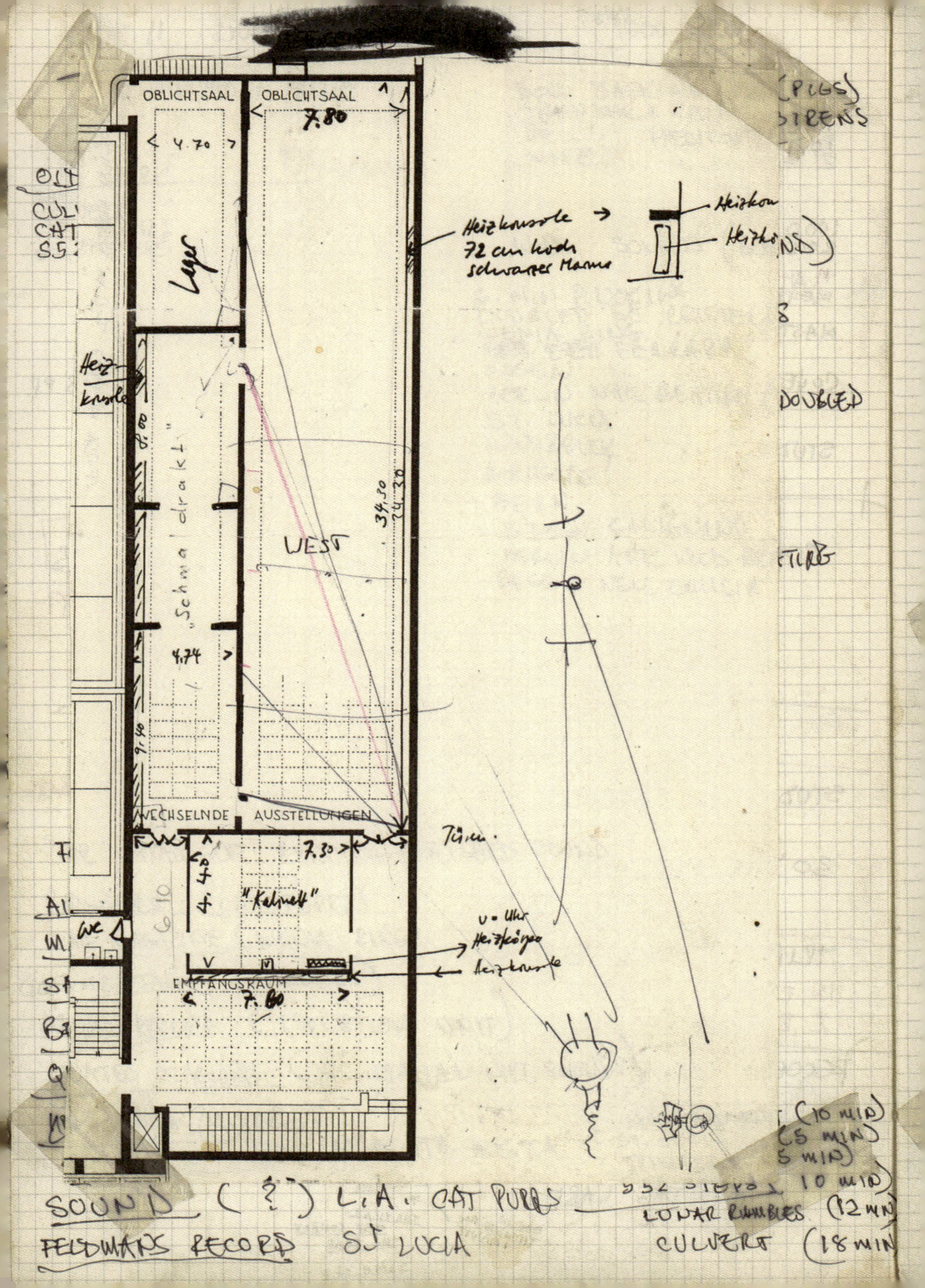

OBLICHTSAAL
OBLICHTSAAL
7.80
4.70
Lager
Heizkonsole
72 cm hoch
schwarzer Marmor
Heizkonsole
"Schmal drakt"
WEST
4.74
WECHSELNDE AUSSTELLUNGEN
Türen
7.30
"Kabinett"
Heizkörper
Heizkonsole
EMPFANGSRAUM
7.80
SIRENS
DOUBLED
SOUND (?) L.A. CAT PURRS
FELDMANS RECORD
ST LUCIA
(10 MIN)
(5 MIN)
10 MIN)
LUNAR RUMBLES (12 MIN)
CULVERT (18 MIN)

HEAD (OF OBSERVER) [FROM THE KABINET]

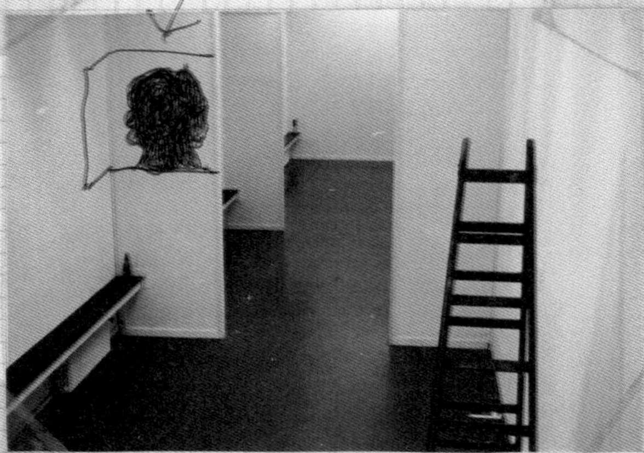

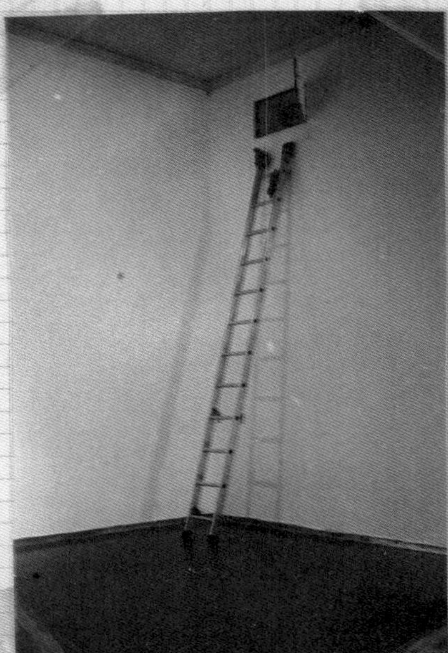

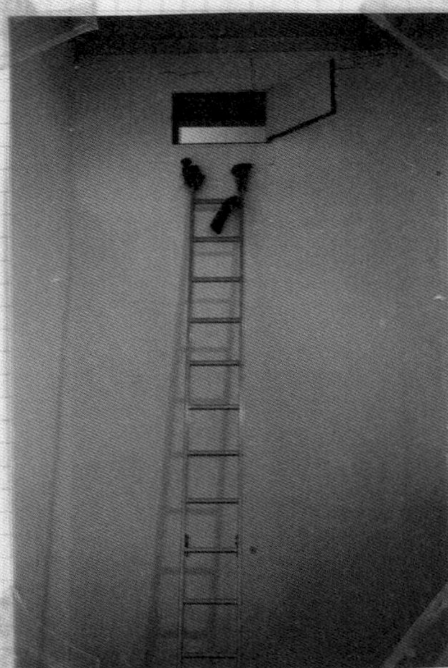

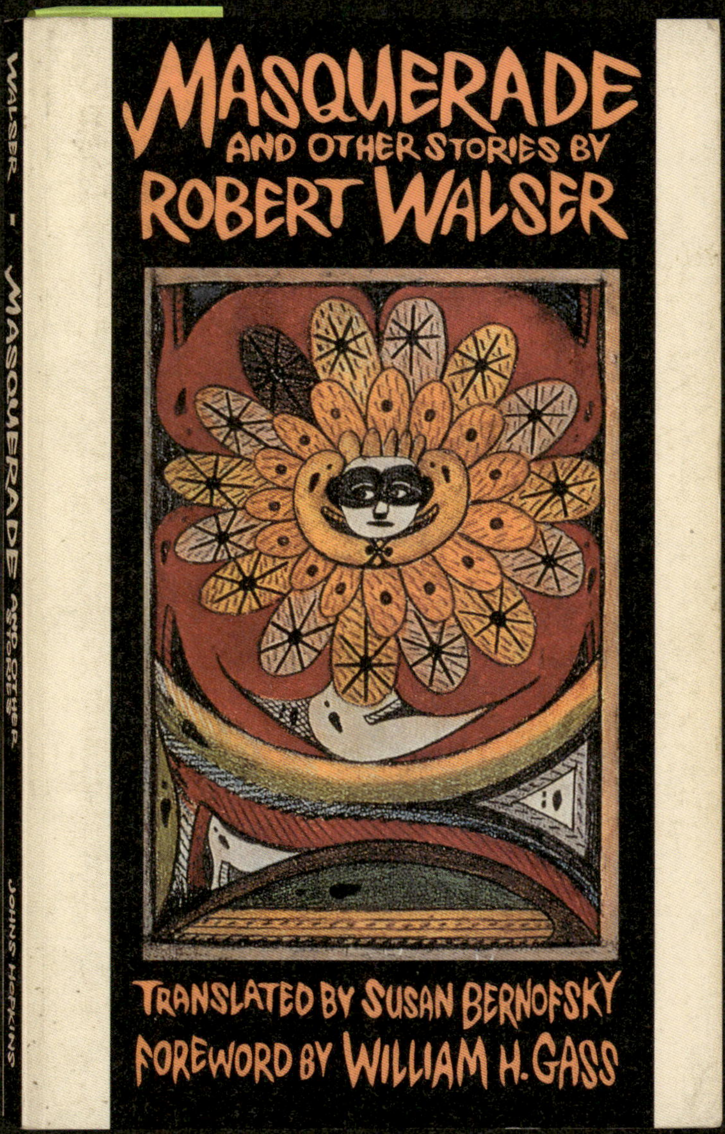
MASQUERADE
AND OTHER STORIES BY
ROBERT WALSER
TRANSLATED BY SUSAN BERNOFSKY
FOREWORD BY WILLIAM H. GASS
WALSER · MASQUERADE AND OTHER STORIES
JOHNS HOPKINS

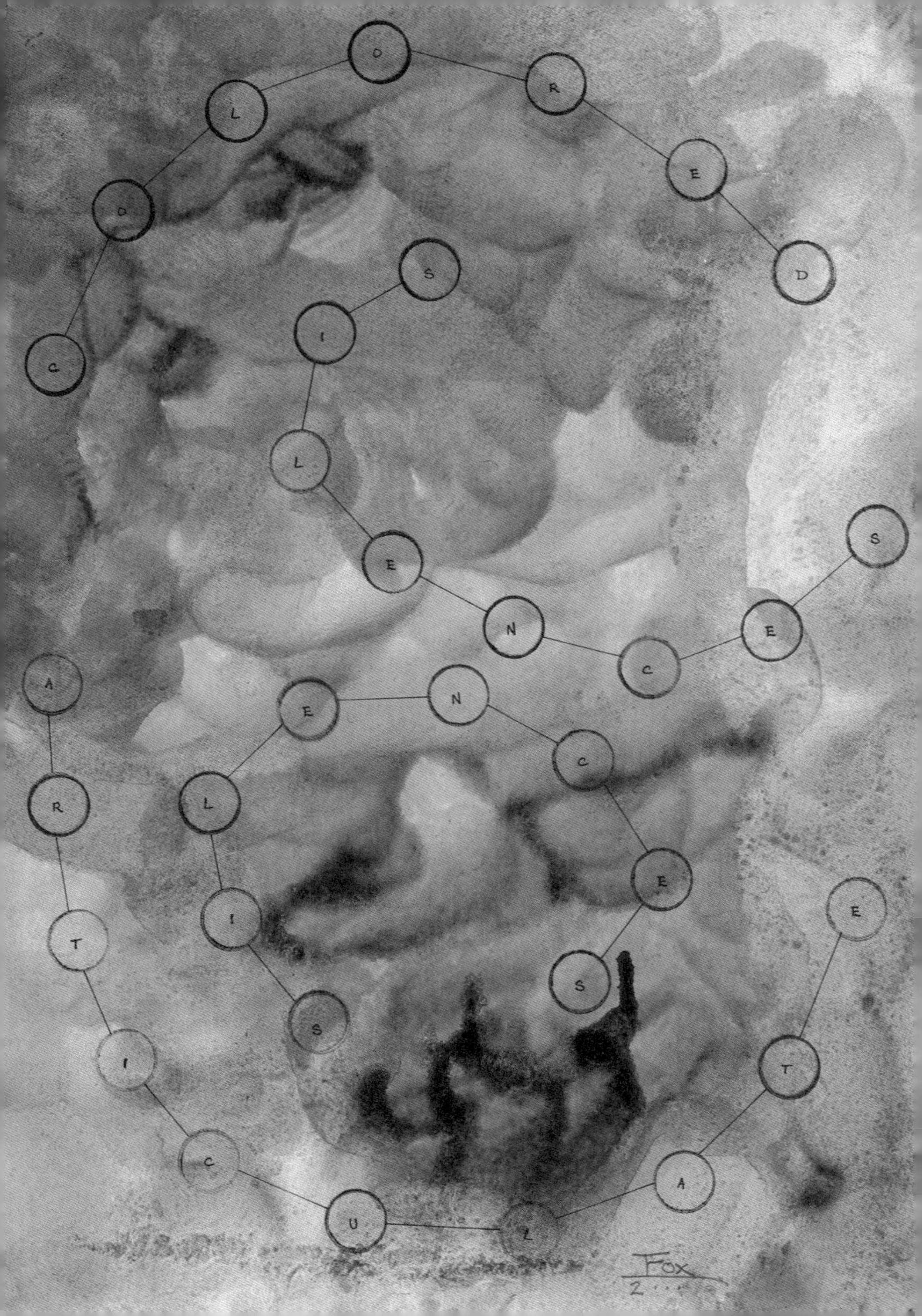
COLORED
SILENCES
SILENCES
ARTICULATE
FOX

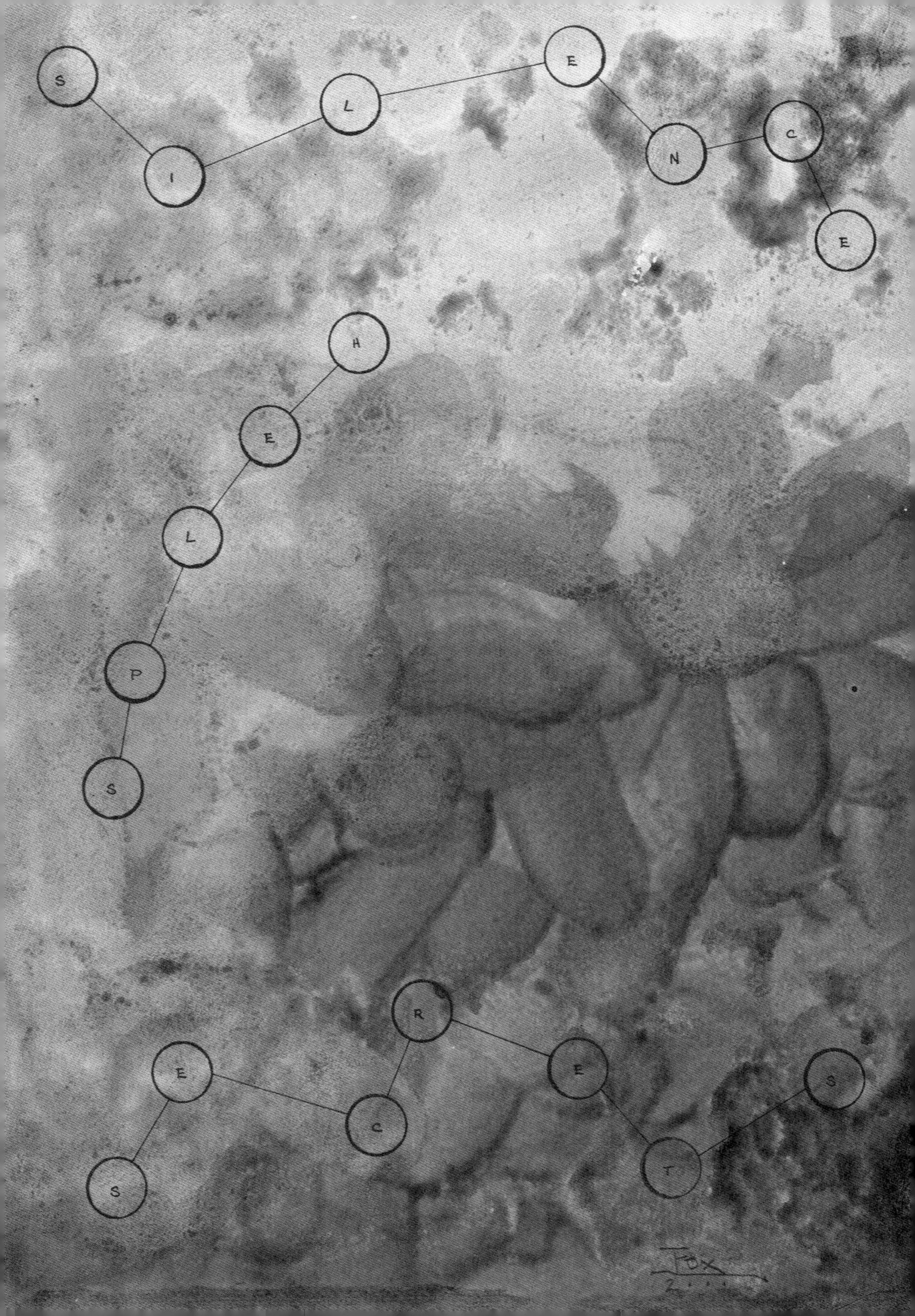

SILENCE
HELPS
SECRETS
FOX

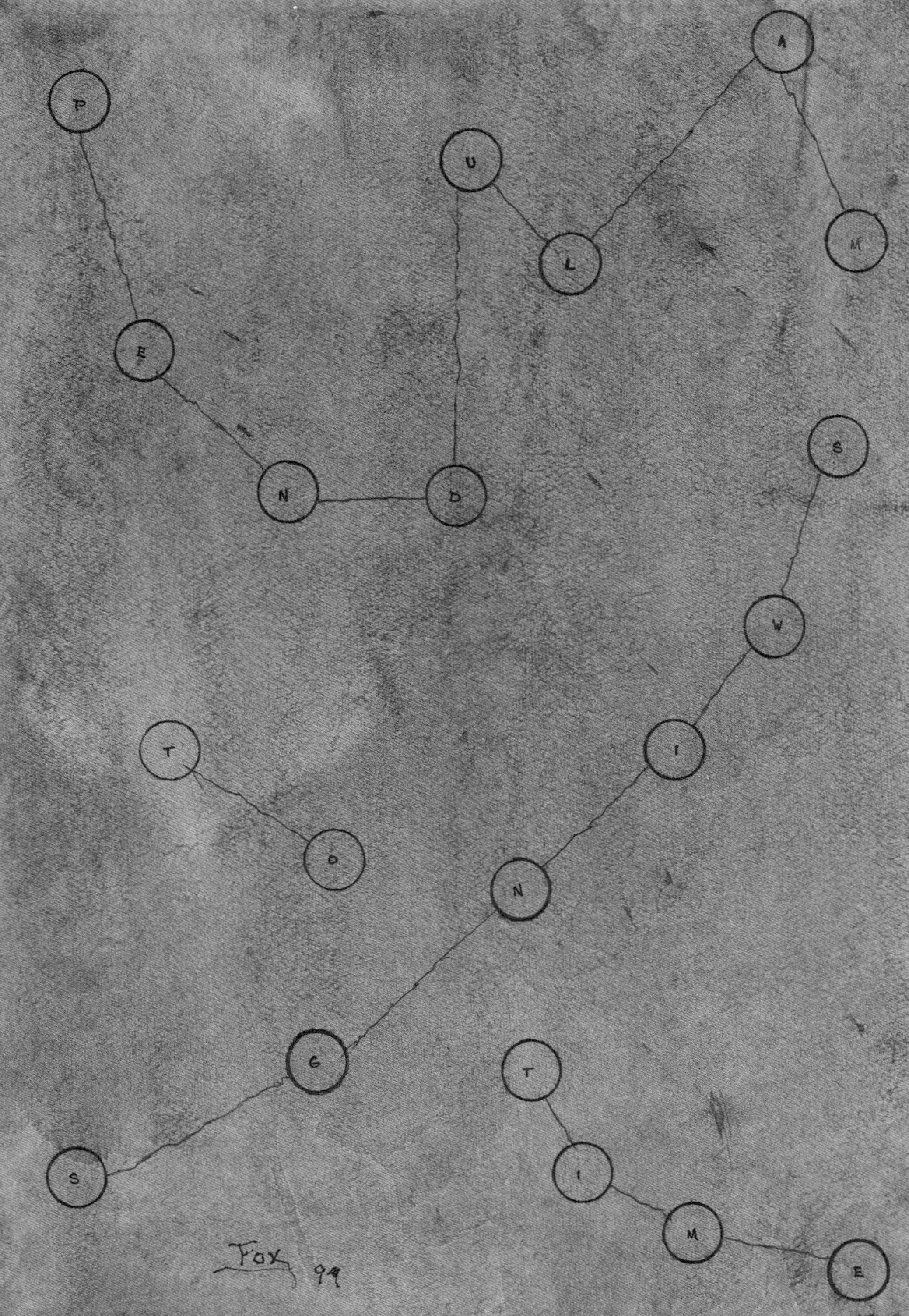
P
E
N
D
U
L
A
M
S
W
I
N
G
S
T
O
T
I
M
E
Fox 99

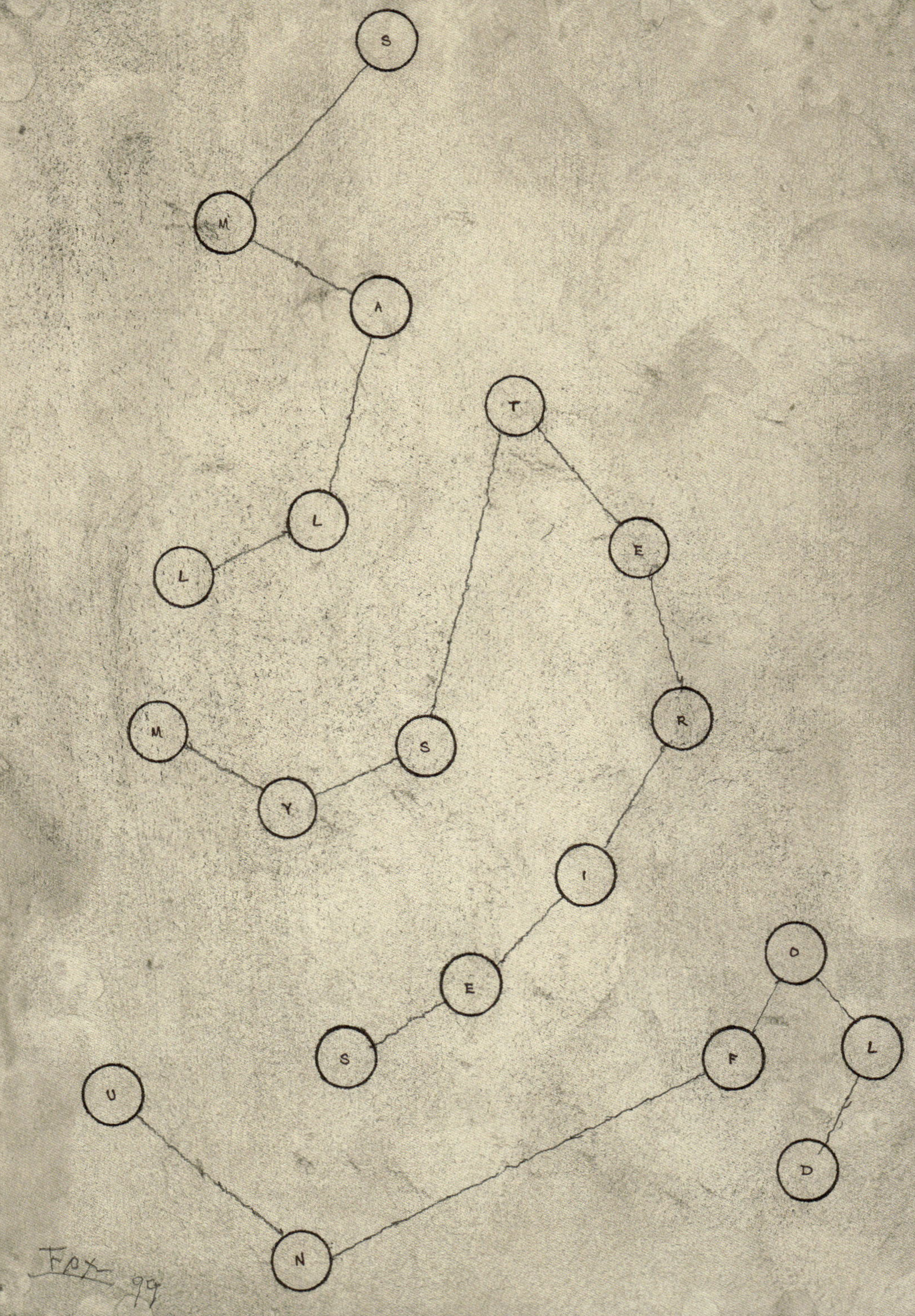
SMALL
MYSTERIES
UNFOLD
Fox 99

Dear Peter Petre ptre ptr...
thank you for your wonderful letter with so much information!! and of course for the photographs you sent which were very imbued with a feeling of the performance. Its good to move to New York because of the enviroment and for no other reason. the art alternatives are the same here as anywhere but the physical city offers me something i can find in no other u.s. citx. we live in a small apartment on Houston conner of elizabeth, next to the Bowerey boyry bowry which is only loo dollars per and we sblit it 3 ways (me my brother romaine, Romaine Perine, Larry Fox and Terry Fox ((twin brothers))),si u so it is an incredible delight it is ama-ing to be here and also the political,cultural climate_is intérresting here altho8gh the desire for money is ama inhl6 amazingly stronger herethan in.... I am enclosing a tape of some sounds from some performances I have done. On side one is a 15 minute excerpt from a 90 minute tape attempting to render the sound of the labyrinth at chartres by using 11 purrs of 11 different cats to represent the 11 concentric rings in the labyrinth and the 552 steps from the outside to the center of the labyrinth become 10 second time intervals, the 552 lo second int4rvals become 90 minutes of time. at each the of the 34 turns the purrs from one ring overlap with the purrs from another for 10 seconds. the center is represented by the simultaneous purrs of all 11 cats at once, the tape moves from right to left speaker as the labyrinth turns left to right.xxxxxx I made this rubberstamp and the dots on the plan follow the dots on the excerpt of tape you have in this cassette, each dot on the plan= lo seconds of purr, the plan beginning at the first of this excèrpt, so yo7y u can follow this score by following the diagram. the second excerpt is from "lunar rambles" a 5 days in the streets of new york in different locations, all picked beforehand for thier accous tics. there were no invitations and no one knew of the location except the person who went with me to video tape, michael shamberg, who go me this show at the kitchen. the indoor show consisted of the 1 hour color video tape of one hour of uniterrupted performance from the day before, a different tape each day for 5 days, this was the reason i cam to n.y. and they gave me 300 dollars so i took the train roundtrip from s.f. to ny on a 21 day pass and had enough money left over to live and do this work. thie the sound is the bowing, with violin bows, acrooss across 2 metal bowl, one very bulbous and made of aluminum, and the other the iron disc from a plow. I have used these instruments in many many perfor mances all over, they are especially good in the street. I found them both in the street and it is there they find thier voices. this is from lunar rambles and is recorded with just a microphone and no electronics as i am for the accoustic and against the electronic and never use it accept to record. this excerpt is a few minutes from an all day session. the 3rd excerpt is from a piece i did on the top of a mountain near san francisco. i wqs given 100 dollars by the san francisco museum to do a sound piece and i dispise the museum so i offered to do the piece 1200 feet above the museum and 20 miles away and used the money to hire a single engine airplane in which my son foxy flew and directed the pilot to make as many passes as he cofld for the money, over the top of the mountain, but out of sight of the spectators, they could not see the plan

I made a instrument which you hear on THIS excerpt on the tape of a box found on the street and 2 piano wires which i playes with a bow to imaitate the propeller pitch of the airplane as it made itspasses in the clear quiet air of the mountain top. I had a sliding bridge on my instrumen made of a metal bowl and the instrument looked like this and i slid the bowl to obtain the pitch of the airplanel. the audience was not informed about the airplane and few made the conection with the title of "timbre" the performance was 4½ hours of uninteruppted sound. the last pice of tape on the side A is from 552 steps through 11 pairs of strings done in my rose street studio in san franciwsco. It is 11 pairs of piano wires of 11 thichnessess in pairs from 22 feet long to 3 feet long, made to whear the same sounds of the labyringh as mentioned before, the 11 piano wires are the 11 concentric rings (purrs) it was played over a period of 5 hours using a score consisting of a string with 552 knots ties in it for the left hand as the right struck with a mallet in a r3gular rythem the pairs of strings. the audience sat in the room below (my twin brothe5s room, shile i played abo ve) I played unseen above . the instrument wasstreached over a thin wooden floor which was the cieling of m6y brothers room below.

the other side of the tape is from a visiting artist job i did in missoula montana. i looked, together with the students, for sitews arou nd missoula ((high in the mountains, a tiney vil age in the basing of an extinct glacieal lake surrounded by tall mountains like innsbruck with 5 canyons emptying rivers into the bottom of the bowl, so I did a piece in a tunnel half filled with the swiftly flowing water of the clark for river I took a rowboat into the tunnel and asked for help from anybody and 2 students jumped into the boat which i had never met. we releqsed the ropes and drifted halfway into the tunnel(100 feet) and tied up the boat and proceeded to produce the sounds on this tape for 3 hours using only voices, glass bowls, glass and metal food covers, musical saw, and other found objects. the distortion in the sound is caused by the length and the reflextive power of the tunnel. then i rowed these 2 students out and returned and played in the boat a continuous sound for 24 hourz. this tunnel was next to a freight train track, whose 2whistle you can hear every so often. this was a place favored by the bums and not a p7ublic place. this side contains a few excerpts from this initial 3 hours.

and so love to you and i am so sorry we cou ld not see ea ch ofhter mosr in san francisco. i think it was toms fauslt. I am happy here and begin to a new work. write me again all love and greetings to you and your friedns!!

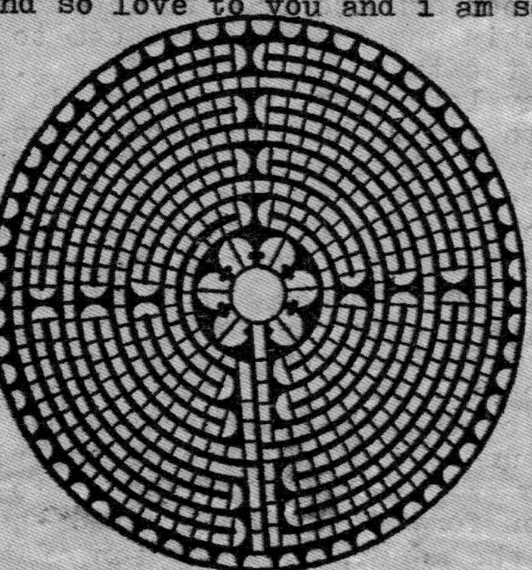

All thoughts!

terry'

P.O. BOX 528
CANAL ST. STATION
N.Y.C. N.Y. 10013
NEW PHONE! 212 431 9304

PETER –

THIS MAY HELP YOU VISUALIZE THE SOUND:

SIDE A

1.

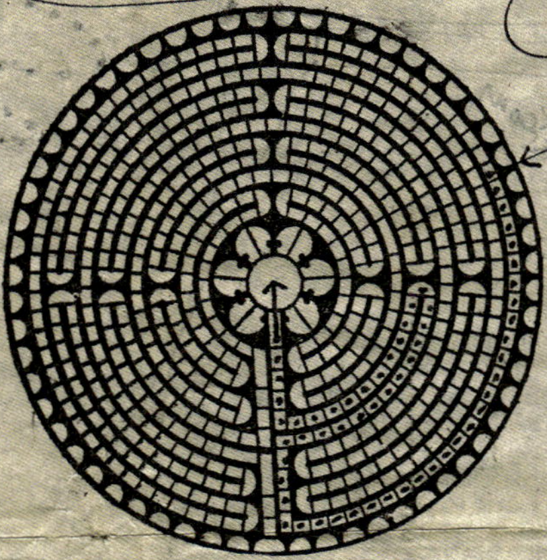

THE CAT PURR EXCERPT BEGINS HERE & FOLLOWS THE DOTS TO THE CENTER WHERE YOU HEAR ALL 11 CATS
REMEMBER EACH STEPS IS 10 SECONDS LONG.

2.

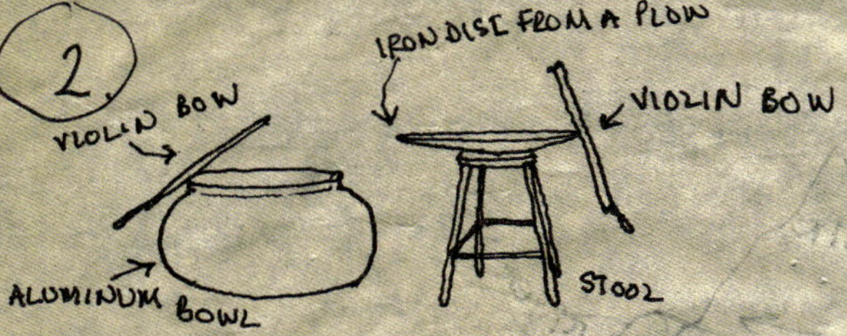

THE MICROPHONE THAT RECORDED THIS EXCERPT WAS INBETWEEN THE BOWLS. I PLAYED WITH MY BREATHING, A BOW IN EACH HAND.

3.

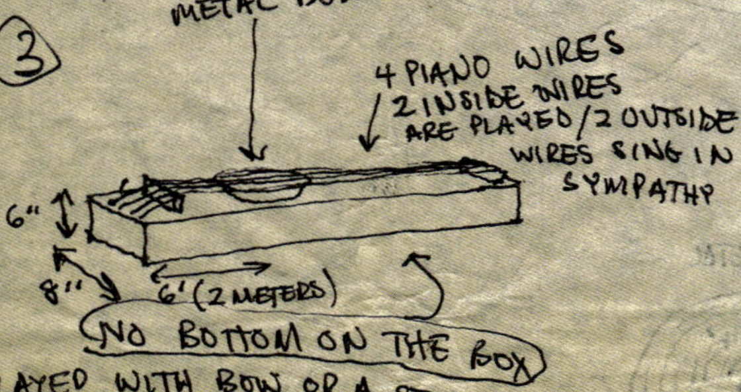

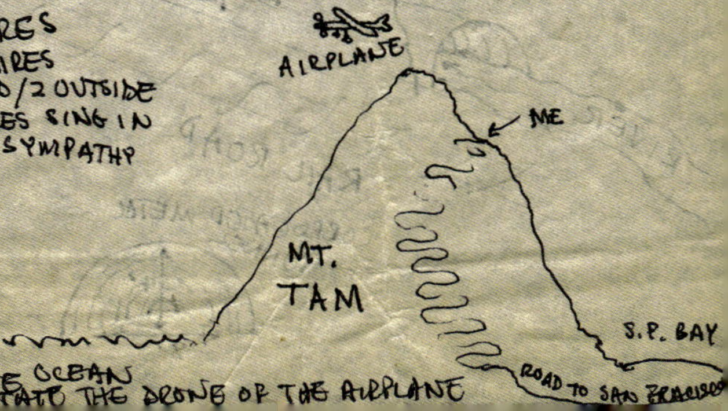

PLAYED WITH BOW OR A STICK 4 1/2 HOURS CONTINUOUSLY FROM ONE END OF THE BOX TO THE OTHER TO IMITATE THE DRONE OF THE AIRPLANE

4

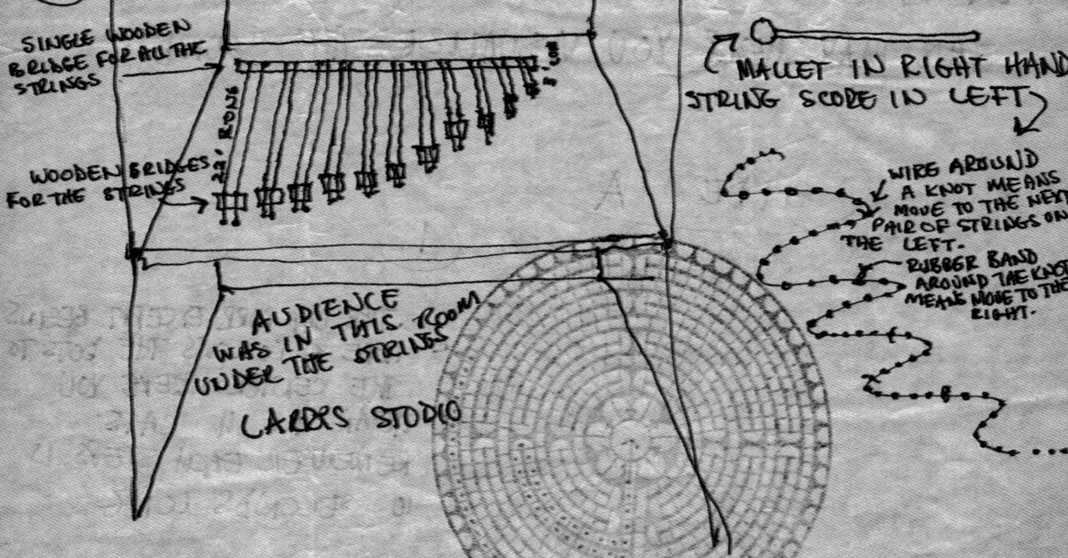

SIDE B

"CULVERT!"

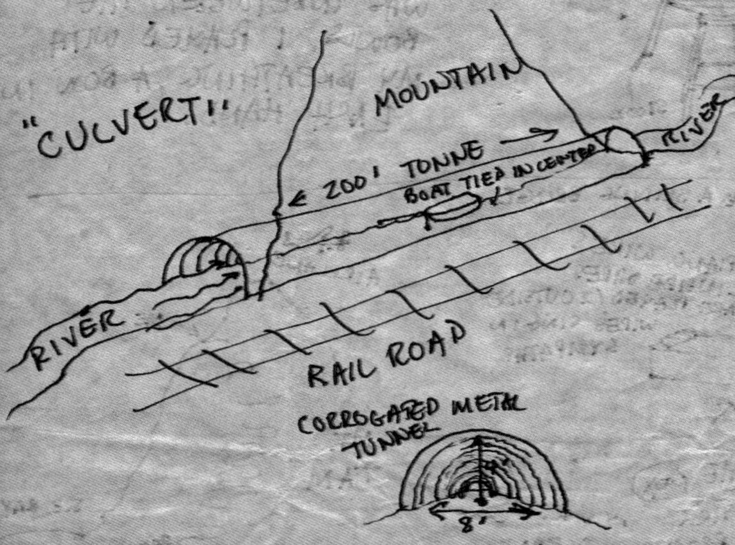

INSTRUCTIONS FOR INSTALLATION OF A METAPHOR

TEMPORARY TEXT ATTACHED TO THE WALL WITH ATTACHED NAIL.

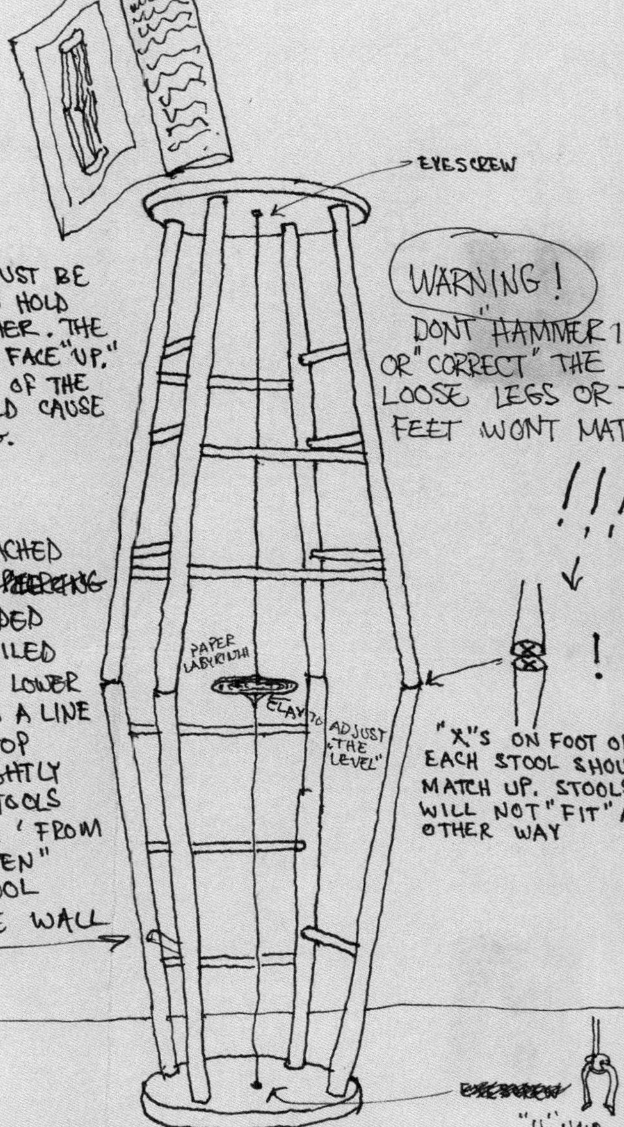

THE STRING MUST BE STREACHED TIGHT TO HOLD THE STOOLS TOGETHER. THE LABYRINTH SHOULD FACE "UP." THE IRREGULAR SEAT OF THE LOWER STOOL SHOULD CAUSE A PLEASENT ROCKING.

WARNING!

DONT "HAMMER IN" OR "CORRECT" THE LOOSE LEGS OR THE FEET WONT MATCH! !!!

THE TEXT SHOULD BE ATTACHED TO THE WALL BY A ~~WALL PIERCING~~ NAIL PIERCING THE PROVIDED HOLE. IT SHOULD BE NAILED TO THE WALL SO THAT THE LOWER EDGE OF THE TEXT IS ON A LINE WITH THE SEAT OF THE TOP STOOL, BEHIND AND SLIGHTLY TO THE LEFT OF THE STOOLS WHICH SHOULD BE 1–2 ' FROM THE WALL WITH THE "OPEN" SIDE OF THE WHITE STOOL FACING AWAY FROM THE WALL AS SHOWN HERE

"X"'S ON FOOT OF EACH STOOL SHOULD MATCH UP. STOOLS WILL NOT "FIT" ANY OTHER WAY

WHITE STOOL WITH "BOTTOM" + SIGNATURE

ANY QUESTIONS ?
CALL OR WRITE

TERRY FOX (PHONE 621 3479)
16 ROSE
SAN FRANCISCO 94102

Hans Peter Kuhn, Ron Meyers

A Talk

Hans Peter Kuhn: Ron, you know Terry quite a bit longer than I do—so I want to ask you, "How did you meet and how did you become friends? What happened"?

Ron Meyers: So, I met . . . I was a student at The San Francisco Art Institute, and The San Francisco Art Institute at that time, in the late eighties, had as faculty in the Performance/Video department all of the major conceptual and performance artists in the San Francisco Bay Area from the seventies, which had included Terry. So, Paul Kos, David Ireland, Howard Fried, Tom Marioni, a lot of these artists, they came together and they taught at the San Francisco Art Institute—it was—they called it an easy gig.
It paid well and you didn't have to do much. Especially in the Performance Art department—What is that? I did not know what it was . . . but someone at the school said, "Oh, you have got to take this class. You'd like it a lot." So I met this artist, Paul Kos, and also in the film department was a professor, Al Wong, who was a very close friend of Terry's from San Francisco.
He said, "You have got to take Terry Fox. Terry Fox is going to be visiting as a professor in your class for six weeks, 1987." So, I immediately went to the library and got all the catalogues—well, I'm sorry, all the **catalogue** [*laughter*] they had of Terry—*Metaphorical Instruments*. Al Wong said, "Okay . . . you have been exposed to artists here, but Terry is a real artist." Okay—wow—**wow**—I have got to take this . . .
So, I waited twelve weeks until this event. The Art Institute—there is a little ghetto, where the Performance Art department was . . . it was way off [*laughter*]. All the other students in the departments got studios, but not the Performance Art department students. "You don't need a studio" . . . that's what the school thought anyway . . . (I am sorry for my English, I really apologize . . .)
[*laughter*]
So, the day came, Terry Fox arrives, and I was standing with a friend of mine on a roof, overlooking where he started to walk into the department—and he had on a big leather coat, with the collar up, like this, and all buttoned up, and very short hair. And I thought, "Oh my God, this guy is tough, oh man, he's a gangster or something!" [*laughter*] And I thought, "What have I got myself into? Oh, Jesus!" So we arrived in class, and everybody was terrified, TERRYfied . . . [*laughter*] . . . yes, it was Terryble, it was Terryfying. And of course we all wanted to impress this **real** artist. So he showed his work, in slides, and the main thing the first day was to introduce himself; and Terry didn't really like teaching, I have to say, he was against teaching . . . perfect circumstances for everyone.

But he was a great teacher nevertheless, though he didn't enjoy the pedagogy, he didn't enjoy teaching . . . and he thought—by the way he was very democratic—he thought anyone who signed up for his class should get an A automatically . . . If you are paying that kind of money, you should get an A . . . This is an **art** school . . . what kind of qualifications are you going to be judged by in the outside world, it's an art school, you can't really teach art anyway . . . which I believe. You can learn, but you can't get a **degree** in art . . . my God . . . also I got the second and third degrees in art . . .
So he turned out to be the sweetest, kindest, most intelligent, warmest person I have ever met in my life. You know, maybe everything else is an exaggeration, but that is not an exaggeration. Terry was amazing—"maze"—really a-mazing, and not a labyrinth, because there is a difference. I listened in German, I mean I listened in—**what**? I listened in American trying to listen in German, since 2 o'clock—and it occurred to me that that's how I met Terry. It was like learning a language that I didn't know. I saw his pictures in a catalogue—oh, this is all answering your question, by the way—I saw pictures in a catalogue and immediately they were like legendary to me. Wow, these pictures are so **strange**, I don't know anything about it, nothing. I went to the Art Institute knowing nothing about the history of art . . . Picasso and Duchamp, okay, but every illiterate schoolboy knows Picasso and Duchamp.
And, by the way, Ivar, I first found out about Chris Burden through our friend Kevin O'Sullivan [American writer] . . . [pointing to Ivar Smedstad, Norwegian artist, in the audience]: that's for Ivar.
So I knew nothing about performance. Performance, I thought it was theater. What is this, an acting class, what's going on? And it turned out to have changed my entire direction of my life. I mean completely, without my knowing it . . . that was—in my adult life—I think that was the most important time of my life, taking a class at the Art Institute which led me to meet Terry Fox. Because, even if he had turned out to be as tough as I thought he was, it would have been worth it.

Hans Peter: But you collaborated later . . .

Ron: We did not collaborate. He was proposing collaborating on a project, when I got cancer and we couldn't go through with it. And by the time I was recovering, he died. So, it just didn't work out. But I had seen him last in the United States in 1994. And 1994, he had—there was a very unfortunate series of events with a bypass surgery he had in Belgium. And I was in touch periodically with him, but from San Francisco, on the telephone.
In 1998, I had a show in Göteborg in Sweden. When I got back, after ten days, I got a call from Terry and Marita, and Terry said, "How would you feel about coming to Cologne, and maybe being my assistant, because I need a studio assistant?" And I said, "okay!"—so I got back on a plane and I went to Cologne and we both said, "let's see if it works out," and I ended up staying like six to seven months there. Then I was Terry's assistant—whenever he needed me, I would fly back to Cologne. We just had a blast—wonderful, just amazing. And I always felt it to be a great privilege—I mean, who am I? Really . . . and to be friends with Terry was just amazing, mind-blowing. So I don't know quite what to say—there were a lot of funny things that happened.

Hans Peter: I am wondering, I would like to ask you about this: when you see his work, it has this extreme range between being extremely serious, sometimes even political, and on the other hand being funny and light, and in the same piece. Of course, everybody tries to do this. But, how was your experience when he came up with this work? Did you have this . . .

Ron: Okay, so, I lived . . . when I met him, he invited me after his six weeks of teaching . . . "Why don't you come visit me in Liège?" (in Lüttich?) in Belgium? So . . . yeah, why **not**!? No, I immediately made plans to go visit Terry, of course, I mean it was incredible. He told me he had this four-story-house that he just bought—and it was. But it was very thin, also [*laughter*]. It was more like a four-story-chimney [*laughter*]. So, I went there, and Arnold Dreyblatt [American artist, in the audience] lived there—I guess, Arnold, you told Terry about Lüttich, right?—[Arnold: Yeah]—Because it was very cheap and central.
[Arnold: And Terry could speak Italian] Exactly, he came from Florence, right and [interruption by Arnold] . . . Oh, yeah—wait till I tell you what Arnold had! So, Arnold had this place up a winding medieval street . . . yeah, same street, just up the street from Terry—it's kind of like Montmartre.

Arnold Dreyblatt: It was kind of a hole you had to go through to get up to this "casa" up there—and you lived in it . . . I gave it to you . . . not quite a gift . . . but I'm really sorry about that, I hope you forgive me. It had an electric shower, that I brought from Berlin, which I tried to get you to pay me for . . . and then it didn't really work, did it? [*laughter*].

Ron: I've been waiting for this apology for so many years . . . [*laughter*]
So I took over Arnold's apartment—well, hovel—it's too complicated to go into . . . and it would take hours to explain what 74 Rue Pierreuse was . . . but it involves someone named "Dede," but I cannot go into that . . .
So I lived up the street—I was a neighbor of Terry's: from my back terrace—and it was a pretty big terrace, too, that was a good thing about it—I could see down the street into Terry's backyard [Arnold: The terrace was kind of filled with garbage, wasn't it? What was up there?] . . . More than that . . . [*laughter*] it was also a burial place in the winter for cats. So we strung a string from Terry's backyard up to my terrace, so we could signal one another [Hans Peter: A telephone] . . . a primitive telephone, like kids make with cups. So I eventually took over Arnold's gift (**luckily** the shower never worked . . .) [*laughter*].

Arnold: So I have to tell this story: I met Sabisha Friedberg, who studied at Bard College, a young sound artist whom I met in New York—we were talking, and she said, "I know that you know Terry Fox" . . . she actually had lived there after you, and she started talking about the shower to me—and this was after you . . . this was only two years ago).

Ron: Well, it was a portable electric shower—the bottom is electrified, a heater, and it heats a volume of water; it goes through a pipe and comes out **potentially** as a shower. But I used to shower at Terry's . . . In fact, I went to the bathroom at Terry's . . . [*laughter*] because the so-called bathroom that I had, was a . . . okay [*laughter*].

Hans Peter: Thank you, Ron for answering my question about Terry's . . . how he managed to do these works [*laughter*]

Ron: I'm coming to that, I'm coming to that . . . Well, we have three hours, don't we? [*laughter*].

So, I was living on that street . . .
Terry had a studio next door to him, and it was like a storefront, but empty—very, very beautiful — and Terry every night would . . . what do you call it, “fire up a doobie,” would smoke some hash, and if it wasn’t a night that we would go out drinking, all night, then he would work on his art—so he’d be working—he had an office (he called it an office). And he **worked**, he didn’t want to be disturbed, he was working, but what resulted from that work came down into the studio, and he would invite me in, and I would see these—like *Cynosure* up in the exhibition, is like the sculptural schematic for a wheelbarrow, or for a cart, what’s up there with two semi-wheels and a text. So he was making that while we were there . . . and a bunch of those pieces all went into one show in Mönchengladbach—so I saw all those pieces in genesis. And I would come in, and they’d be half-made, and they were astounding . . .

Hans Peter: They were—as we heard also before that he planned everything precisely. So they look basically as he drew them?

Ron: The drawings . . . right, are necessarily—I don’t mean it badly—cartoons of them . . . [Hans Peter: Sketches] . . . sketches is a good word . . . and precise—and he was very, very rigorous and precise with his notations about exactly how big the dimensions were, where it would be—and he worked all that out in his office, and he worked that all out.
And he loved to draw—very carefully, very, very carefully . . . I think the hash helped that kind of concentration.
Then I would go down—he said come over and smoke something and look at this . . . But to answer your question about politics and all that . . .

Hans Peter: There was this enormously wide range between being really deep into something like *Catch Phrases* and then, on the other hand, being very light and funny sometimes . . . and this is great, you have this kind of big range in one piece . . . that’s amazing.

Ron: Yeah, but that was **Terry**—I would say he embodied that whole range . . . I don’t know, I can’t explain it. But the politics that Terry had were left-leaning from the sixties, and he was in Paris in May 1968. And he always talked about how this was a critical, key moment in his life. And that’s when he said he learned what sculpture is and what art is. He really learned or solidified them . . . and—I have to say: okay, when I came to visit Terry, I was his American oasis. Because he really longed to speak American English; it was really essential to him. I think he needed to speak his own language, but he needed to **live** away from it. So, when I came or when we talked on the phone, it was really a kind of mineral springs for him. But he came out of the sixties politics. So, when he tried to listen to American speech on the radio in Europe, all he could get was American Armed Forces Radio, and that fed into his political disgust, but he put it into amazing verbal and visual form that came flowing out of him.

Hans Peter: For me it is touching, because today you have all these only political works and that is so boring, because there is no humor in it—I really cannot get it . . . and this is great with his work which has both in it—it is grounded but also light at the same time.

Ron: Yeah, he was very funny . . .

Hans Peter: You just said this keyword, which I also like very much: he saw sound as a sculpture. Because for me sound and space or room, whatever we call it, is always totally connected. I cannot speak sound without space... and that makes... sculpture.

Ron: It is sculptural and he always referred to drawing as more sculptural than painting. You can feel the rasp of the pencil cut into the fibers of the paper. And that's sculpture, that's material... and he also saw sound that way, sound as material, as something coming into the ear. I don't think he would see it as wave and particle in that sense. I think it is material coming into any ear and affecting the body with vibrations. Whatever comes out of that, whatever interpretation that person has, is their own, and he's not responsible for that. He's responsible for setting it into action in a certain way, in a very rigorous way, in response to the particular place he was in. That's all; he would study the place he was in and then make a work that suited that place... but that's the way it works. Okay, I say all this, but **I** can't do it. Terry was able to do it, because... I think that's were talent comes in, where the person comes in. It's still amazing to me to see those works of art.

Hans Peter: I think it works well in the exhibition, too—it's such a big range and still open and light to see and experience... but you know him better...

Question from the audience: One last question?... I met him at the beginning of the 1980s, and everything was kind of exciting and effervescent, and Terry was kind of angry about things... and whatever, and then I lost contact with him... and so I am really happy to be back in this exhibition to see all the work I have never got to see. And I was just curious—a kind of stupid curiosity—about the last time I met him at Hans Peter's party up on top of his tower... and he was really happy that he stopped drinking alcohol. He said, "I feel wonderful, life is beautiful"... I don't think that he said that, but he said I feel wonderful and everything is great... But did he smoke dope until the end of his life?

Ron: No, no, but not that he didn't want to... But his physical condition, his medical conditions... He had problems with his eyes also, had operations for the lenses in his eyes... it would have been unhealthy for him to continue. He did do it now and then—**very** now and then, very separated—but I know he loved doing it... Because that's what we spent most of the time in Liège doing.
As for the drinking... that was always detrimental, that was never a good thing for him, after the stroke, and before, too. It served its purpose, but it wasn't a good thing. But smoking was great. Though not for **me**: I get very paranoid when I smoke. Even though it was **extremely** uncomfortable for me, I did it every night for two years, because of the privilege of going out on the town with Terry, just walking and exploring... it was amazing. You know, going to the local Spanish bar there—that we called the Spanish bar. My God, what an experience... I mean, I'll never get over it, I'll never be **able** to get over it; but it was so much fun... But I miss him so, God I miss him SO much.

Hans Peter: Thank you very much!

Transcription by Ingrid Beirer of the audio recording of an artist's talk on November 6, 2015, at the conference "Terry Fox—Situations," organized by the Terry Fox Association e. V., Cologne, at the Akademie der Künste, Berlin (Hanseatenweg).

William Wiley (Poem for Terry Fox), 11/10/2008

& so Terry Fox of ancient
tongue .. a circle of
words .. some which
stung .. with accurate
pressure .. for art &
life .. which contained
ample love .. & salve
for the knife.

[signature]

11/16/08

Thanks Terry!

[signature]

Appendix

Acknowledgments

Our gratitude is extended to the Kunstmuseum Bern and the sponsors of this publication, the authors, photographers, designers, translators, publishers, and the volunteers at the Terry Fox Association e. V., especially Marita Loosen-Fox and Ingrid Beirer, for their support of and collaboration on this publication. We are grateful to the artists, museums, and galleries who opened their archives for this book and so generously released image material. Special thanks go to Sebastian Cremers, Annelie Lütgens, Ron Meyers, Lily Pearsall, Wilfried Prantner, Tania Prill, Angelika Schulz, and Jill Sterrett.

M.G. / C.S.

Authors

Kathleen Bühler (Bern), curator for contemporary art, Kunstmuseum Bern

Chris Dercon (Berlin), curator, theater scholar

Michael Glasmeier (Berlin), art historian, publicist, exhibition-maker

Hans Peter Kuhn (Berlin), sound artist

Marita Loosen-Fox (Cologne), filmmaker, oversees the Estate of Terry Fox

Sabine Mainberger (Bonn, Berlin), literary scholar, lecturer in Bonn

Reinhard Manz (Grenzach-Wyhlen), artist, lecturer, producer

Ron Meyers (Los Angeles, California), artist, former assistant to Terry Fox

René Pulfer (Rheinfelden), artist, curator, lecturer

Seraina Renz (Chur, Zurich), art historian, curator

Bernd Schulz (d. 2017 in Berlin), curator, publicist

Ulli Seegers (Düsseldorf), art historian, lecturer in Düsseldorf

Carsten Seiffarth (Berlin), curator, producer, publicist

Lisa Steib (Baden-Baden), art historian, curator

Konrad Tobler (Bern), publicist

Käthe Walser (Basel), artist, technical curator, lecturer

Max Wechsler (Lucerne), art publicist, translator

William Wiley (Woodacre, California), painter, graphic designer, sculptor, filmmaker

Abbreviated references

Metaphorical Instruments
Terry Fox: Metaphorical Instruments, exh. cat. Museum Folkwang, Essen, and daad-galerie, Berlin (Essen and Berlin, 1982).

Works with Sound
Terry Fox: Works with Sound, Arbeiten mit Klang, ed. Bernd Schulz, exh. cat. Stadtgalerie Saarbrücken (Heidelberg, 1999).

Ocular Language
Terry Fox, Ocular Language: 30 Jahre Reden und Schreiben über Kunst / 30 Years of Speaking and Writing about Art, ed. Eva Schmidt (Cologne, 2000).

Elemental Gestures
Terry Fox: Elemental Gestures, ed. Arnold Dreyblatt and Angela Lammert, exh. cat. Akademie der Künste, Berlin, Musée des Beaux-Arts (BAM), Mons, Von der Heydt-Museum, Wuppertal, and Kunstmuseum Bern (Dortmund, 2015).

Image credits

Cover illustration (front and back), Frontispiece:
© Estate of Terry Fox, Cologne

Glasmeier, Meyers, Seiffarth
THE EYE IS NOT THE ONLY GLASS THAT BURNS THE MIND
1, 3–6 © Estate of Terry Fox, Cologne
2 Hrabanus Maurus, *LIBER DE LAUDIBUS SANCTAE CRUCIS,* facsimile *CODEX VINDOBONENSIS 652,* Austrian National Library (Vienna and Graz, 1972)

Zwischentitel: Terry Fox, Switzerland...
© Estate of Terry Fox, Cologne

Glasmeier, *The Museum as a Resonating Chamber*
1, 2 © Adolf-Wölfli-Stiftung, Kunstmuseum Bern
3–5, 7–9, 15 © Estate of Terry Fox, Cologne
10 Excerpt from Reinhold Hammerstein, *Von gerissenen Saiten und singenden Zikaden: Studien zur Emblematik der Musik* (Tübingen and Basel, 1994), fig. 48
11, 12 Excerpt from Stephanie Buck and Peter Hohenstatt, *Raffaello Santi, genannt Raffael* (Cologne, 1998), fig. 104, 105
13, 14 Author

Steib, *C E N T E R O F A T T R A C T I O N*
1, 6, 10 © Estate of Terry Fox, Cologne
2–5, 7, 9 © Galerie Löhrl, Mönchengladbach
8, 12 © Von der Heydt-Museum, Wuppertal
11 © Crown Point Press, San Francisco

Wechsler, *Terry Fox at Furk'art*
1–10, 14–26 © Max Wechsler
11–13 © Aufdi Aufdermauer
27 © Estate of Terry Fox, Cologne
28 https://upload.wikimedia.org/wikipedia/commons/5/57/Courbet_Die_Forelle_1871.jpg

Pulfer / Walser, *The Intervention of Video and Sound in an Artificial Landscape*
Selection of images and montage: René Pulfer, 2017
© *Videowochen im Wenkenpark*, Reinhard Manz and René Pulfer

Renz, *They are the strangest creatures*
1 © Valerian Maly
2–4, 6–10 © Estate of Terry Fox, Cologne
5 © bpk / Stiftung Museum Schloss Moyland / Ute Klophaus
11 http://a142.idata.over-blog.com/4/01/70/45/pologne/Planche-naturaliste-et-labyrinthe.jpg

Zwischentitel: ... and "Elsewhere"
© Estate of Terry Fox, Cologne

Schulz, *Ointment for the Knife*
1 © Estate of Terry Fox, Cologne

Seegers, *The World as a Labyrinth…*
1–3, 5, 6 © Estate of Terry Fox, Cologne
4 © Von der Heydt-Museum, Wuppertal

Glasmeier, *The Hardly and the Specific: The School of Velocity ...*
1–12 © Estate of Terry Fox, Cologne

Mainberger, *Word—Body— Art*
1–3, 5, 6 © Estate of Terry Fox, Cologne
4 © Galerie Löhrl, Mönchengladbach
7 © Anglim Gilbert Gallery, San Francisco

From the Archives
I–XXIV © Estate of Terry Fox, Cologne
XXV © San Francisco Museum of Modern Art

Wiley, *(Poem for Terry Fox)*
© Estate of Terry Fox, Cologne

Imprint

"THE EYE IS NOT THE ONLY GLASS
THAT BURNS THE MIND"
Terry Fox, Switzerland, and "Elsewhere"

A publication by the Kunstmuseum Bern
and the Terry Fox Association e. V., Cologne
Edited by Michael Glasmeier and Carsten Seiffarth

Editing: Ingrid Beirer, Michael Glasmeier,
Marita Loosen-Fox, Ron Meyers, and Carsten Seiffarth
Translation: Dawn Michelle d'Atri, Catherine
Kerkhoff-Saxon, Andrea Lerner, Andrea Scrima
Copyediting: Dawn Michelle d'Atri
Proof reading: Elias F. Quijada Link
Concept and design: Prill Vieceli Cremers, Zurich
Printing and binding: ruksaldruck, Berlin

Supported by
Swisslos. Kultur Kanton Bern

SWISSLOS
Kultur Kanton Bern

Cover illustration (front and back):
Terry Fox, (*Untitled*), n.d., drawing, on both sides,
pencil on paper, 25.4 x 20.3 cm, Estate of Terry Fox,
Cologne

Frontispiece:
Terry Fox (design), *Instruments to be Played by the Movement of the Earth*, Capp Street Project, San Francisco,
1987, invitation card, front (detail), 10.3 x 16.2 cm,
Estate of Terry Fox, Cologne

KUNST
MUSEUM
BERN

Kunstmuseum Bern
Hodlerstraße 8–12
CH – 3000 Bern 7
www.kunstmuseumbern.ch

Terry Fox Association e. V.
Auerstraße 8
D – 50733 Cologne
www.recalling-terryfox.de

Published by
Spector Books
Harkortstraße 10
D – 04107 Leipzig
www.spectorbooks.com

ISBN 978-3-95905-204-7

The German version of the book was also published by
Spector Books under the following ISBN 978-3-95905-224-5

Distribution:
Germany, Austria: GVA, Gemeinsame Verlagsauslieferung
Göttingen GmbH&Co. KG, www.gva-verlage.de
Switzerland: AVA Verlagsauslieferung AG, www.ava.ch
France, Belgium: Interart Paris, www.interart.fr
UK: Central Books Ltd, www.centralbooks.com
USA, Canada, Central and South America, Africa, Asia:
ARTBOOK | D.A.P. www.artbook.com
South Korea: The Book Society, www.thebooksociety.org
Australia, New Zealand: Perimeter Distribution,
www.perimeterdistribution.com